END THE BEGINNING

Mark DeWayne Combs

Splinter
In The Mind's Eye

END THE BEGINNING

Cover design by: Mark DeWayne Combs

Published in the United States of America

Library of Congress Control No: 201492631

ISBN: 978-0-9909695-0-1
1) Angelology/Demonology
2) Ancient Mysteries/Controversial
3) Biblical Criticism and Interpretation

To my mother, whose personal sacrifice opened so many windows of opportunity.

"There is a principle which is a bar against all information, which is a proof against all argument, and which cannot fail to keep man in everlasting ignorance.
That principle is condemnation before investigation."

- Edmund Spencer

Now all the writers of barbarian histories make mention of this flood, and of this ark; among whom is Berosus the Chaldean. For when he is describing the circumstances of the flood, he goes on thus: "It is said there is still some part of this ship in Armenia, at the mountain of the Cordyaeans; and that some people carry off pieces of the bitumen, which they take away, and use chiefly as amulets for the averting of mischiefs." Hieronymus the Egyptian also, who wrote the Phoenician Antiquities, and Mnaseas, and a great many more, make mention of the same. Nay, Nicolaus of Damascus, in his ninety-sixth book, hath a particular relation about them; where he speaks thus: "There is a great mountain in Armenia, over Minyas, called Baris, upon which it is reported that many who fled at the time of the Deluge were saved; and that one who was carried in an ark came on shore upon the top of it; and that the remains of the timber were a great while preserved. This might be the man about whom Moses the legislator of the Jews wrote."

The Works of Flavius Josephus
Antiquities of the Jews
Book 1 Chapter 3 Paragraph 6

Table of Contents

Preface

The underlying goal of this text is to neither prove nor disprove any known, commonly accepted, or presumed factual details regarding the legendary accounts of Noah and the Ark.

This is, for all intents and purposes, a work of data collection that has been woven together using recorded stories, various legends, and ancient documentation to provide the backdrop for a detailed examination of an age old saga that, if true, may very well be the most significant happening in human history.

It is not designed to be a novel, but rather a think-out-loud and write it down journal of how such events may have transpired. The story of Noah, the ark and a devastating worldwide flood has troubled me for some time. Studying through details, as they have been recorded in the biblical record, leaves me with numerous questions that are not only worthy of being asked, but also deserving of being answered.

Some scientific data will be included, but only to serve as markers of the things that we have learned and currently understand about our present world. Does science refute or advance the storyline? We shall see.

I would suppose that this is one of the most widely known tales in the history of the world and those who have heard it, either as a child or as an adult, fall sharply and distinctly into the rank and file of those who believe or those who scoff.

After years of reading and pondering that which I've read, it is my contention that regardless your allegiance to the story being one of fact or one of fiction; your verdict demands more evidence. And for that reason, I challenge you to open your mind and critically think.

"Gentlemen, all I have done is make a bouquet
from flowers already picked,
adding nothing but the string
to tie them together."

- Michel de Montaigne

Introduction:
Less Answers, More Questions

The general story of the great flood and a small group of survivors is common legend to almost every known culture. The fact that the basic story is practically universal in nature would lead us to believe that the tale must in some way, at some point, be traceable back to a solitary source.

"Noah is but one tale in a worldwide collection of at least 500 flood myths, which are the most widespread of all ancient myths and therefore can be considered among the oldest.
Stories of a great deluge are found on every inhabited continent and among a great many different language and culture groups."

- Robert Schoch, Voyages of the Pyramid Builders, 2003, pg. 249

"In 95 percent of the more than two hundred flood legends, the flood was worldwide; in 88 percent, a certain family was favored; in 70 percent, survival was by means of a boat; in 67 percent, animals were also saved; in 66 percent, the flood was due to the wickedness of man; in 66 percent, the survivors had been forewarned; in 57 percent, they ended up on a mountain;

*in 35 percent, birds were sent out from the boat;
and in 9 percent, exactly eight people were spared."*

*- James Perloff, Tornado In A Junkyard:
The Relentless Myth of Darwinism, p. 168*
(taken from: LaHaye & Morris, The Ark on Ararat, pg. 237)

That a story of such immeasurable consequence, which detailed the survival of one man and his family through the perils of a global extinction level event, would be preserved from generation to generation, crossing cultural and geographic boundaries as time separated each newly developing society farther and farther from the point of origin is not only possible, but also logical.

Whereas specifics may vary from society to society, the foundational structure remains constant. In the biblical account, the morality of mankind is also a pivotal feature. The entirety of the human race has declined into hopeless debauchery and violence. God, the creator god, is disheartened to the point of remorsefulness that he fashioned man at all. Just before wiping the entire slate clean and leaving the earth void of any life (other than sea creatures presumably), the creator is remarkably taken with one man who finds favor. Thus the initial plans of annihilation are amended.

All life on earth will be destroyed. This one man, however, will be given advance notice of what is to come, as well as the opportunity to safeguard himself and his family. The man will also be charged with the preservation of the animal kingdom. Sea life will somehow persevere on its own, but all land animals and fowl will need a safe haven if they are to survive.

The man is given specific instructions as to what to build and how to build it. He is told that he is to collect animals in mating pairs. He is also told that he can bring his wife, his sons and their wives.

Most versions of the biblical tale include a period of time wherein the man pleads for others to join him on the ark. He warns all who will listen of the coming judgment, but is ridiculed for his efforts.

Once sealed safely inside the ark, the rain begins to fall and the flood waters begin to rise. Sometimes the telling of the story includes the cries of help from those who are trapped in the rising torrents outside the ark. The water rises above the highest mountain peak and the rain continues to fall non-stop for forty days and nights.

Finally, the rain stops. The water subsides. And the ark comes to rest in the mountains. A window is opened and a dove is released. When the dove later returns to the ark with an olive leaf, the man finally opens the door. Preserved through the devastating storm, man and animal set foot on dry land once again.

The creator god puts a rainbow in the clouds as a solemn promise to never again flood the earth with water.

While I'm sure we can draw many lessons from the story; my primary interest here is not in morals, but in reality or at least the potential of reality. Is this a fable that lives in every culture as a bedtime story for kids? Is it a story of destruction and recovery to plant the seeds of ever present hope? Or, could it possibly be the account of a historical event that actually happened?

If the first two questions sufficiently answer the mystery as to where this story came from and why it has been passed down in every generation and in every tongue, then please plug in my nightlight and pull up my blankets. And, for the record, pick another book tomorrow night. *The Princess Bride* has a lot more twists, turns and character plots.

But, if there's any way that this thing is a historical event that actually happened, I've got a few questions before you fluff up my pillow and kiss my cheek. I've got more than a few actually and I hope you don't mind if I toss and turn for a few more pages while we go in search of answers.

You Want Me To Do What?

As we explore the possibilities of this story, we'll rely on a number of resources for information. Some will be ancient manuscripts that may or may not be familiar. As we introduce each of these resources along the way, we'll attempt to give some validity as to why it was chosen as a resource that could be trusted to provide insightful information.

When looking at the story as a whole, there are a number of key elements in the story that tend to set off their own flashing red lights. This is a story that has become quite easy to dismiss as illogical and even easier to scorn as a preposterous fable. Although it is a part of the cultural legacy of at least 175 different civilizations, it's commonly referred to by the accepted terminology of "Flood Myth," predisposing it as fiction. It's so easy to ridicule that perhaps the one, crucially important question is no longer even considered: Is there any way it could possibly be true?

Over the next few pages, we'll look at each element, attempt to ask honest questions, and search for well-reasoned answers. But, before we go anywhere, there's one question that just has to be explored:

Having been assigned the mission of building the ark, how would someone go about achieving such a daunting task?

Stepping back to look at the overall scope of the project, there are a number of questions that need careful consideration. In the South someone might put it this way, "If you're gonna cook up a big dinner, ya gotta go fetch yer groceries first."

That being said, let's put a few questions on the table that are begging to be answered:

- How big is this boat?
- Where would you build something this size?
- Where would you get the materials to build it?
- Who's involved in the project?
- Are they qualified to build this thing?
- How long is this going to take?
- Do you have the resources to finish the job?
- How does this affect daily family life?
- Do you tell your friends what you're doing?
- If so, what do you tell them?

In reality, is it even feasible that something like the ark could be built by a single human being and his three sons in the proposed era of time? Would the end product be adequate for the proposed workload? Would it possess the structural integrity and seaworthiness to survive for a lengthy period of time under extreme conditions? Is there any way possible, any reasonable, logical, and believable way at all, that it could be done?

If the answers to these questions can't be moved from the realm of "no way!" to the land of "just maybe," then no other questions regarding this ancient tale need to be explored.

Your End Is Off by Two Cubits

Since the story is regarded primarily as a Biblical tale, it seems reasonable to rely on the Old Testament text as a primary source for details. We'll supplement along the way with narratives from other valued resources, but Genesis will be the informational hub for our base elements.

The length, width and height dimensions of the ark are given in Genesis 6:14-16. It's there that we are first introduced to the ancient measurement term of cubit. The English word "cubit" comes from the Latin word for elbow, *cubitum,* and is commonly described as being the length from the point of a person's elbow to the tip of the person's middle finger.[1] If you're describing the size of the catfish you pulled out of Aunt Bea's backyard pond, this measurement might suffice. But for a building project, it's a recipe for disaster!

Using the catfish analogy, it's a pretty good bet that everyone in Floyd's barbershop would know that Opie's one-cubit mud minnow isn't going to take up nearly the same space on the dinner plate as Andy's. Grab your tape measure and gather your friends. It won't take long for the obvious to sink in: everyone's "cubit" is different. Even in the smallest of building projects, measurements can play a critical role and "it's about as long as your arm" is gonna make for a mess.

We don't have the preserved bones of Noah himself on hand and we could probably dismiss them if we did. Unless he stopped what he was doing to go lay his forearm on a board every time something needed to be cut, the measurement from his elbow to fingertip is of no great significance. This leaves us to argue the validity of modern-day conversions. Which is accurate? And how much does it really matter?

A length of 18 inches appears to be the most commonly accepted conversion of the Biblical cubit.[2] Some conversions point to the involvement of Moses in the compilation of the story and gravitate to the Egyptian Royal Cubit (ERC) as the most accurate measurement. With the standing testament of the pyramids casting shadows across the sands, it would seem that the ability to accurately measure something in Egypt for the purpose of building would be highly valued. The length of the ERC has been documented at 20.6 to 20.8 inches,[3] which still leaves us with a slight variance. Applied to an object of great size, such as the ark, this difference of two-tenths of an inch really does add up. And the 2¾-inch difference between the 18-inch proposal and the ERC is considerable.

If we take 18 inches as our constant, the ark measures out at 450 feet long (18 inches multiplied by 300 cubits, divided by 12 inches), 75 feet wide (18 inches times 50 cubits, divided by 12 inches) and 45 feet tall (18 inches times 30 cubits, divided by 12 inches). (See figure #1.)

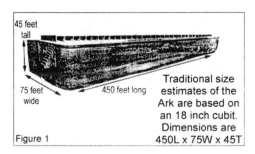

45 feet tall
75 feet wide
450 feet long

Traditional size estimates of the Ark are based on an 18 inch cubit. Dimensions are 450L x 75W x 45T

Figure 1

If we adopt the maximum Egyptian Royal Cubit of 20.8 inches as our benchmark, then we've got a vessel that spans 520 feet in length, 86⅔ feet wide and 52 feet tall. (See figure #2.)

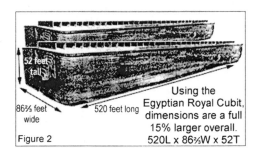

52 feet tall

86⅔ feet wide

520 feet long

Using the Egyptian Royal Cubit, dimensions are a full 15% larger overall.
520L x 86⅔W x 52T

Figure 2

The difference between the two proposed measurements is some 70 feet in length, 11⅔ feet in width and 7 feet in height. That's over 5,700 cubic feet, or nearly twice the storage capacity of a typical 45-foot semi-truck cargo trailer.[4] In fact, it's enough space to store 475 washing machines.[5] (See figure #3.)

Figure 3

27in

43in

27in

I've got 475 of these.
Where do you want them?

The typical two-car garage measures 18 feet deep and 20 feet wide, with approximately 8½ feet of head room. This adds up to 3,060 cubic feet of storage capacity. (See figure #4.) By comparison, the typical 45-foot cargo trailer has 3,083 cubic feet of

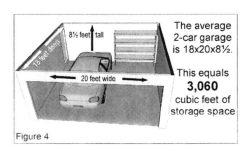

8½ feet tall

18 feet deep

20 feet wide

The average 2-car garage is 18x20x8½.

This equals
3,060
cubic feet of storage space

Figure 4

capacity.[6] Empty your two-car garage. Then, pack it as full of washing machines as you possibly can. Use every inch you can. Even the best package organizing savant will find that they have 220 machines left sitting outside on the front lawn.

Using either previously defined cubit, we've got a really big boat. But the difference between the two options leaves a lot of room for extra canary cages or much needed food supplies or living and sleeping quarters or make-up, nail polish and shoes, or... well, you get the idea. We're talking about more cubic feet than my daughter's New York City apartment, circa 2010. If the goal is to search for satisfying answers to reasonable questions, then we probably have to admit that this difference in size needs resolution.

As a point of reference, comparisons have been drawn to the size of a football stadium or a cruise ship. Since neither of those things is present in my general neighborhood, I'm still left up to my own visual imaginations. However, I do make it to the airport a few times each year, and that may provide an excellent visual.

The Boeing 747 is 231 feet in length and has 20 feet of side-to-side cabin space inside. The dimensions given for the ark are more than twice that long and four times as wide. Hmmm. Boeing lists the height of the tail tip at 63 feet, 5 inches; the ark was at least 45 feet tall (about the height of the cabin). Again, hmmm.

Trim off the tail fin and the wings from eight 747' bodies (don't get caught doing this); then line up four plane bodies side by side and position two groups of four end to end. Now, we're closing in on a comparable visual illustration. (See figure #5.) Getting the ramp agent at the local airport to drop the wings on eight planes and line them up in formation might sound like fun, but it's probably a little too much to ask. Visual lost.

Let's settle on a logical designation for the cubit. Then, we'll calculate a more accurate length and width footprint for the ark. Having our dimensions in place, we'll go in search of a visual that's a little easier for each of us to find and actually tour.

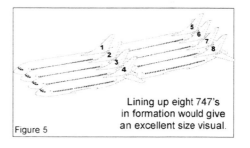

Lining up eight 747's in formation would give an excellent size visual.

Figure 5

Sometime around the middle of World War I, in 1916, the German Assyriologist and curator of the Archeological Museum of Istanbul, Eckhard Unger, found a copper-alloy bar while excavating at the lost city of Nippur. As a worship center for the Canaanite god Bel (Ba'al), Nippur was a thriving city, and modern archeology places it among the very first established cities in ancient Sumer.[7] It was located about 100 miles southeast of present-day Baghdad, Iraq. The bar that Unger found was dated circa 2650 BCE.[8]

This region of the world is about 450 miles south-southwest of where the ark is said to have come to rest in the Ararat mountain range. The ancient city of

Nineveh would be midway between Ararat and Nippur (Baghdad). The region to the south of Nineveh, closer to Nippur, was known as the Plain of Shinar (Gen. 10). The area is bordered to this day by a pair of famed rivers, the Tigris and the Euphrates.

The infamous Tower of Babel was built in this general area (Gen. 11). The ancient cities of Erech (also called Eruk) and Ur (Gen. 10) were to the south, near where the two rivers empty into the Persian Gulf. The ancient cities of Accad (or Akkad) and Calneh (Gen. 10) were to the north, near where the rivers run most closely together. (See figure #6.)

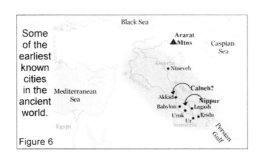

Some of the earliest known cities in the ancient world.

Figure 6

These cities are identified in Genesis 10 as being the earliest cities built after the flood and, to date, all but Calneh have been located.[9]

The ark came to rest in the mountain range to the north, and early civilizations and cities were established along the river and in the valley to the south and southwest. We commonly refer to this area today as Mesopotamia or the Fertile Crescent.

The notation, BCE, has replaced the use of BC in contemporary scholarly work. It means Before Common Era, whereas BC indicated a period of years Before Christ. The notation AD signifies the Latin designation Anno Domini or Year of Our Lord. It has been replaced in present-day scholarly work with the notation, CE, meaning Common Era. The designations BC and AD will be used in this book, due to their more common familiarity. BCE and CE may, however, appear from time to time when direct quotes are being given.

It was the foundation of ancient Sumer and the Sumerian culture.

With this historical backdrop, the copper-alloy bar found in Nippur appears to be a credible measurement standard. In fact, Unger identified the irregularly marked graduated rule as such and defined the Sumerian cubit as an accepted measurement of 518.6 millimeters (mm) or 20.4 inches.[10]

Using the measuring bar that was excavated from a city that is recognized as a premier civilization in the ancient world as the source for measurement, we can reasonably propose accurate proportions of the ark to be 510 feet long,

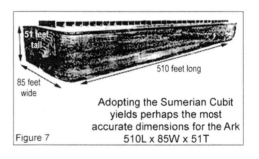

Figure 7

Adopting the Sumerian Cubit yields perhaps the most accurate dimensions for the Ark 510L x 85W x 51T

85 feet wide and 51 feet in height. (See figure #7.)

You're Gonna Need a Smaller Boat

Now let's try to find a way to put ourselves inside of the length and width footprint of the ark. Take some time to find the nearest parking lot that is reasonably large. A grocery store lot might suffice, but most likely the parking lot associated with the nearest shopping mall would be a better starting point, or perhaps even a movie theatre complex.

If you take a tape measure with you, you'll find that the average width of a parking space is about 8½ to 9 feet.

(See figure #8.) Do a little bit of math and you'll find that at 8½ feet, the length of the ark would be equal

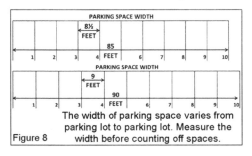

Figure 8

to the width of 60 parking spaces. If your lot is home to parking spaces that are 9 foot wide, the conversion comes out to 56⅔ spaces.

If you chose the parking lot of the nearest grocery retailer, you may find (as I did) that the lot is home to rows of parking that are only 18 to 20 spaces deep. This is only about one-third of the overall length of the ark. You're going to need a bigger parking lot or a smaller boat. If you take the time to find a suitable parking lot and step it off with a partner, I think you'll be surprised at how far it would actually be from one end of the ark to the other.

This little field trip is worth the effort. If you take the time to put yourself inside the footprint of the ark's actual size, it will make quite an impression. Trust me, you can't get this visual any other way.

Now let's add some width to that footprint. Most lots are designed to park cars nose to nose in a perpendicular arrangement. The depth of these parking spaces is typically 18 feet, making the

Nose to Nose Parking Lots are designed with multi-directional driving lanes & 36ft wide parking zones.

Figure 9

combined length of the nose to nose style spaces 36 feet. The driving lane is designed to allow sufficient passing room between cars. As such, it is typically 20 feet wide. (See figure #9.)

If you visit a lot that is set up for angled parking, the measurements for the parking spaces and driving lane will be significantly different. (See figure #10.)

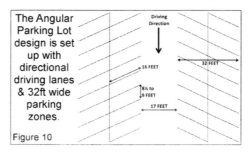

The Angular Parking Lot design is set up with directional driving lanes & 32ft wide parking zones.

Figure 10

In a lot designed for straight-on parking and multidirectional traffic lanes, the painted nose-to-nose parking grid represents about 36 feet of width. Include the driving lane on either side and you've added another 40 feet, for a total of approximately 76 feet. This is 9 feet short of our proposed overall width of the ark. To make up for this difference, you can include about half the length of a

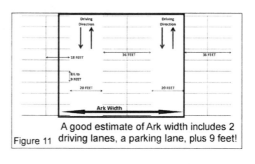

A good estimate of Ark width includes 2 driving lanes, a parking lane, plus 9 feet!

Figure 11

space, extending into the next set of parking spaces on one side of the driving lane. (See figure #11.)

Again, in lots designed for angled parking spaces the measurements will lay out a little differently. (See figure #12.)

Searching for an accurate illustration of height can be tricky. Going through a short list of commonly

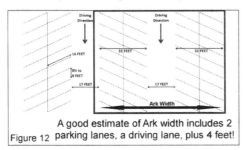

seen structures that stand out above the surrounding landscape, I came up with three visual images.

A good estimate of Ark width includes 2 parking lanes, a driving lane, plus 4 feet!

Figure 12

The standard length of a utility or telephone pole in the United States is 35 feet. That seems fairly tall, but the pole is buried at least six feet in the ground and sometimes more.[11] Our height visualization just shrunk to less than 30 feet, which means that most telephone poles are going to stop stretching skyward a full 20 feet short of the 51-foot target for a visual.

How about a standard highway overpass? Some of those seem really tall. A little bit of research provided a standard requirement of 14 feet of clearance in urban areas (vertical measurement from road below to the lowest point in the underbelly of the overpass) and 16 feet of clearance in rural zones.[12]

Let's balloon that clearance number to a standard of 20 feet, for the sake of illustration, and add on another five feet for structure above the clearance zone. Twenty feet of clearance below, plus five feet of actual highway and barrier railing only gives us about 25 feet. Highway overpasses do seem fairly tall when you're standing next to one, but this is only half as tall as the proposed ark measurement at best.

The third option that comes to mind is a building more than four stories tall. If you or your companion is at least six feet tall, you can get an idea that becomes useful for visual measuring. Stand with your back against a tall building like a movie theatre and visually count upwards by eight and a half times the height of the person (6 ft x 8½ = 51 ft). I tried this in front of a theatre complex, which seemed sufficiently tall, but ran out of building. (See figure #13.)

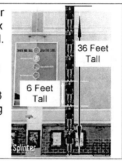

The building that houses our local movie theatre complex tops out at about 34 feet tall.

It seemed like a pretty tall building, but the Ark would have been about 17 feet taller. That's equivalent to 3 more copies of me standing on top of the 6 that are already in the picture.

Figure 13

36 Feet Tall

6 Feet Tall

Splinter

If you can find a section of the building that has some sort of consistent decorative brick pattern, it may help you keep track as you stack imaginary images of your partner on top of each other in your mind's eye. When you get to 51 feet, you're probably going to be surprised by how tall that actually is. It looks particularly towering when you stand next to the building and look straight up. If you can get to that height and look straight down, it's also pretty impressive.

Location, Location, Location

The completed size of the ark played a monumental role in project planning. From the moment the initial measurements were given to Noah, it was easy to see that the overall magnitude of the project made the question of where to build the ark one of extreme significance. A number of aspects would have factored into the decision-making along the way. When you're undertaking the construction of a structure that's more than four stories tall, some 500 feet long and over 80 feet wide, you know right away that it can't be built just anywhere.

A steady supply of building materials for such a massive project would have to be readily available near the worksite. A reliable method of getting materials from the supply site to construction site would have to be considered. Making certain that production, once underway, could proceed uninterrupted by the opposition of outside interests, protestation or even curious passersby would be a priority.

Location would also be of utmost significance, if the various stages of construction were going to move methodically from ground clearing to launch (flotation). It's easy to see to see that this was no weekend warrior backyard project. This was a colossal undertaking. Rome wasn't built in a day and the ark wasn't built over a four-day weekend.

We've actually got two separate problems to resolve before we start chopping away at the nearest clump of trees. We need a better idea of how much building material is actually going to be needed, and we need to settle on a construction site that not only gives us sufficient room to build, but also provides the potential for the safe launch of our floating apartment complex. Let's take a stab at the materials first.

Cutting 'em Down to Size

If we were to propose using a board that was 12 inches wide, 16 feet long and 8 inches thick, we'd probably be underestimating the durability needed for the outer hull, but we have to start somewhere.

Our floating box is 510 feet long. So, we'll need 32 boards that are 16 feet in length just to reach from one end to the other (they would total 512 feet). We'd need an additional 5⅓ boards to span the width from side to side (85 feet). At this pace, it would take all or part of 75 boards to complete one trip all the way around the ark (the two long sides and two 85-foot-wide ends).

Our previously established height of the ark was 51 feet tall, which is why we proposed planks that are 12 inches wide. The math is pretty easy here. We'd need 51 planks stacked on top of each other to reach from the bottom of the ark to the top. Sharpen the pencil one more time and we can easily estimate the amount of lumber needed to panel the exterior walls. A trip around the outside takes 75 boards. And 51 trips around the outside will get us from top to bottom. It looks like 3,825 boards that are 8 inches thick, 12 inches wide, and 16 feet in length will be needed to complete the exterior walls.

If you're a "Sheldon"[13] and you only relate to exact measurements, you may find yourself anxious to point out that our estimate is a little bit high. The actual circumference of our giant houseboat is equivalent to 74.375 boards, not 75, which means we only need

3,793 boards for the outer walls. For the record, this is equivalent to 489,600 board feet for just the outer paneling. Feel free to research the calculation of board feet if you want to really bog down in the details. The goal here is reasonable estimates for visualization purposes only. We don't actually have plans to build.[14]

I don't know about you, but my imagination could benefit from another close-to-home, hands-on visual at this point. A standard 25.5-cubic-foot kitchen refrigerator is approximately 36 inches wide by 34 inches deep and about 69 inches tall.[15] It would take an unfinished round log nearly 51 inches in diameter to produce a "refrigerator-sized"

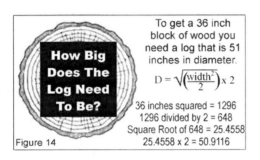

How Big Does The Log Need To Be?

To get a 36 inch block of wood you need a log that is 51 inches in diameter.

$$D = \sqrt{\left(\frac{width^2}{2}\right)} \times 2$$

36 inches squared = 1296
1296 divided by 2 = 648
Square Root of 648 = 25.4558
25.4558 x 2 = 50.9116

Figure 14

block of wood. (See figure #14.)

Stack three refrigerators on top of each other to get a visual image of the height of this block of wood, that's 207 inches or 17¼ feet tall (long). If you could perfectly slice this block four times across into 8-inch segments (32 inches) and three times across into 12-inch segments (36 inches) without losing any useful lumber to the sawdust of your cuts, you would be able to harvest

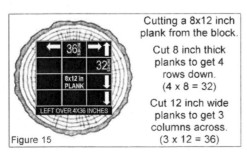

Cutting a 8x12 inch plank from the block.

Cut 8 inch thick planks to get 4 rows down.
(4 x 8 = 32)

Cut 12 inch wide planks to get 3 columns across.
(3 x 12 = 36)

36
32
8x12 in PLANK
LEFT OVER 4X36 INCHES

Figure 15

a dozen useful boards out of each refrigerator-sized block. (See figure #15.)

At this conversion rate, Noah would need 319 trees that were greater in circumference than the refrigerator from our example, and more than three times the height of that same refrigerator before they began to taper off. That's 319 blocks of wood, which having been properly cut, would provide a total of 12 planks that are 8 inches thick, 12 inches wide and 16 feet long. Having trimmed out and planed all 319 tree trunks, we're left with a total of 3,828 beams. The previous calculations indicated that we'd need somewhere between 3,793 and 3,825 precisely cut boards to get the job done.

We may have a few full-sized planks left over and perhaps some scraps, but I'm sure we'll find good use for them as this calculation only takes into account the materials needed to panel *the exterior wall area* of the ark. We didn't erect a single support beam or lay down any flooring.

At this point, it's easy to see that there would be multiple cries of "Timber!" in that stack of timber. So, how many trees are there in the average forest? Better yet, how many of them have reached the sufficient girth to qualify as useable? According to the California Forest Foundation (CFF), it's reasonable to anticipate that the typical northern California growth environment would support 32 Redwood trees per acre in the average forest. This would include 10 trees that are approximately 40 inches in diameter, two trees of 50 inches and one trunk of nearly 90 inches.[16]

The tree diameter used in our example was 50 inches. If Noah lived in an area that supported growth at a rate of 50 trees per acre that had reached adequate girth and height, it would take almost six and a half acres of sufficiently sized tree trunks to produce our minimum requirement of 319.

Using the CFF projections of approximatly 32 total trees per acre, only 13 of which would be anticipated to have reached a trunk diameter of 40 inches or more, we could make 40 the new 50 and the overall projected yeild per acre still drops considerably (from 50 to 32). Working from the CFF projections, Noah and sons would have to clear at least 24½ acres of trees to obtain enough trunks to panel the exterior walls of the ark. *Twenty-four acres and a half!*

A standard acre of land is 43,560 square feet. The footprint of the ark was equivalent to 43,350 square feet (510 feet long and 85 feet wide). Considering that it would require almost one complete acre of land just to house the structure and possibly as much as 23½ additional acres of old growth forest just to provide the minimum amount of lumber needed, we're looking at a pretty substantial worksite.

If you'd like to get a good visual of that, just revisit the parking lot where you originally stepped off the measurements of the ark. Now, try your best to imagine that amount of space times 24. Maybe the lot you used has enough parking and driving lanes available or maybe not. The one I used came up a little short.

For those of you who are silently screaming "Gopher wood! The Bible says, 'Gopher wood!'" we are using the California Redwoods for the purpose of illustration only. Genesis 6:14 is the only place that the word "gopher" is used in the entire King James text and it's actually the original Hebrew word, "gopher." In other words, it's the only non-translated word in the entire King James Bible.

The New Living Translation and the New International Version translate the word as "cypress," presumably because the trees grow abundantly in Chaldea and Armenia. Most other mainstream translations do not attempt to translate the word at all, choosing to leave it as it is – gopher. The Greek translation of the Old Testament scriptures, The Septuagint, circa 300-100 BC, translates the word as "squared timber." The Latin Vulgate, dating back to the 5th century AD, translates it as "smoothed wood."

There are also those who believe that the term "gopher" is more of a description of the woodworking process, as opposed to a specific type of wood. It has been suggested that "smoothed wood" could also be a reference to planed or layered wood.

We can't say with any certainty what type of wood was used and I'm not sure that the type of wood is actually important. It's entirely possible that the ark was built from a mixture of different types of woods from different trees for different construction uses. The only thing that is clear is that Noah had to "go for wood" and he had to go for a lot of it.

Just in case it's gotten swallowed up by the sawdust, remember that our previous lumber calculation was for the wood needed to panel the outside walls of the ark only. It doesn't include any framing of the outer structure, which would certainly be needed: the exterior paneling has to be attached to something.

Interior walls, base flooring, decks and either stairways or ladders (possibly both) would still need to be built. Noah would also need some stalls, cages or coops so the animals would have a place to call home and certainly there would be a need for massive amounts of storage. Have you ever been in a home that had too many closets or cabinets? *Ever?!?*

While we're on the topic of the general build of the ark, let's take the time to nudge a sleeping pooch as we walk by. Much has been made about the structural integrity of the ark and the qualifications of its builder. The common dismissive accusations are:

1. A wooden boat wouldn't survive in rough seas for very long, particularly not one of this size.

2. A structure of this size and complexity couldn't be built by the finest craftsmen today with even the best of technology. How could an ignorant man with primitive tools possibly build it?

In 1942 the United States faced a perplexing dilemma when it came to transporting and supplying troops during World War II. German U-boats were making crossing the sea by boat a treacherous journey, but the

U.S. War Department still needed to transport troops and supplies to Europe. To make matters even more difficult, wartime priorities mandated that, due to the limited amount of resources, any newly constructed aircraft could not be made primarily of metal.

Challenge: transport mass numbers of troops across the ocean safely, but don't construct any new aircraft using metal. Enter Henry J. Kaiser, a ship builder, and an aircraft design specialist named, Howard Hughes. Together they came up with the design for a massive cargo plane that was made primarily of wood – the HK-1 Hercules.

The plane was capable of transporting 750 fully equipped troops or one M4 Sherman tank. At the time, the massive design eclipsed the size of any other transport available to the military. Although it was made from Birch, the media nicknamed it the "Spruce Goose." Some critics of the design also referred to it as the "Flying Lumberyard."

The Goose was 218 feet long and had an impressive 321-foot wingspan. It boasted a cruising speed of 250 mph and a projected flight range of 3,000 miles. Although it was never mass produced, the prototype was fully constructed and made its maiden flight on November 2, 1947. To comply with government restrictions regarding the use of metal, the vast majority of the massive aircraft was fabricated of planed, laminated wood, which proved to be sufficiently strong for the projected workload. The completed prototype is currently on display at the

Evergreen Aviation & Space Museum in McMinnville, Oregon.[17,18]

Before we become so dismissive of technological achievements in the ancient world, maybe it would serve us well to consider a few questions:

1. What scale is being used to evaluate the overall knowledge and skills that Noah and his sons possessed? And who has the sufficient qualifications to impose such a scale? How do we know what they didn't know?

2. By what standard are we evaluating the tools that they had at their disposal? Someone clearly built the astonishing megalithic structures of the ancient world, and today we are still at a loss in many cases to explain how they built them with such precision. Maybe we should lighten up just a tad in our own criticism until we're able to understand and mirror their incredible craftsmanship.

3. Are we so certain that we can casually dismiss the source of the general project blueprint and the divine instruction that was apparently given as to how to accomplish the task? Maybe the design was incredibly suited for the task at hand. The *SS Great Britain* was lauded as a revolutionary engineering marvel for its use of a 30:5:3 ratio scale (the same ratio used in the building of the ark) and that ratio was hailed as the prime ratio for seaworthiness.[19, 20] The *SS Jeremiah O'Brien* was built for World War II using the same ratio and, as of this writing, it is still a functioning, seafaring vessel. In fact, it's the only ship that was present during the Normandy Invasion and later sailed back to the 50th anniversary in Normandy in 1994 under its own power.[21]

4. We must keep in mind that the ark wasn't designed to go anywhere. It was designed to do one thing and one thing only – *float*.

Some Room... With a View

Our focus, so far, has been centered on the amount of building materials needed for a project the size and scope of the ark. That spins the conversation now to the overall land mass that a project of this scale would need.

Although the actual requirement might exceed our best guess, we settled on a plot of extraordinarily well-forested land no less than 10 acres in size. We then put forth a legitimate argument that as much as 25 total acres of old growth forest would be required to satisfy the demand.

Perhaps a conservation specialist could get by on 18 to 20 acres of prime timber by squeezing usefulness out of every splinter and limiting waste, but even at that, we're still a long way down the road from a quiet cul-de-sac in the suburbs. And that brings us to another curious question: how big is an acre anyway?

As long as we're working in the realm of real-world visualization, we might as well roll this stone over and take a peek underneath. Previously, we defined the dimensions of an acre as 43,560 square feet. It seems like it would be much easier to estimate the size of a gallon of milk, a shoebox, a queen-sized bed, or even a school bus than to project what portion of any given parking lot would be equivalent to an acre. In this instance, "you'll know it when you see it" doesn't always work.

If you live somewhere near a recreational softball complex, then we've got a suitable resource with which to work. Typically, from home plate to the fence down both the first base and third base lines measures out at about 285 to 300 feet. Add some room for bleachers behind home plate, dugouts for both teams and a little bit of walking space between fields and you're working on a 350-foot by 350-foot plot of ground for each field.

Although there are stand-alone fields and a multitude of two-field duplexes across the United States, most softball complexes play host to at least three or four fields that are designed with home plate near the center of the complex and outfield fences spanning the circumference. (See figure #16.) A single field would measure out at 122,500 square feet or 2.81 acres of land. Put four of these together in a complex with a little room to roam in between each field and you've got a plot of ground that is somewhere between 11 and 12 acres, not including the parking area.

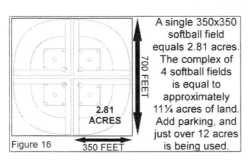

A single 350x350 softball field equals 2.81 acres. The complex of 4 softball fields is equal to approximately 11¼ acres of land. Add parking, and just over 12 acres is being used.

Figure 16   700 FEET   350 FEET   2.81 ACRES

So, we want to build a floating building the projected size of the ark? Okay, we need to locate a fairly isolated area that is home to an old growth forest and we need to make sure the forest extends to at least the size of not one, but two typical softball complexes. Cakewalk! Anything else?

Well, there's at least one other factor that may be of extreme importance. It stands to reason that if the sole purpose for building this boat in the first place is to survive the soon-to-arrive catastrophic flood, we wouldn't want to build it in a low-lying area. If we're on board this thing, we're building it with the intention of feeling it slowly lift with the rising level of the water as we set sail.

We've got no interest in being broadsided by a 73-foot-tall tidal wave that just came crashing through the valley because a natural water break was over-stressed and gave way. That kind of exposure would most likely tumble our masterpiece of engineering technology (and best hope of survival) along the ground violently until it crashes against the nearest mountain range. No thank you to the complete and fullest extent of a loud "*No, thank you!*"

There are a variety of disastrous conditions to consider. If we go too high into the mountains, we're separating the project from the naturally growing materials that we'll need to build the ark. We're also putting the entire project at risk of potentially quaking earth that could send us plunging off of our unstable but lofty perch and down a slope to ruin. If we build in the valley, we're exposed to the potential of a wall of rushing water that may result from a buildup and collapse of a basin several miles away.

This is beginning to sound like history's first

Goldilocks conundrum. Finding a location that was "just right" would have been a crucial component that no doubt played heavily into the plans. Not only would it need to satisfy the question of necessary overall worksite space and provide access to sufficient building materials, but it would also have to serve as the optimum place to launch, or wait for launch to happen as the case may be.

Keep Your Head Above Water

This brings us to another facet of the build that seems imperative, but often goes without consideration. We've explored the overall enormity of the project and we'll get to the occupants (both animals and humans), as well as the life-sustaining provisions needed for such a voyage in later chapters, but floatability and stabilization need to be addressed.

As stated earlier, the ark was not designed to go anywhere. From the basic information we can derive from the instructions, as given in Genesis 6, navigation and maneuverability really don't seem to be much of a consideration at all. Even in my best efforts to read between the proverbial lines, I just don't see it. The only thing that the ark was designed to do was float. But even if that was the only objective, it still needed to float with optimum stability.

The ability to ride aloft on the surface of the rising water would have been the most simplistic goal to achieve. Being able to do so, without the occupants being beaten to death by turbulence, would have been the greater challenge. There's no way to project a complete and utter global devastation without the implication of stormy seas.

In 2005, Katrina, a category 3 hurricane, assaulted the Gulf Coast of the United States with 130-mph sustained winds and a storm surge that approached 28 feet in some portions of Mississippi.[22] In March of 2011, horrific video footage streamed out of Japan showing a wall of water that raced inland from the coast as far as six miles, leveling everything in its path. The tsunami was caused by an 8.9-magnitude earthquake just off the coast of the island nation, and the destruction from the ensuing wave affected 250 miles of Japan's coastline.[23]

The Indian Ocean tsunami of 2004 was attributed to a 9.0-magnitude quake off the coast of Sumatra. It sent a series of devastating waves rushing away from the epicenter and crashing into the coastlines of 11 countries. It was estimated that more than 150,000 people lost their lives, many of them dragged into the ocean by the power of the receding waves.[24]

There are many more examples that could be cited of immense devastation from overpowering flood waters. Photos of the Japan tsunami show tidal whirlpools that resulted from withdrawing torrents of water. An article about the Indian Ocean tsunami included a complete section about the aftermath, including the massive floating patches of rotting corpses.

None of these dreadful incidents, or any others that one might call to memory, could possibly compare to the devastation of a flood that would be global in scope. Those aboard the ark knew full well that the ride would not be smooth.

There's an interesting passage found in an ancient Jewish history book called the Book of Jasher, where a precursor to the worldwide flood is recorded. In a later chapter we'll go into more detail as to why the Book of Jasher has been considered as a useful and reliable resource. But for now, consider this reference:

Jasher 2:3-6

> *(3) "And it was in the days of Enosh that the sons of men continued to rebel and transgress against God, to increase the anger of the Lord against the sons of men.*
>
> *(4) "And the sons of men went and they served other gods, and they forgot the Lord who had created them in the earth: and in those days the sons of men made images of brass and iron, wood and stone, and they bowed down and served them.*
>
> *(5) "And every man made his god and they bowed down to them, and the sons of men forsook the Lord all the days of Enosh and his children; and the anger of the Lord was kindled on account of their works and abominations which they did in the earth.*
>
> *(6) "And the Lord caused the waters of the river Gihon to overwhelm them, and he destroyed and consumed them, and he destroyed the third part of the earth, and notwithstanding this, the sons of men did not turn from their evil ways, and their hands were yet extended to do evil in the sight of the Lord."*

Enosh was the son of Seth, who was a son born to Adam and Eve when Adam was 130 years of age. The passage relates that he was named Enosh specifically because of the nature of the prevailing culture at the time he was born – mankind as a whole had turned away from worshipping the Creator and initiated the practice of fashioning idols from brass, iron, wood and stone.

These are descendants of Adam, the same Adam who was formed from the dust by the Creator himself. Yet his grandsons and great-grandsons are consumed with idol worship. Adam's son, Seth, is so appalled by this behavior that he names his son, Enosh (Enos in Genesis). The name means "mortal man" or "man is mortal."[25] Maybe this was intended as a reminder to others of who man was. Or, maybe it was a condemnation of their widespread inclination to deliberately separate themselves from the Creator and chase the serpent's promise of godhood (Gen. 3:5).

Verse 5 indicates that this prevailing apostasy continued all of the days of Enosh and his children, perhaps a reference to his son Cainan. According to Genesis 5:11, Enosh (or Enos) passed away at the age of 905. This was 1,140 years from the creation of Adam. Genesis 5:14 states that Cainan died at the age of 910. This was 1,235 years from the point of creation.

Verse 6 seems to imply that it is at some point after the passing of Enosh and his children that the flooding of the river Gihon takes place. If this is a reasonable and reliable time stamp, then we can place this flood event somewhere in the early life of Noah. We'll see later that Noah was born 1,057 years from the point of creation and would have been alive to witness this event.

You might also recognize the name of the river Gihon as being one of the four rivers that were said to flow from the Garden of Eden (Gen. 2:13). This river encompassed a land that is referred to as Ethiopia, but there's nothing to verify that it would be the land we know as Ethiopia in the modern world.

Verse 6 also makes it clear that this flooding of the river Gihon destroyed one-third of the world. It could easily be presumed that the Garden of Eden was destroyed as a part of this flood as well.

The point of the reference is simple: Noah was very aware of the devastation that could be associated with a massive flood. It's entirely possible and perhaps more than probable that he would have been eyewitness to the aftermath. Make no mistake; Noah knew without any question what uncontrollable devastation the flood waters would bring. He also knew that stability of the ark was a crucial point of emphasis, not an afterthought.

In 2009, National Geographic aired a special entitled "The Truth Behind the Ark."[26] The special featured a segment designed to test the stability of the ark design when faced with imposing swells on the open sea. The tests were performed by a shipbuilding engineer and his crew. The group not only built a scale model of the ark, but tested how the design performed under extreme open sea conditions in their facility, tracking motion data with electronic motion sensors.

In the special, the model ark rolled violently in the waves, nearly capsizing at times. When the test crew removed the airtight sealed lid of the model, to simulate projected leakage, the model lasted only a short time before sinking to the bottom of the wave tank. National Geographic concluded that the ark would have never been able to withstand the extended exposure to the flood waters, as the Bible describes.

In 2010, an interesting video was posted on YouTube[27] that showed additional testing that was performed by the same shipbuilding engineer and his crew. Apparently, this segment was not aired by National Geographic. The additional test was done to illustrate the use of weighted ballast that some propose would have been suspended below the ark to enhance stabilization.

The testing demonstrated a marked improvement in stability, even in the face of much larger swells being generated by the wave machine. It has been theorized that the suspension of "drogue stones" along the length of the ark would have accomplished two things: 1) Minimize the side-to-side rolling effect that would have been otherwise experienced. 2) Give the ark a certain amount of drag, which would have allowed prevailing winds to position the ark head-on into the swells, as opposed to taking them broadside. (See figure #17.)

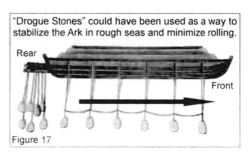

"Drogue Stones" could have been used as a way to stabilize the Ark in rough seas and minimize rolling.

Rear

Front

Figure 17

49

It has also been suggested that the addition of suspended stone weights would have been useful as the ark came to rest. Those suspended to a greater degree would begin to drag first, thus indicating that the ark had reached shallower water and land was underneath. If the dragging stones created too much turbulence and stress for the ark, they could easily be cut loose as needed.

There is quite a bit of information available on the subject, if you're interested in researching additional details.[28,29]

The Need to Get Away

A long-standing and inseparable part of the flood story, as it has been told and passed down, is a portion in which Noah devotes time to warning those around him about the coming judgment of God – the impending flood.

As this portion of the tale is recounted, a picture is painted of a single man, pleading with all who would listen, to make preparation, collect their things, gather their family, and join him on the ark. His proclamations are met with bitter ridicule and mockery. Nonetheless, Noah is said to have continued his pleading, in an attempt to reason with all of those who are soon to be subjected to the atrocity on the horizon.

Justification for this segment of the story may stem from a reference to Noah in the New Testament writings of Peter, who referred to Noah as "*a preacher of righteousness,"* (2 Peter 2:5). This certainly makes for good storytelling, but I've always wondered about its accuracy.

According to the Biblical record, Noah was told to build a structure of a predetermined size. He was specifically told that it is a place for him, his wife, his three sons and their wives. He was also informed that it will be a safe haven for animals, a mating pair of each kind of animal known to exist at that time. He was *not* told to lay out the welcome mat for any other living creatures, man or beast, and encourage them to come inside.

There may have been other specific artifacts, which are not identified in the ancient text, that Noah was expressly told to take on board, but I can't find any indication anywhere in the Biblical text that Noah was instructed to make any effort at all to persuade others to join him on the ark, and the Genesis account doesn't offer any evidence that he did so of his own accord.

There is, however, an interesting tidbit, found in the Book of Jasher, that records a commission given to Noah and his grandfather, Methuselah (Jasher 5:6-11). The two are told to proclaim a coming judgment and reveal that the judgment will be repealed if men renounce their idol worship and return to worshipping the Creator. A timetable of 120 years is given as a period of leniency before the judgment, but it is not stated that Noah and Methuselah pleaded with men for the entire length of time. Jasher indicates that once the message is rejected, Noah retreats into solitude.

The reference in Peter specifies that Noah was the eighth person to board the ark. Noah's three sons, plus their wives (presumably one each) would equal six. Noah's wife would bring the head count to seven, and Noah himself would be the final person – number eight. So, even though Noah is referred to as a preacher of righteousness, it would seem that the maximum occupancy anticipated was indeed eight human beings.

When pressed by his disciples to disclose insider information regarding the end of the world, Christ himself referenced the flood (Matthew 24:36-39). By doing so, he puts himself unquestionably among those who believe the ancient account to have actually taken place. In addition, by his own testimony, Jesus declares that those outside of Noah's immediate family, *"knew not until the flood came and took them all away."*

Far be it from me to put words into the mouth of the one hailed as the King of Kings, Lord of Lords and the very Son of God himself, but he does clearly say that no one, other than Noah and his family, knew about the coming flood judgment until it happened.

It would seem that Noah didn't spend any time at all telling anyone about anything. Not a single word was spoken. Not a single warning was chiseled into a rock. Not even a friendly little game of "guess what I know that you don't?" *Nothing! Zilch! Nadda!*

This brings another detail that seemingly would impact the choice of location – the absolute necessity of isolation.

Having a heavily wooded area and the proper elevation would be prerequisites for sure, but you're never going to stay on schedule with an endless parade of interruptions shuffling through your worksite. Although it's sometimes suggested that Noah was mocked by those around him as he worked to build the ark, no Biblical texts give any indication that Noah had interaction on any level with those outside of his immediate family once construction started. From every conceivable angle, it would seem that solitude would be preferred over continuous social interaction, "I'm quite busy here. I've got a deadline looming. *Leave me alone!!!*"

Isolation would not only be a distraction issue, it would also fall under the category of a safety issue. We'll dig deeply into the culture of the time period in the next chapter, but suffice it to say that at this point not everyone walking the face of the earth was sporting a coexist tattoo.

Genesis 6:5 spells it out pretty plainly, "*And God saw that the wickedness of man was great in the earth....*" Not only was it bad, it was award-winning bad. By the time Noah had logged 500 years of "What's for breakfast?" civilization had taken a decided downturn.

Aside from himself, Noah had a wife to care for and there were three sons that would be added to the family tree at some point after Noah's 500th birthday. Since we're going to devote an entire chapter to Noah's family and even spend a little bit of time exploring the old-age thing that was pretty prevalent prior to the flood, I don't want to invest too much ink in the details at this point. While isolation may have been critically important, Noah was not alone. He had a family and it would appear that he was an excellent father.

There are quite a number of different pieces to this puzzle. We've looked at the finished size projections, the massive amount of materials needed, the overall geographic room required for such a monumental undertaking, the optimum conditions needed for an under-control launch, and also the family factor. It seems hard to imagine that the decision of where to build the ark was not one of great significance and lengthy deliberation.

So When Do We Get Started?

There's a big question with regard to the kids and the general construction of the ark that revolves around timing and possibly how involved the three sons were in the overall project from start to finish.

What we know from the Biblical narrative is that Noah was 500 years old before the first son was born (Gen. 5:32). The sons were born at separate times (Gen. 9:22-24 & Gen. 10:21). And Noah was 600 years, one month and 17 days of age when the flood began (Gen. 7:11).

What isn't spelled out explicitly is the point at which Noah began building the ark. Some, who have written about the flood in great detail, express the opinion that Noah began building the ark 120 years before the first raindrop fell. These authors reference Genesis 6:3 as the foundation for their supposition,

> *"And the Lord said, 'My spirit shall not always
> strive with man, for that he also is flesh;
> yet his days shall be an hundred and twenty years.'"*

In this scenario, the sons would be born as the construction on the ark develops. Having never known their father outside of this mammoth building project would make it easier for all three of the sons to become wholly committed to the family business. If Dad is committed to the daily task of building this gigantic structure for a future time when it will be the only means of preservation, then the sons would most naturally follow in his footsteps as soon as they're able to drag a board or carry some nails. This really has video camera moment written all over it.

On the other hand, having to wait for the toddlers to get past diapers and teething would seemingly back the project up quite a bit and shorten the overall time span for building. It also means that each of the sons had to leave home at some point to find a wife who would look forward to life on the open seas.

Our last possibility would be saddling Noah with the responsibility of convincing three adult sons (and their wives) to give up their established lives and make a complete personal commitment to Daddy's latest obsession. This scenario seems like a really tough sell.

The Biblical narrative doesn't clearly say whether Noah was given the assignment before or after his sons were born. Neither does it specify when he began to build, or how long it took from start to finish. The only indications are that Noah fathered three sons and that all three sons were destined to be occupants on the ark.

Genesis 6:18

> *"But with thee will I establish my covenant;*
> *and thou shalt come into the ark, thou, and thy sons,*
> *and thy wife, and thy sons' wives with thee."*

This verse falls smack dab (expressive Southern term) in the middle of the step-by-step instruction conversation between God and Noah. That being the undeniable case, we are left with a pair of alternatives when it comes to our construction initiation timetable: 1) The commission to build the ark is given at the 120-year mark as some suggest, and God is foretelling the birth of Noah's yet-to-be-born sons and their yet-to-be-wooed wives. 2) The commission to build the ark comes a number of years after Noah's three sons had been born and possibly even a few years after each of them had found wives.

Trying to sort out the logical details of these two options brings us back to one mysterious phrase in the ancient text. The narrative of the interaction between God and Noah begins in Genesis 6:9 with the acknowledgement, *"These are the generations of Noah...."* This statement is an indication that we're about to read something specific that pertains to that particular person and his family tree.

The phrase is commonly used in the early chapters of Genesis, but it's the closing phrase of this verse that stands out *"...and Noah walked with God."*

This walking with God phrase is only used of one other person in the pre-flood world and, no, it's not Adam. We're told that God walked in the Garden of Eden in the cool of the day (Gen. 3:8), but the Noah statement is different. As it is recorded, this is an indication of a continual activity. It's not as if God and Noah took a walk around the block one afternoon as the sun was setting. On the contrary, the indication is that of a habitual, physical activity as if a reference to a person's vocation.

For instance, if Herman worked for a shipping company unloading freight from cargo ships down at the port, you might say: "Herman unloads freight." Or, if Bill worked for a software design company and wrote programs for them to market to businesses, you might say: "Bill designs computer programs."

The only other person to whom this "walked with God" phrase is attached is a man named Enoch. He's the son of Jared and father of Methuselah. We're told in Genesis 5:22 that after the birth of Methuselah, Enoch "walked with God" for 300 years. This is a reference to a habitual physical activity.

"What's Herman do?"

"He unloads freight down at the port."

"And what does Bill do?"

"Oh, that guy is a software designer."

"How about this Enoch character?"

"Enoch? He walks with God."

Could it be that Noah "walked with God" for 120 years prior to the flood (Gen. 6:3) and that at some point during that time he was given the step-by-step instructions as to how to build the ark and why he should build it?

We'll settle a few of these unanswered questions when we take a closer look at Noah and his family. For now, we'll just designate this portion as, "To be continued..."

There Goes the Neighborhood

It's said that "the devil is in the details," and I suppose that's true in some instances. I tend to lean more heavily towards a belief that it's actually significance that's hiding in the details. Maybe hiding isn't the right description. It's more likely that significance is screaming at us from the details, but just can't get our attention.

Details are easily missed and often purposely skipped over for the sake of time. We're in a hurry to get from point A to point B and tend to place heavy emphasis on the destination, thus sacrificing the journey. Honestly, when was the last time you carefully read every word of a Terms of Service or Licensing Agreement before you agreed to abide by things you didn't have the time, or take the time, to read?

I'm sure that somebody, somewhere at some point in time, has read one or two paragraphs, perhaps even a page, but have you ever read each word and phrase prior to signing? What if your cell phone contract stated that you agreed to pay the provider $3 a month for life for each phone covered by the contract even if you switched carriers at some point in the future? Would you consider that a significant detail?

I'm usually in a rush as well when I read through such things. "Scan over" might be a more accurate description than "read through." Perhaps it would be best if I confessed to flipping past page after page just looking for the places I need to initial on my way to the place where I need to sign. Been there? Done that?

It's easy to treat familiar Biblical passages in much the same way. We've heard the story. We're familiar with the scene. We've been told what to think about it and we've agreed to do so without the slightest hint of questioning. As a result, we often rush past details that matter and critical information that might cause us to rethink our perspective.

Eighteenth-century English author Samuel Johnson is credited with saying, "The two most engaging powers of an author are to make new things familiar and familiar things new."

That will be the challenge as we explore the life and culture that led up to the flood. We'll take a look at the first 1,000 years of human history, as it's presented in the Biblical text. We'll also introduce texts from other highly regarded ancient manuscripts to draw additional information and corroborate the testimony of the Biblical text.

If there truly is significance in the details, then let's give the details an opportunity to convey their often-overlooked information. We'll look at pieces and attempt to discover where these pieces fit together. And, we'll ask questions... lots of questions.

Meet Cain's Wife and Son and Grandson and...

How long had man lived on the earth prior to the flood? Did these ancient people roam aimlessly and live in caves? Before the flood, did people really live for hundreds of years before dying? What knowledge could they possibly have had in the areas of construction, industry, astronomy and the arts? Where did this knowledge come from? Was there law, order and government? And, the ultimate question: What led to God's decision to annihilate mankind through the means of a worldwide catastrophic event?

If we are to take the Biblical record as historically accurate, then it's fairly easy to piece together a timeline from Adam to the flood. The question becomes, do we trust our current perception of ancient history, or can we trust the documentation we have at our fingertips and allow it to shape our understanding, free from superimposed culturally accepted bias? As we will discover, the two options are fairly contradictory.

HistoryWorld.net describes the basic elements considered necessary for a civilization to emerge and progress in the following manner:

> "Many different elements must come together before a human community develops to the level of sophistication commonly referred to as civilization. The first is the existence of settlements classifiable as towns or cities. This requires food production to be efficient enough for a large minority of the community to be engaged in more specialized activities — such as the creation of imposing buildings or works of art, the practice of skilled warfare, and above all the administration of a centralized bureaucracy capable of running the machinery of state."[1]

So our key components are: settlements (towns or cities), food production (organized farming), specialized activities (industry and arts), militia (skilled warfare), and above all administration of bureaucracy (government). A group of people, regardless of the number of people in the group, which lacks any one of those ingredients apparently does not meet the modern-day obligatory standards to be regarded as a civilization.

According to History World, the earliest recognized civilizations emerged between the Tigris and Euphrates rivers in an area known as Mesopotamia around 3100 to 3200 BC. These two predominant empires are known as Sumer and Egypt.[2]

With our defining blueprint in place, let's see what we can discover about the ancient, pre-flood world and its occupants.

Genesis 4:1-2

> *(1) "And Adam knew Eve his wife;*
> *and she conceived, and bare Cain,*
> *and said, I have gotten a man from the Lord.*
>
> *(2) "And she again bare his brother Abel.*
> *And Abel was a keeper of sheep,*
> *but Cain was a tiller of the ground."*

Organized farming? Check. Domestication of livestock? Check.

Genesis 4:16-17

> *(16) "And Cain went out from the presence of the Lord,*
> *and dwelt in the land of Nod, on the east of Eden.*
>
> *(17) And Cain knew his wife;*
> *and she conceived, and bare Enoch:*
> *and he (Cain) builded a city,*
> *and called the name of the city*
> *after the name of his son, Enoch."*

Let's get this straight. When Cain left home, he journeyed to a known area (the land of Nod), as opposed to wandering off to see what else was out there. Really now?

Referring to outlying areas by name would seem to indicate some sort of division of the surrounding territory, possibly even rudimentary mapping and marking of the landscape.

If you say, "Cain went east," then you're just identifying a general direction of travel. But, if you say, "Cain went to the land of Nod," you're identifying an area with a commonly accepted and recognizable name. If the question is asked, "Where did Cain go?" and the response is, "He went to Nod," that implies that others not only had heard about the land of Nod, but were also able to find it without too much difficulty. One might even raise the question of whether others frequented the land of Nod or resided there on a permanent basis.

The noted first-century Jewish historian, Flavius Josephus, states that Cain traveled over many countries before coming to the land known as Nod.[3] Whereas Josephus is most likely short on eyewitnesses to verify his statement, he's within historical tradition to the point of not being questioned regarding the assertion. The idea of there being "many countries" for Cain to pass through on his way to the land commonly known as Nod certainly paints a different mental image of culture in which Cain lived.

Easton's Bible Dictionary describes Nod as a land of unrest, noting that the word itself means "wandering." Perhaps Nod is the name given to the unsettled area that is just beyond the outskirts of settled lands, making it a heretofore unsettled wilderness.[4]

According to Genesis 4:17, once he settled into the land of Nod, he began a family and built a city. This is beginning to sound more and more like an intelligent people who exhibit the traits of a civilization. Check.

Genesis 4:18

> *"And unto Enoch was born Irad:*
> *and Irad begat Mehujael:*
> *and Mehujael begat Methusael:*
> *and Methusael begat Lamech."*

Genealogical record-keeping and documentation of family lineage? Would uncivilized people keep records? This organizational structure is starting to sound a bit administrative. Check.

Genesis 4:19

> *"And Lamech took unto him two wives:*
> *the name of the one was Adah,*
> *and the name of the other Zillah."*

We've seen several mentions of "wives" thus far. Eve was commonly known as the wife of Adam (Gen. 4:1 & 23). Genesis 4:17 speaks of Cain's wife, and here, Cain's great-great-great-grandson, Lamech, is said to have taken two wives.

Not a lot of information has been recorded about the methods of marriage at this point. We don't know if Lamech asked for their commitment or was gifted them as a part of a trade agreement. Maybe Lamech was in the market for a wife and couldn't decide between the blonde and the brunette, so he opted to purchase one of each. Facetious? Yes, I know. But, the point is, we don't know by what process a man and a woman of that day married.

We do, however, have documentation that they did indeed marry and, once married, someone somewhere kept a record of the authorized and recognized union. We're not told why they kept records or to what extent and purpose the records were used, but there was a record. This continues to sound more and more like the administration of bureaucracy and government. Check.

Genesis 4:20

> "And Adah bare Jabal: he was the father of such as dwell in tents, and of such as have cattle."

Here we have the domestication of livestock again and documentation of people dwelling in tents, not caves, which suggests purposeful mobility. Is this a group of ranchers or an indication of mobile military outposts?

Josephus also mentions that Jabel "loved the life of a shepherd" and Tubal-cain, Jabel's half-brother, was "very expert and famous in martial performances," and refers to these particular descendents of Cain as being "intolerable in war."[5]

It looks like we definitely have continued domestication of livestock and quite possibly we can check "the practice of skilled warfare" off of the list of requirements for the existence of a civilization as well.

Genesis 4:21

> *"And his brother's name was Jubal: he was the father*
> *of all such as handle the harp and organ."*

Okay, wait a minute now. Didn't primitive man take a stick and pound on a log to produce something rhythmic? A harp is a stringed instrument and an organ would produce sounds and tones by the movement of air through different-sized reeds (the woodwind section). If we have music, and it seems as if we do, then we can put a checkmark next to the arts.

Genesis 4:22

> *"And Zillah,* [Lamech's other wife]
> *she also bare Tubal-cain, and instructer*
> *of every artificer in brass and iron:*
> *and the sister of Tubal-cain was Naamah."*

We met Tubal-cain a few paragraphs earlier, but here we find a detailed disclosure of his particular skill set. The word that has been translated "instructer" (Old English spelling) is used only four other times in the Hebrew text: 1st Samuel 13:20, Job 16:9, Psalm 7:12, and Psalm 52:2. In these four occurrences the word is translated as either "sharpen" or "whet."[6] The implication is that of putting the finishing touches on a blade so that it becomes useful.

At first glance it appears that Tubal-cain was a teacher of sorts: an instructor. Although he clearly specialized in working with metals, he was not just a teacher. The use of this particular word points to his advanced skill in working with metals.

There's additional insight provided by the phrase, "every

artificer in brass and iron." The word "artificer" indicates that there were those who already worked with metals. They were known as artificers or metal craftsmen.[7] These people apparently came to Tubal-cain so that they could sharpen their skills. It seems clear that Tubal-cain's knowledge of metallurgy was advanced.

Were they producing metal tools to be used for agriculture or weapons and armor to be used in battle? It's entirely possible that they produced both. They most likely made pots to cook with, as well as utensils, and probably even decorative stuff.

Maybe they even fashioned long brass tubes for Jubal's organs or some sort of framework for his harps. What about horns and trumpets? If you've got elaborate stringed instruments such as a harp and already understand the principles of passing air through tubes to make sound, as would be done with an organ, then why not metal tubes that you could blow into?

We are several generations and most likely hundreds of years removed from Eden at this point. We're seeing construction, agriculture, and the beginnings of industry. Things are starting to look more and more like History World's laundry list of required ingredients to recognize a group of people as a civilization.

As a bit of a side note, I'd like to call attention to the last part of Gen. 4:22, "and the sister of Tubal-cain was Naamah." It's rare that females are listed in Biblical genealogies. When they are, most often it is to identify them as someone's wife and/ or mother. While this is certainly the case with the mention of Adah and Zillah, in this instance there's an even greater significance.

Adah and Zillah are identified in the Book of Jasher as the daughters of Seth's grandson, Cainan (Jasher 2:16). The passage identifies Cainan as a ruling monarch in verses 12-14 and reveals that Lamech became related to Cainan by this marriage. This entry in the ancient Jewish history book appears to be a record of a political union of sorts between descendants in the lineage of Cain with those in the lineage of his brother, Seth, through the legally binding agreement of marriage.

This type of arrangement would certainly seem to fall under our requirements for a group of people to be considered as a civilization. In fact, these ancients seem to be much more civilized that we might have initially expected.

Naamah, the daughter of Lamech and Zillah, is mentioned as Tubal-cain's sister, but no additional information is given about her. Some scholars have misidentified her as the wife of Noah.[8,9] The Book of Jasher identifies Noah's wife as Naamah, but specifies that she is the daughter of Enoch through the lineage of Adam's son, Seth. The Book of Jubilees, another ancient Jewish book of history that is highly regarded for its content, but sometimes questioned regarding precision, identifies Noah's wife as Emzara, the daughter of Noah's uncle, Rake'el (Jubilees 4:33). We'll dig more deeply into the mystery of Noah's wife a bit later.

Naamah is featured in early art and can be seen pictured with her half-brother, Jubal, in a bas relief in Orvieto Cathedral, a 14th-century Roman Catholic cathedral in Orvieto, Italy.

Jubal is recognized as the father of music and Naamah is said to be a teacher of reading.

It's certain that she's mentioned because she is significant, but there is no record, other than the Jasher reference regarding her mother being the daughter of Cainan, that identifies with certainty the nature of her importance. But suppose that she was a teacher of reading, as the bas relief suggests: to have reading, we must first have writing and writing would certainly qualify as a cornerstone ingredient for any developing civilization.

We Are Not Alone

The record seems to indicate that Adam and Eve's son, Cain, carved out quite the legacy after leaving home. The narrative describes architecture, agriculture, the arts and industry. The descendants of Cain appear to be craftsmen with a wide range of skill and intellectual knowledge.

The opening verses of Genesis chapter 4 mentioned a pair of sons who were born to Adam and Eve, and it seems that almost anyone would recognize their names – Cain and Abel. Verses 3 through 15 tell the story of a history-altering event that happened at some point after the two brothers had reached adulthood.

We are told that Cain was a tiller of the ground, a gardener, and that Abel was a shepherd. Evidently both had been taught by Adam to observe sacrificial offerings to God, but when the time comes, each brings a different offering. Cain brings a collection from the harvest. Abel's offering is the firstborn lamb, chosen from the "fat" or best of his flock.

Of the two offerings, only Abel's is found to be acceptable. There's no indication that Cain's offering was not the best that he could bring, only that it wasn't the type of offering required. Cain took the rejection very hard and his bitter disappointment turned to burning anger. Genesis 4:8 tells of a post-offering altercation that ended with Cain taking the life of his younger brother. This is the first documented act of violence between humans, and Cain is ultimately banished by God himself because of his deed (Gen. 4:11-12).

No specific time line is given as to the ages of Cain and Abel when this incident happened, and nothing in the text indicates that this was the first time the two had brought sacrificial offerings to God. Sometimes identifying what we don't know can be a very important part of coming to an understanding of things that we do know.

Genesis 4:6-7a

> (6) "And the Lord said unto Cain, Why art thou wroth? and why is thy countenance fallen?"

> (7a) "If thou doest well, shalt thou not be accepted?"

From this we can see that Cain knew what to do and how to do it. The rhetorical question, "Shalt thou not be accepted?" seems to indicate with very good probability that Cain had brought offerings to God in the past that had been accepted. This Q&A between Cain and God takes place prior to Cain's confrontation with Abel.

Genesis 4:13-14

> *(13) "And Cain said unto the Lord,*
> *My punishment is greater than I can bear.*
>
> *(14) "Behold, thou has driven me out this day*
> *from the face of the earth; and from thy face*
> *shall I be hid; and I shall be a fugitive and a vagabond*
> *in the earth; and it shall come to pass,*
> *that everyone that findeth me shall slay me."*

This conversation takes place after Cain has confessed to Abel's murder and been sentenced by God. It's the last phrase of Cain's response that is particularly interesting. To this point in the Biblical record, we have the mention of Adam, Eve, Cain and Abel. Abel is dead and buried, but Cain's assertion of "everyone that findeth me shall slay me," is a clear acknowledgement by Cain that by this point in time there is an abundance of people living on the earth. Although the Old Testament text has only named the four previously mentioned, this statement pulls back the curtain and makes us aware of the fact that they are not alone.

There is a collection of ancient Hebrew manuscripts known as the Apocrypha. Whereas some of these writings were considered to be a sacred portion of the ancient Hebrew Scriptures at some point in the past, they were separated as manuscripts of uncertain origin and thus excluded from the canon of Old Testament books during the Reformation of the 1500s.[10]

The manuscripts were, however, considered to be from highly esteemed sources and thus continued to be recommended reading by most scholars. There is a secondary group of ancient historical manuscripts known as the Pseudepigrapha. Although these manuscripts are regarded as having been initially recorded by ancient Jewish patriarchs and prophets, most of the texts currently available cannot be traced back beyond 200 BC.[11] It's among these texts that we find a collection of writings known as the Book of Jubilees, which may offer some additional insight.

Genesis 5:3-4 tells us that in his 930 years of life, Adam had many children – both sons and daughters. The ones of great magnitude are mentioned by name, but we are assured that there were many others who go unnamed and unreferenced.

The Book of Jubilees indicates that Adam and Eve had enjoyed seven wonderful years of bliss in the Garden of Eden before the serpent began calling to Eve from the forbidden tree. In fact, we're told that the big event happened on the 17th day of the second month of the eighth year (Jubilees 3:17). How's that for putting an anniversary date on when things went south?

Again, let's take a moment to clarify what we know that we don't know. We don't know if Adam and Eve had any children before the fall. A valid argument can easily be made to support either point of view. There's no definitive proof to support either perception, only conjecture. (I cover this topic in greater detail in *My End of the Circle*, a companion book to this volume.)

When it comes to the birth of children prior to the fall, we just don't know. We do know, however, that before the close of the sixth day of creation (Gen. 1:28), they were commanded by God to *"be fruitful and multiply."* It seems evident that this commandment clearly precedes the seduction of Eve by the serpent, as God said that everything was *"very good"* at that point in time (Gen. 1:31).

We also don't know with certainty that Cain was the first son born to Adam and Eve. In essence, Adam and Eve may have had a number of children in that seven-year period before being driven out of the Garden of Eden, even though none of them are specifically mentioned by name.

The Book of Jubilees commonly speaks of a period of seven years as a "week" and states in Jubilees 3:34 that Adam and Eve did not have a son until after the first week of the first Jubilee had passed (years one through seven). It does not specify that they had no children at all during that first seven years in the garden. Jubilees 3:17 identifies year eight as the first year outside of the garden and mentions that the first son was born afterwards.

In Jubilees 4:1, a window of time is given for the birth of Cain, as opposed to an exact year, *"the third week of the second Jubilee"* (between years 64 and 70). This window separates his birth from the garden expulsion by at least 56 years, leaving plenty of room to question whether he was indeed the firstborn son, as commonly assumed. Jubilees 3:34 does not say that Cain was Adam and Eve's first son. It simply states that their first son (whomever it may have been) was born outside of Eden.

Genesis 3:16 outlines a specific judgment for Eve as a result of the fall. From that moment, moving forward, Eve (and all women presumably) would experience intense pain when giving birth. Had she previously brought children into the world without experiencing such pain?

The forbidden tree was, after all, the Tree of Knowledge of Good *and Evil*. Perhaps Adam and Eve had only the knowledge of good prior to the fall.

Jubilees 4:1 says the following, with regard to Eve:

> *"...in the third week in the second jubilee*
> *[years 64-70 A.M.] she [Eve] gave birth to Cain,*
> *and in the fourth [years 71-77 A.M.]*
> *she gave birth to Abel,*
> *and in the fifth [years 78-84 A.M.]*
> *she gave birth to her daughter Awan."*

A.M. is the designation Anno Mundi, which is Latin for "In the Year of the World" or "Year after Creation."[12]

In the Book of Jubilees, years are recorded in brackets of seven and referred to as a week of years. Seven weeks of years is equal to 49 years in all and is designated as a Jubilee. So, the first Jubilee is the grouping of year 1 through year 49. The second Jubilee begins with year 50 and continues through year 98. (See Chart #1.)

Overall Jubilee #	Overall Span of Yrs	Wk in the Jubilee	Overall Wk of Yrs	Yrs w/in the Week
1	1-49	First	First	1-7
		Second	Second	8-14
		Third	Third	15-21
		Fourth	Fourth	22-28
		Fifth	Fifth	29-35
		Sixth	Sixth	36-42
		Seventh	Seventh	43-49
2	50-98	First	Eighth	50-56
		Second	Ninth	57-63
		Third	Tenth	64-70
		Fourth	Eleventh	71-77
		Fifth	Twelfth	78-84
		Sixth	Thirteenth	85-91
		Seventh	Fourteenth	92-98

Chart #1

The count of weeks starts anew with each Jubilee, thus the first week of a Jubilee year is a reference to the first seven years of that particular Jubilee. When reference is made to the third week of the second Jubilee, the document is identifying a period of time that includes years 64 through 70. (See Chart #2.) Cain is said to be born during this period of time. This is at least 56 years after Adam and Eve are expelled from the Garden of Eden.

Overall Jubilee #	Overall Span of Yrs	Wk in the Jubilee	Overall Wk of Yrs	Yrs w/in the Week
1	1-49	First	First	1-7
		Second	Second	8-14
		Third	Third	15-21
		Fourth	Fourth	22-28
		Fifth	Fifth	29-35
		Sixth	Sixth	36-42
		Seventh	Seventh	43-49
2	50-98	First	Eighth	50-56
		Second	Ninth	57-63
		Third	**Tenth**	**64-70**
		Fourth	Eleventh	71-77
		Fifth	Twelfth	78-84
		Sixth	Thirteenth	85-91
		Seventh	Fourteenth	92-98

Chart #2

Abel is born during the fourth week of years (years 71 through 77). Jubilees doesn't specify the exact year. At some point during the fifth week (years 78 through 84), a daughter is born. Her name is Awan.

According to Jubilees 4:9, she becomes the wife of Cain, at some point in the seventh week of the fourth Jubilee (years 190 through 196).

Jubilees 4:2 indicates that the confrontation between Cain and Abel occurred in the first week of the third Jubilee. This places it somewhere between year 99 and year 105. That's a rather large time window in our terms, but it does give us some perspective. This is more than 90 years after being expelled from Eden.

The timetable places Cain's age somewhere in his 30s. The youngest he could be is 29. (See Chart #3.) The oldest he could be is 41. (See Chart #4.)

Event	Jubilee Year	Actual Year
Murder	First Year of	
of Abel	Jubilee 3 Wk 1	Year 99
Birth	Last Year of	
of Cain	Jubilee 2 Wk 3	Year 70
Length of Time		
Between Events		29 Years Old

Chart #3

Event	Jubilee Year	Actual Year
Murder	Last Year of	
of Abel	Jubilee 3 Wk 1	Year 105
Birth	1st Year of	
of Cain	Jubilee 2 Wk 3	Year 64
Length of Time		
Between Events		41 Years Old

Chart #4

Using the same calculations, we can figure that Abel is at least 22 years old (See Chart #5.) and could not be older than 34. (See Chart #6.)

Event	Jubilee Year	Actual Year
Murder	First Year of	
of Abel	Jubilee 3 Wk 1	Year 99
Birth	Last Year of	
of Abel	Jubilee 2 Wk 4	Year 77
Length of Time		
Between Events		22 Years Old

Chart #5

Event	Jubilee Year	Actual Year
Murder	Last Year of	
of Abel	Jubilee 3 Wk 1	Year 105
Birth	1st Year of	
of Abel	Jubilee 2 Wk 4	Year 71
Length of Time		
Between Events		34 Years Old

Chart #6

If there were other children born to Adam and Eve before the births of Cain and Abel (and there may have been many), the youngest child would be at least 29 years of age (the minimum calculation of the age of Cain when he killed Abel). At this age, it would not be unreasonable to presume that they were able to produce children of their own and at least some of them were most likely doing so.

The dates given in the Book of Jubilees confirm that Cain and Abel's sister, Awan, was at least in her teens by this time, and there certainly could have been other siblings who were born in the time period between the birth of Cain and the fatal confrontation.

Cain's fear that someone, possibly even an entire group of people, would track him down and seek to avenge the death of Abel is clearly justified. He's not imagining ghosts or demons. He's thinking of his other brothers and sisters, or possibly even nephews and nieces. (Cain would not have had uncles, aunts or cousins.)

To Heir Is Human

Finding that the Biblical account gives such detail of Cain's lineage is absolutely remarkable. Cast aside after taking the life of his younger brother, it would be understandable for the heritage of Cain to be largely ignored following his banishment, yet just the opposite is true.

It's evident that Cain is not the only branch in the family tree. But did Adam and Eve give birth to anyone else who left a documented legacy?

Genesis 4:25

> "And Adam knew his wife again; and she bare a son,
> and called his name Seth: For God, said she,
> hath appointed me another seed instead of Abel,
> whom Cain slew."

The Book of Jubilees notes that Adam and Eve mourned the loss of Abel for nearly 30 years (Jub. 4:7). It identifies this time period as years 99 through 127. Eventually the mourning comes to an end and life returns to some form of normal. Then, in the year 130, Seth is born (Jub.4:7) and Eve rejoices exceedingly.

A daughter is born to Adam and Eve a few years later. She is named Azura (Jub.4:8). At some point between years 225 and 231, Seth takes Azura to be his wife (Jub.4:11). In year 235, Seth and Azura give birth to a son and name him Enos (Jub.4:11). Seth is 105 years of age when Enos is born. This same timeline is documented in Genesis 5:6.

Thus begins the narration of Genesis 5, which details more than 1,000 years of family lineage traceable through Seth all the way back to Adam. Being Seth's family records, it's likely that most of it was personally witnessed and recorded by Seth himself. The inclusions of the time of death for both Adam and Seth make it clear that another prominent family member, possibly Enoch, takes on the responsibility of preserving the record in the latter years of Seth's life. It's also noteworthy that in this lineage the age of the father at the time of the son's birth is listed, as opposed to the loosely defined "week" of years we saw with Cain, Abel and Awan.

As the lineage unfolds, we see the birth of several dynamic individuals:

- Enos – In whose time people began to seek knowledge from God (Jubilees 4:12).
- Cainan – Previously referenced as the highest ranking monarch and father of Adah and Zillah (Jasher 2:10-16).

- Enoch – Noted as a person who "*walked with God*" (Gen. 5:21-24), wrote about many mystical revelations and apparently never died.

- Methuselah – Famous as the one who lived longer than any other person in world history (969 years, according to Gen. 5:25-27).

- And eventually, Noah – the builder of the ark.

The lineage is also spelled out in great detail by the Book of Jubilees. We'll use both the Book of Jubilees and the Biblical text as we work our way through the documented dawn of human history. Genesis provides an accurate time stamp of both the births and the deaths of each person listed. The Book of Jubilees adds insight as to each person's wife and even gives her heritage. All listed dates are A.M. (Anno Mundi) or the "Year of the World" (from the creation of Adam).

Sometime between years 309 and 315 (third week of the seventh Jubilee) we find that Enos, the son of Seth, takes a woman named Noam to be his wife (Jub.4:13). Noam is identified as the sister of Enos, presumably his blood sister as opposed to half-sister.

Genesis 4:26 states that during the time period into which Enos was born, men began to call on the name of the Lord. No specific year is given as to when this began to occur, but it is noteworthy and the Book of Jasher adds that Seth names his son Enos for this very reason (Jasher 2:2). The word translated "call" in the Genesis passage is used in a variety of ways, including the concept of crying aloud for help.[13]

Although God once walked in the Garden with Adam during the cool of the day (Gen. 3:8), now there are a multitude of people living on the earth, and apparently personal communication with God had become a thing of the past.

In year 325, Enos and Noam give birth to a son whom they name Cainan. His name is spelled Kenan in the Book of Jubilees, but the reference is to the same person. Enos is 90 years old when Cainan is born (Gen. 5:9).

You may remember the name Cainan from the family of Cain. In fact, you may see several names over the next few paragraphs that look familiar. Don't let it become confusing. The names mentioned in Seth's genealogy are completely different people from those mentioned in the genealogy of Cain.

Sometime between years 386 and 392, Cainan takes his sister, Mualeleth, as his wife. In year 395, they give birth to a son that they name Mahalaleel. Cainan is 70 years of age (Gen. 5:12).

> **SIDE NOTE:** This is the same Cainan who later fathers Adah and Zillah, the two wives of Lamech in the previously reviewed lineage of Cain. He is also noted in the Book of Jasher as the ruling monarch (Ch. 2:11-14). Thus, the rest of the names that are listed in this lineage are a part of a royal line of descendants.

Sometime between years 449 and 455, Mahalaleel takes a woman named Dinah as his wife. She is identified as the daughter of Mahalaleel's uncle, making her a first cousin. The practice of marrying the daughter of an uncle (never an aunt) continues from this point. In year 461, the couple give birth to a son and name him Jared. Mahalaleel is 65 years old (Gen, 5:15).

If you've been doing your own math and counting the years as we go along, you'll notice that an extra year has been gained. Keep in mind that Genesis only lists the age of the father at the birth of the son, while the Book of Jubilees has been identifying a specific year. Since neither text specifies a month in which someone was born, there is no real discrepancy at this point. The extra year, as specified in Jubilees, has been added here, but the dates listed in Jubilees begin to break down from this point forward.

For those of you who would like sharpen a pencil and work your way line by line through the spine-tingling details of the genealogy as it is given in the Book of Jubilees, we've included the unabridged version in Appendix 1.

Jared takes a woman named Baraka as his wife sometime between years 519 and 525. As you may have guessed, she is identified as his first cousin through his uncle, Rasujal. (Yes, the names of the uncles are also meticulously recorded. It is after all a royal bloodline.) Jared and Baraka give birth to a son in year 623 whom they name Enoch.

Enoch becomes a mysterious central figure of early world history. His writings, once thought by some to be forever lost, have become particularly relevant within the last 75 years. Later, we'll look into some of Enoch's writings as we seek to gather additional insight about some of the unusual happenings in the years before the flood. Genesis states that Jared was 162 years of age when Enoch was born (Gen. 5:18).

Enoch marries his first cousin, Edna, and the couple give birth to a son that they name Methuselah when Enoch is 65 years of age (Gen. 5:21). Born in year 688, Methuselah enjoys a longer recorded life span than any other person who ever lived. He dies at age 969. The great flood begins in the same year that Methuselah died. That would be Year of the World 1657 for those who are itching to jump ahead. Writers know who you are!

The name given for Methuselah's wife is also Edna. I'd mention that she's his first cousin, but you've probably already filled in that blank. Methuselah is said to be 187 years old when he and Edna give birth to a son they name Lamech (Gen 5:25). This brings us to year 875 and Adam still has 55 golden years ahead of him before he finally passes away at age 930 (Gen. 5:5). It seems doubtful that he personally knew all of his grandchildren and their children, etc. But logistically, it's a very realistic possibility. At the very least, it would seem that they were uniquely aware of the living, breathing, first man – Adam.

Lamech takes Betenos as his wife. When Lamech is 182 years old, the couple gives birth to a son whom they name Noah (Gen. 5:28). This is year 1057 AM. The birth of Noah is a very unusual event and we'll look at it in detail when we come to the chapter on Noah's life. Late in his life, Noah becomes the builder of the ark. The flood begins 600 years, one month and 17 days after Noah is born.

> **SIDE NOTE:** Genesis 7:11 plainly states that the flood begins in the 600th year of Noah's life, in the second month and on the 17th day. This is Year of the World 1657. Jasher 4:13 indicates that Noah was born on the

first day of the new year. The Book of Jubilees gives a precise calendar date for the fall of man in the Garden of Eden – the 17th day of the second month of Year of the World 8 (Jub. 3:17). Could it be possible that the flood began exactly 1,650 years from the fall of man to the day?

The documented lineage of Seth precisely spells out the first 1,000 years of Earth history. It spans the entire 930-year lifetime of Adam. According to Genesis 5:8, Seth lived 912 years. Having been born in year 130, that takes us to year 1042. If the count of years is correct, then both Adam and Seth lived to see the birth of Lamech, but neither lived to see the birth of Noah.

Methuselah also lived over 900 years and, as previously noted, he died in the same year that the great flood began. We'll uncover a few interesting details about the impact he may have had in a later chapter. From the birth of Noah in year 1057 to the great flood in year 1657, the only additional births that are noted are those of Noah's three sons, all of whom are born after Noah reaches 500 years of age (Gen. 5:32).

In Seth's lineage, we meet some individuals of world renown and impact: Enos, Cainan, Enoch, and Methuselah. We have a direct record of an uncorrupted bloodline from Noah back to Adam, which will prove to be of vital consequence. We also have a significant change of tradition from the practice of marriage between siblings early on, to the act of marriage between first cousins. This maintains a very strict and direct descendant bloodline. We're told of a period of time in which the interaction between God and man changed in the days of

Enos. And, as we shall see, we have a period of time in which supernatural revelation is ordained during the days of Jared and his son, Enoch.

Beware the Others

With the exception of the Cain and Abel incident, life outside of the garden has rocked along pretty smoothly to this point, but things are about to get a little rocky over the next few pages. Actually, things are about to get wildly out of hand and you might want to buckle up. This is the stuff of which legends are made.

Let's revisit Genesis 4:25,

> *"And Adam knew his wife again; and she bare a son,*
> *and called his name Seth: For God, said she,*
> *hath appointed me another seed instead of Abel,*
> *whom Cain slew."*

It seems evident that Adam and Eve had a large number of children. Jubilees 4:10 refers to the births of nine additional sons after Seth. Couple these sons' own offspring with the activity of their children producing children, and it would be well within reason to project an ever-expanding family tree. That being said, the last phrase of this verse is absolutely astounding: *"For God, said she, hath appointed me another seed instead of Abel...."*

The birth of Seth, in the eyes of Eve, was the express fulfillment of an ancient prophecy that was initially unveiled by God while Adam and Eve were still living in the Garden of Eden.

The prophecy is given as a part of the serpent's judgment for his role in the fall.

Genesis 3:14-15

> *(14) "And the Lord God said unto the serpent,*
> *Because thou hast done this, thou art cursed above all cattle,*
> *and above every beast of the field;*
> *upon thy belly shalt thy go, and dust shalt thy eat*
> *all the days of thy life:*
>
> *(15) "And I will put enmity between thee and the woman,*
> *and between thy seed and her seed;*
> *it shall bruise thy head, and thou shalt bruise his heel."*

Apparently Abel was to be the progenitor of the Adamic bloodline. No wonder Adam and Eve mourned so when Cain took Abel's life. The promised seed of the woman, which Eve saw passing through Abel, was cut off before Abel could extend the bloodline. The heel had been bruised!

For nearly 30 years Adam and Eve continued to mourn the loss of Abel, until the birth of Seth breathes new life into the mysterious Garden of Eden Prophecy.

The royal bloodline of Adam was now alive in Seth. Hence, we see the reason that the lineage of Seth is so carefully documented. From the birth of Seth to the future birth of Noah, the bloodline is meticulously traced, verified and recorded. As we shall see, it is the future of this bloodline that comes under attack.

All seems right with the world, but it most certainly isn't. Genesis 3:15 references the existence of an alternate seed, the seed of the serpent. We traditionally trace bloodlines through the father, but it's Eve who recognizes and proclaims the significance of the birth of Seth, and the Genesis reference calls attention to her seed, not Adam's. This is a prophetic statement, as it was yet to happen, and it seems clear that the message was not lost on Adam and Eve, particularly Eve.

There are some who identify Cain as the seed of the serpent, but this can't be a reference to Cain. Even though he has been banished and apparently cut off, he is unquestionably a permanent part of the bloodline of Adam and Eve.

Many hours of reading and a wide variety of sources were consulted in an effort to research information for this section. Having pored over the accounts given from so many different authors, both ancient and modern, it would be easy to get caught up in the descriptive language and begin to dramatize the revelations of what apparently transpired.

If you gravitate towards something sensational, search keyword "giants" on YouTube and you'll find a rich supply of audio and video clips, ranging from riveting to unwatchable.

For our purposes, we're solely interested in what the cross-referenced testimony of the ancient documents support. Are the tales of human-angelic hybrids legendary fiction? Or could these stories be built upon the preserved eyewitness archives of actual events that transpired before the flood?

Christ himself referred to the horrifying days of Noah to illustrate a time of future calamity. He then went on to declare that no one would survive the perilous time to come if the days were not shortened (Matthew 24). Was he confirming the report of the ancient scribes as accurate and trustworthy?

Or was Christ embellishing his personal portrait of the end of days in an effort to emotionally motivate his audience?

Daniel, a Hebrew captive of Babylon circa 606 BC, points to a "time of trouble such as never was," in the 12th chapter of his prophecy. This time period, according to Daniel, will arrive just before the end of days. In chapter 4 of his manuscript, Daniel identifies the source of his information as "one of the watchers," an angelic messenger-being whose role it was to impart knowledge and spiritual wisdom to mankind (Daniel 4:13 & 17). Who were these watchers? Where did they come from? When did they get involved in the events of human history? What was their agenda?

There is a multitude of reference material on the Watchers. They show up in ancient literature from nearly every culture and in almost every known language. Sometimes they're referred to as Fallen Angels or Sky Gods. Some have suggested that the Watchers are the famed Annunaki or possibly the Igigi that are written about in ancient Sumerian and Assyrian lore. A person could literally spend years doing nothing but reading manuscripts and commentary of what others have already written on the subject.

Most agree that it is the Watchers who are the focal point of Genesis 6:4,

> *"There were giants in the earth in those days:*
> *and also after that, when the sons of God*
> *came unto the daughters of men,*
> *and they bare children to them, the same became*
> *mighty men which were of old, men of renown."*

That small reference in Genesis opens the door to a multitude of speculation and conjecture. Some have argued that these "sons of God" were the violent, war-mongering descendants of Cain. But, as we have already noted, Cain and his descendants were irrevocably of the bloodline of Adam and Eve. Cut off, banished, rejected and disinherited though he might be, Cain was still without question the flesh-and-blood child of Adam and Eve.

The description given in Genesis 6:4 discloses something that was much more substantial than the return of a vanquished son to raid the inner circle and steal away the fairest of the fair.

Noted scholar and author of numerous volumes of biblical commentary, Matthew Henry, presents the "sons of God" as the godly descendants in the lineage of Seth and portrays the "daughters of men" as seducing women from the lineage of Cain.[14] But, as we shall see, there is ample documentation to identify the "sons of God" and none of it supports the idea that they are descendents of Seth.

Genesis 6 introduces the title reference "sons of God" as a known designation. Hence, there should be no real mystery as to their identity. This curious distinctive phrase is used elsewhere only in the Book of Job (commonly pronounced: Jōbe):

Job 1:6

*"Now there was a day when the **sons of God** came to present themselves before the Lord, and Satan came also among them.*

Job 2:1

> *"Again there was a day when the **sons of God**
> came to present themselves before the Lord,
> and Satan came also among them
> to present himself before the Lord.*

Job 38:4-7

> *(4) "Where wast thou when I laid the foundations of the earth?
> Declare, if thou hast understanding.*
>
> *(5) "Who hath laid the measures thereof, if thou knowest?
> Or who hath stretched the line upon it?*
>
> *(6) "Whereupon are the foundations thereof fastened?
> Or who laid the corner stone thereof:*
>
> *(7) "When the morning stars sang together,
> and all the **sons of God** shouted for joy?"*

In each of these passages it would seem abundantly clear that the phrase "sons of God" does not reference flesh-and-blood human beings, but rather a group of spiritual beings that are uniquely acquainted with the presence of God. In fact, according to the Job 38 passage, it seems evident that these beings were unquestionably present when the initial creation of the world took place.

The first human being (Adam) wasn't present until the sixth day, and this was after everything else had been created and set into motion (Gen. 1:24-31). As we discovered previously, Cain wasn't born until at least 64 years after creation and Seth wasn't born until year 130.

It seems conclusive that the reference "sons of God" applies to a group of beings that were in existence before Adam was formed from dust and long before either Cain or Seth was born. The "sons of God" are not flesh-and-blood humans and they most certainly are not the descendants of Cain or Seth.

The "sons of God" are also referenced in Genesis 6:2. Once again, they're identified as having found the daughters of men, the flesh-and-blood female children of Adam and Eve's family tree, desirable. Genesis 6:2 says that the daughters of men were so desirable that the sons of God "*took them wives of all which they chose.*"

The Hebrew word that is translated as "took" in Genesis 6:2 is the word "*laqach*" (lä•kakh'), which means to take something by force, to seize, snatch or take away.[15] It's the same word that is used in Genesis 2:21 in reference to God taking a rib from Adam's side and using it to fashion Eve.

The picture could very easily be painted of these women being abducted or taken by force from their homes and families. Genesis 6:2 says that the sons of God "*laqach*" (took by force) "all of which they chose," and nowhere in the record does it indicate that anything was done in an effort to stop them.

Allow yourself to think for just a brief moment of the efforts you would make if your child was taken by force from your home. There would be no end to the limits you would push in your effort to get her back home safe and sound, especially if you knew who took her or where she had been taken. If these were the descendants of Cain, it would seem reasonable to find records of battles between the two warring groups of people. On the contrary, nothing is said with regard to such a confrontation.

So if they weren't flesh-and-blood humans, where did they come from? And, how, why and when did they get involved in the affairs of mankind?

Genesis 6:4 directs the reader's attention to appearance of "giants" in the earth. It goes on to state that these giants were evident during two distinct periods of time: "in those days" and "also after that." The cause or source is clearly identified as being because "the sons of God" became physically involved with "the daughters of men" and offspring were produced as a result of the union.

There's a whole lot of stuff in that one short passage. And, quite frankly, there's a complete genre of modern literature that is dedicated to proposing hypothetical scenarios. It would be so easy to redirect the focus towards such a rabbit hole and chase a seemingly endless array of storylines.

In an effort to gain a little clarity and to avoid interjecting our own imagination as to what happened; we'll rely on additional information from the Book of Jubilees, the Book of Enoch and the Jewish historian, Flavius Josephus.

Jubilees 4:15

> *"And in the second week of the tenth jubilee*
> *[years 449-455 A.M.] Mahalalel took unto him to wife*
> *Dinah, the daughter of Barakiel the daughter of his father's brother,*
> *and she bare him a son in the third week*
> *in the sixth year, [year 461 A.M.] and he called his name Jared,*
> **for in his days the angels of the Lord descended on the earth,**
> **those who are named the Watchers, that they should instruct the**
> **children of men, and that they should do judgment and**
> **uprightness on the earth."**

Mahalalel and his wife, Dinah, gave birth to a son in Year of the World 461 and named him Jared, which means "descent" or "descending."[16] It would seem that Jared was born and named shortly after the initial arrival of the Watchers from the heavens.

With respect to the growing number of proponents of Ancient Astronaut Theory, these were not "flesh-and-blood extraterrestrials" and they were not misidentified by our ancient ancestors.[17] It's very clear that people knew who they were, where they came from and why they came.

According to Jubilees 4:15, the Watchers were to instruct the children of men (Adam's descendants, including the lineage of Cain) for the purpose of sound judgment and uprightness. They did not come of their own accord as an invading force, they were sent. And they were sent to teach good things!

Jubilees 4:16-21

> (16) "And in the eleventh jubilee [years 512-518 A.M.] Jared
> took to himself a wife, and her name was Baraka, the daughter
> of Rasujal, a daughter of his father's brother, in the fourth week of
> this jubilee, [year 522 A.M.] and she bare him a son
> in the fifth week, in the fourth year of the jubilee,
> **and he called his name Enoch.**

> (17) "And he [Enoch] was the first among men that are born
> on earth who learnt writing and knowledge and wisdom
> and who wrote down the signs of heaven according to the order of
> their months in a book, that men might know the seasons of the
> years according to the order of their separate months.

> (18) "And he [Enoch] was the first to write a testimony
> and he testified to the sons of men among the generations
> of the earth, and recounted the weeks of the jubilees,
> and made known to them the days of the years,

*and set in order the months and recounted the Sabbaths
of the years as we [the Watchers] made (them), known to him.*

*(19) "And what was and what will be he [Enoch] saw in a vision
of his sleep, as it will happen to the children of men throughout their
generations until the day of judgment;
he saw and understood everything, and wrote his testimony,
and placed the testimony on earth for all the children
of men and for their generations.*

*(20) "And in the twelfth jubilee, [years 582-588 A.M.] in the seventh
week thereof, he [Enoch] took to himself a wife, and her name was
Edna, the daughter of Danel, the daughter of his father's brother,
and in the sixth year in this week [year 587 A.M.] she bare him a son
and he called his name Methuselah.*

*(21) "And he [Enoch] was moreover with the angels of God these six
jubilees of years, and **they showed him [Enoch] everything which is
on earth and in the heavens, the rule of the sun,
and he wrote down everything."***

Enoch is born about 60 years after the initial arrival of the Watchers and becomes the prize student of their teaching during the early portion of his lifetime. We are told that they taught him writing and that he was instructed to write down all the things that he was being taught, presumably so that it could be preserved and passed down to future generations.

Enoch wrote about the history of the world prior to his birth and the happenings of his lifetime. He also wrote in prophetic detail about the full record of human history, beginning with his time period and stretching forward beyond our present day.

The writings of Enoch were discovered as a part of 972 texts uncovered in modern times, between 1946 and 1956, in caves overlooking the Dead Sea at Khirbet Qumran. Though difficult to verify its authenticity, one of the scrolls found in the cave is acclaimed as a copy of the legendary Book of Enoch.

More complete copies of the text have been found in Ethiopia. The Ethiopian copies are commonly accepted by the Ethiopian Orthodox Tewahedo Church as a sacred part of their biblical text. In the first century AD, the writer of the New Testament book of Jude quotes directly from the Book of Enoch. Verses 14 and 15 of the single-chapter book of Jude are almost a direct word-for-word quotation of Enoch 1:9, depending on which translation of Jude and Enoch are being matched up.

At some point in the early years of Enoch's life, the interaction between mankind and the Watchers take a turn. In the sixth chapter of his book, Enoch notes that the children of men (a reference to all of the descendants of Adam and Eve) had multiplied greatly in the earth and that their daughters were beginning to attract the interests of the Watchers.

Enoch 6:1-2

> *(1) "And it came to pass when the children of men*
> *had multiplied, that in those days were born unto them*
> *beautiful and comely daughters.*
> *(2) "And the angels, the children of the heaven,*
> *saw and lusted after them (the daughters of men),*
> *and said to one another: Come, let us choose us wives*
> *from among the children of men to beget us children."*

Nowhere do we have indication that fathering children was ever a part of the original mission. The Watchers were to instruct men in the ways of sound judgment and uprightness. They were sent to guide men and to help men fulfill their mission on the earth, which was to be the righteous custodian or steward of God's creation (Gen. 1:26).

The holy, appointed position of man was somewhat forfeited and damaged when Eden was lost. Mankind's intended status suffered even more when Abel was slain. Now, four and five generations later (a little over 450 years after creation), man was in need of personal tutorage on a higher level.

Apparently the Watchers fulfilled that role for more than 160 years, with the birth of Jared being the time period of their arrival and sometime after the birth of Enoch being the time period when some abandoned their primary mission.

There is evidence, as seen in the Daniel passage, that many of the Watchers stayed true to their original mission as designated emissaries and continued to provide guidance and wisdom for mankind. In fact, Daniel even credits the Watchers for providing insight to the Babylonian king, Nebuchadnezzar (Dan. 4:23). Daniel's historical point of reference is nearly 2,000 years after the great flood.

Enoch's writings, chapters 6 and following, reflect the actions of small group of the Watchers who had turned their attention to their own desires. In so doing, their objective takes a distinct shift from being the supernatural mentors of the children of men to the commitment of fathering children of their own.

Enoch 6:3 gives the name of their leader as Semjaza and indicates that he was somewhat hesitant to enact this plan out of fear that he would be held solely responsible for the deeds. The next verses indicate that Semjaza is reassured by his chief captains that they're on board with the plan, will instruct their subordinates to follow through and will stand with him in the event of judgment.

The names of 19 of Semjaza's leaders are listed in Enoch 6:7. Each is said to be the chief of a group of nine additional Watchers. These leaders and their charges, added to Semjaza and the nine directly under his charge, make for 200 in all. Together they vow allegiance to the proposal.

Enoch 6:4

> *"And they all answered him and said: 'Let us swear an oath, and all bind ourselves by mutual imprecations not to abandon this plan but to do this thing.'"*

The plan was in place and the oath had been taken. Genesis 3:15 forewarned of the coming seed/bloodline of the serpent and with 200 Watchers now expressly dedicated to a new mission, it seems as if the serpent's bloodline is on the horizon.

There's New Kids on the Block

There's a multitude of information available in Biblical and non-Biblical literature about the Watchers. Knowing who they were and what their mission was (and apparently still is to this day) will prove helpful as we take a detailed look at the actions of a band of 200 that are identified by Enoch.

The word that is translated as "watcher" in the prophecy of Daniel is the Aramaic word, "`iyr," (pronounced: ēr) and it's only found in the fourth chapter of Daniel.[1] According to *Strong's Hebrew Lexicon*, it comes from the root word, "`uwr," (pronounced: ür), which is used 81 times and most often translated as "lift or stir up" (40 times) or as "awake or wake" (31 times).[2] The concept, according to *Strong's Hebrew Lexicon*, is that of having one's eyes opened by being aroused from slumber.

The serpent used a similar term in Genesis 3:5,

> *"For God doth know that in the day ye eat thereof,*
> *then your eyes shall be opened, and ye shall be*
> *as gods, knowing good and evil."[3]*

The words of the serpent from Genesis 3 speak to the attainment of knowledge that had to this point remained hidden from Adam and Eve. Their eyes would be "opened" or "awakened" to it. They would be aware of things in the world around them that they had not previously perceived. It was the ability to know and experience both good and evil. Before this, Adam and Eve knew only of good.

Often the question is asked why a loving God would allow horrific and savage things to happen in our world. It would seem clear that it was never his intention. Throughout the first and second chapters of Genesis, we're told that all things were good. It was a desire to experience more that brought mankind face to face with the knowledge of evil.

It was mankind's thirst for knowledge that paved the way for supernatural interaction with the Watchers. Perhaps the Old Testament book of Job can provide some additional insight as to how this interaction took place.

Job 1:6

> *"Now there was a day when the **sons of God** came to present themselves before the Lord, and Satan came also among them."*

Job 2:1

> *"Again there was a day when the **sons of God** came to present themselves before the Lord, and Satan came also among them to present himself before the Lord."*

In both passages attention is called to an organized presentation of the "sons of God" (angels) before the Lord. This term is also used in the Book of Exodus when Moses entered into the courts of the Egyptian Pharaoh and stood before him. In that case, it is Moses who is forcing the face-to-face meeting (Ex. 5:1). So it is in almost every instance wherein this term is used. It's almost as if the initiator is taking a stand for a particular purpose – to be seen or to be recognized. They are not being "called on the carpet," so to speak.

Satan, also an angelic being, is mentioned by name and the focus is directed to his meeting with the Lord. A conversation between Satan and the Lord takes place. Satan is asked to identify the path of his travels and to state his purpose for "calling this meeting." Satan responds by saying that he comes *"from going to and fro in the earth and from walking up and down in it,"* (Job 1:7). He then begins to rail against the wickedness of man, presumably in an effort to provoke a judgment on mankind from the almighty. (I cover this topic in greater detail in *My End of the Circle,* a companion book to this volume.)

He is then asked by the Lord about a particular person, in this case, a man named Job (Jōbe). His response indicates that he is very much aware of who Job is and of Job's activities. He then questions the Lord regarding Job and is given a personal response on the matter.

Job 1:9-12

> *(9) "Then Satan answered the Lord, and said,*
> *Doth Job fear God for naught?*
>
> *(10) "Hast not thou made an hedge about him,*
> *and about his house, and about all that he hath on every side?*
> *Thou hast blessed the work of his hands,*
> *and his substance is increased in the land.*
>
> *(11) "But put forth thine hand now,*
> *and touch all that he hath, and he will curse thee to thy face.*
>
> *(12) "And the Lord said unto Satan, Behold, all that he hath*
> *is in thy power; only upon himself put not forth thy hand.*
> *So Satan went forth from the presence of the Lord."*

The early portion of the Book of Job gives us specifics with regard to a running conversation between the Lord and Satan that centers on one particular person – Job. But our concerns here are not with the particular story of Job.

The passage also provides a window of insight that details the designed activities of the Watchers, the sons of God, or angels. The Book of Job makes us aware of their dealings with mankind and the documentation of their continued communication with the Lord.

1. Seemingly they move freely between the earth and the presence of the Lord.

2. Seemingly they report to the Lord regarding their activities with mankind.

3. Seemingly they are given specific directions, tasks or guidelines for their interaction.

4. Seemingly they are to request permission to act outside of those guidelines.

Whereas they were quite obviously endowed with unique power, they were also held to specific boundaries. No wonder Semjaza was reluctant to step outside of the directive. His words, as recorded in Enoch 6, make it clear that the temptation to act of their own accord was present and strong, but so also was the knowledge that they would most certainly be held accountable for their treacherous offense.

Of Angels and Men

There is a concept that has become accepted doctrine in theological circles that states that there is a restrictive barrier between angelic beings and mankind, which prohibits their interaction with man on any type of sensual level. The basis for this belief is taken from the very words of Christ himself and, as previously stated, who am I to question the teachings of the one regarded as the Lord of Lords, King of Kings and very Son of God?

Let's be clear. This is not a questioning of the teaching of Christ, but rather our understanding of what he was teaching with regard to the interaction between angelic beings and men.

The premise is that Christ says that it *cannot* happen, implying that it has not happened in the past, nor will it occur at any point in the future. The teaching is taken from Matthew 22:29-30,

> *(29) "Jesus answered and said unto them,*
> *Ye do err, not knowing the scriptures, nor the power of God.*
>
> *(30) "For in the resurrection they neither marry,*
> *nor are given in marriage,*
> *but are as the angels of God in heaven."*

The context of this passage is an exchange between Jesus and a group of religious teachers of his day known as Sadducees. The Sadducees believed in an existence after death, but taught that there was no resurrection of the dead. Jesus taught otherwise, clearly stating that those who had died physical deaths would one day be resurrected to a new existence that would include an immortal physical body.

In an effort to discredit the teachings of Jesus, the Sadducees posed to him a riddle that they based on an Old Testament Law of Moses.

Deuteronomy 25:5-6

> *(5) "If brethren dwell together, and one of them die,*
> *and have no child, the wife of the dead shall not*
> *marry without unto a stranger:*
> *her husband's brother shall go in unto her,*
> *and take her to him to wife, and perform*
> *the duty of an husband's brother unto her.*
>
> *(6) "And it shall be, that the firstborn which she beareth*
> *shall succeed in the name of his brother which is dead,*
> *that his name be not put out of Israel."*

This was a specific law put in place for the nation of Israel to ensure that the family lineage continued. The Sadducees brought it to Jesus with the proposed scenario of multiple deaths by seven brothers and multiple marriages, each one according to the guidelines of the law. Their specific question had nothing to do with angels, but rather the ancient law and how it would affect things if the future resurrection, spoken of by Jesus, was indeed a truthful and accurate teaching.

The question of the Sadducees was, "When this resurrection that you teach takes place, whose wife is she?"

Matthew 22:28

> *"Therefore in the resurrection*
> *whose wife shall she be of the seven?*
> *For they all had her."*

The response of Jesus was to simply say that there was no bond of marriage in the resurrection. He then offered an example that was understood and taught by the Sadducees – *They are as the angels of God in heaven.*

This simple illustration, given by Jesus as a part of his answer to the riddle posed by the Sadducees, has been taken to build the Biblical principle that angels cannot interact with mankind in a sexual manner. If that premise is accepted as the undeniable case, then the sons of God that are referenced in Genesis 6:4 cannot possibly be angelic beings.

Here are some things that we can ascertain from the Old Testament, post-flood passage of Genesis chapters 18 and 19, with regard to the interaction between angelic beings and mankind:

- They appear as men: *"three men stood by him: and when he* [Abraham] *saw them, he ran to meet them...."* (Gen. 18:2)

- Their plans can be persuaded to change: *"if now I have found favor in thy sight, pass not away, I pray thee, from thy servant:"* (Gen. 18:3)

- Their appearance is in accord with their surroundings: *"Let a little water, I pray you, be fetched, and wash your feet and rest yourselves...."* (Gen. 18:4)

- They both eat and drink: *"And he* [Abraham] *took butter, and milk, and the calf which he had dressed, and set it before them; and he* [Abraham] *stood by them under the tree, and they did eat."* (Gen. 18:8)

- They have insight to future events: *"Sarah thy wife shall have a son."* (Gen. 18:10)

- They make decisions and go places with purpose: *"And the men rose up from thence, and looked toward Sodom...."* (Gen. 18:16)

- They can be visually seen even at a distance when present: *"And there came two angels to Sodom at even; and Lot sat at the gate of Sodom: and Lot, seeing them, rose up to meet them...."* (Gen. 19:1)

- They have the ability to reason and can be reasoned with: *"And he [Lot] said, Behold now, my lords, turn in, I pray you, into your servant's house, and tarry all night, and wash your feet, and ye shall rise up early, and go on your ways. And they said, Nay; but we will abide in the street all night. And he pressed upon them greatly; and they turned in unto him, and entered into his house;"* (Gen. 19:2-3a)

- They both eat and drink: *"and he [Lot] made them a feast, and did bake unleavened bread, and they did eat."* (Gen. 19:3b)

- When present, they can physically be seen by everyone and they appear to be regular human beings (they are not the figment of a person's imagination and, evidently, these types of angels do not appear in long flowing robes with wings): *"And they [the men of Sodom] called unto Lot, and said unto him, Where are **the men** which came in to thee this night?"* (Gen. 19:5)

  SIDE NOTE: The Hebrew word translated "men" is the word "'*enowsh*" (en•ōshe'), which is translated 564 times in the Old Testament to imply "mortal men." Although they were clearly angelic beings, they had the physical appearance of mortal men.[4]

- They have supernatural power: *"And they* [the angels] *smote the men* [the `enowsh] *that were at the door of the house with blindness...."* (Gen. 19:11)

- They can forcefully deliver innocents from a perilous situation: *"And while he lingered, the men laid hold upon his* [Lot's] hand and upon the hand of his wife, and upon the *hand of his two daughters; the Lord being merciful unto him: and they* [the angels] *brought him* [Lot] *forth, and set him without the city."* (Gen. 19:16)

The angels that are seen interacting with Abraham and later with Lot in Genesis chapters 18 and 19 are *Watchers!* They're charged with being emissaries between Heaven and Earth. Other types of angels are directly mentioned in the Biblical text, such as cherubim and seraphim. They are given completely different descriptions and have completely different roles to play.

In Genesis 32 we're given the story of Jacob wrestling with someone he perceived at first to be a person, but later recognized as an angel. As the day begins to dawn, the angel pleads to be released from Jacob's grip. Jacob, unwilling to give in until his request for special blessing is granted, refuses to let go.

Finally, the angel touches Jacob's thigh and forces him to kneel. The touch permanently injures Jacob, resulting in a lifelong limp. The request for blessing is granted due to Jacob's persistence and his name is changed from Jacob (meaning "the ankle-grabber") to Israel (meaning "God prevails").[5]

The Watcher type of angel is a specific class of angel. These angels have a prime directive that involves personal interaction with mankind. They're primarily protectors, charged with the care and guidance of mankind, and at times their work crosses over into the physical world. When this happens, they're clearly seen as physical manifestations resembling men.

The record shows that although they are spiritual beings, they have an unmistakable physical presence. Their actions and involvement with mankind can and often do leave physical evidence behind. Today we would refer to them as guardian angels, and those who have seen them have no trouble attesting to the fact that they are very much real.

Stories are told on a regular basis, by people from all walks of life. Sometimes it's the unexplained presence of a person from out of nowhere who offers help in a time of emergency or danger. Sometimes they simply give direction to a person who has lost his or her way. I've even read stories of the reunion of a crying child with a panicking parent. Later the person who brought them together is nowhere to be found, and no one who was caught up in the incident seems to know who the person might have been, where they might have come from, or where they went. The rescuer was there. Then, they were gone. The executive editor of *Guideposts Magazine*, Rick Hamlin, estimates that the magazine receives nearly 5,000 such stories each year.[6]

These interactions no doubt take place amid a variety of circumstances for a number of different reasons. It's possible that they happen much more often than we realize. As the writer of Hebrews informed his readers, there are occasions wherein the communication with an unknown passerby is actually the unrecognized rubbing of shoulders with an angel (Hebrews 13:2).

A Change of Scenery

The information that the Biblical text provides makes it easy to see that the Watchers were able to move freely between the location of their commissioned work in the earthly realm and their original domain, the heavens. There is the question as to whether they were able to transport between realms on their own or if they needed some type of vehicle or craft to do so. When we open our minds to unbiased consideration of the proposal, it becomes a very interesting question.

We have numerous post-flood Biblical passages that could be seen as an indication that there was some type of transport ship used for the purpose of physically moving between the heavenly realm and the earthly.

Genesis 28:12

"And he [Jacob] dreamed, and behold a ladder
set up on the earth, and the top of it reached to heaven:
and behold the angels of God ascending and descending on it."

Exodus 13:20-22

(20) "And they [those who escaped Egyptian captivity with Moses]
took their journey from Succoth, and encamped in Etham,
in the edge of the wilderness.

(21) "And the LORD went before them by day in a pillar
of a cloud, to lead them the way; and by night
in a pillar of fire, to give them light; to go by day and night:

(22) "He took not away the pillar of the cloud by day,
nor the pillar of fire by night, from before the people."

Exodus 24:15-18

(15) "And Moses went up into the mount,
and a cloud covered the mount.

(16) "And the glory of the LORD abode upon mount Sinai,
and the cloud covered it six days: and the seventh day
he called unto Moses out of the midst of the cloud.

(17) "And the sight of the glory of the LORD was like devouring fire
on the top of the mount in the eyes of the children of Israel.

(18) "And Moses went into the midst of the cloud,
and gat him up into the mount: and Moses
was in the mount forty days and forty nights."

Second Kings 2:11

"And it came to pass, as they still went on, and talked,
that, behold, there appeared a chariot of fire,
and horses of fire, and parted them both asunder;
and Elijah went up by a whirlwind into heaven."

Ezekiel 1:4-5

(4) "And I looked, and, behold, a whirlwind came out of the north,
a great cloud, and a fire infolding itself,
and a brightness was about it, and out of the midst thereof
as the colour of amber, out of the midst of the fire.

(5) "Also out of the midst thereof came the likeness
of four living creatures. And this was their appearance;
they had the likeness of a man."

Matthew 24:30 (prior to Crucifixion)

*"And then shall appear the sign of the Son of man in heaven:
and then shall all the tribes of the earth mourn,
and they shall see the Son of man coming in the clouds
of heaven with power and great glory."*

Acts 1:9 (after Resurrection)

"And when he [Christ] *had spoken these things,
while they beheld, he was taken up;
and a cloud received him out of their sight."*

Acts 10:11

"And [Jesus' disciple, Peter] *saw heaven opened,
and a certain vessel descending unto him,
as it had been a great sheet knit at the four corners,
and let down to the earth:"*

Acts 11:5

"I [Jesus' disciple, Peter] *was in the city of Joppa praying:
and in a trance I saw a vision, A certain vessel descend,
as it had been a great sheet, let down from heaven
by four corners; and it came even to me:"*

As of the mid-1960s we had developed our own method of escaping the grasp of gravity, ascending off of the surface of the earth and traveling into the heavens. Since that time we have sent men to the moon and returned them safely to our planet. We have put men in orbit about our planet for months at a time and returned them safely home.

We have even sent unmanned craft to explore the surface of Mars and the outer reaches of our solar system. We do so with the help of a constructed vehicle that produces fire and clouds, and we've only learned how to do this within the last 50 years.

Prior to 1830 our finest mode of rapid transportation was on horseback. July 4, 1828, is listed as the official charter and groundbreaking for the Baltimore and Ohio Railroad. Travel by train emerged swiftly over the next decade, as railways were laid down.[7] Around 1885 or 1886 we developed a steam-driven automobile. Confirmed timelines differ on the exact date. Now, about 130 years later, we send people into space as if it's commonplace. How did our knowledge and understanding of technology advance so far, so fast?

This is space exploration technology and travel. We have also experienced huge advancements in items reserved for everyday use. Basic electronics are far from basic. Technological progress in nearly every conceivable field of science and industry has exploded within the last 100 years and now we're in the midst of genetically engineering our own physical existence. Did modern civilization miraculously crack through a barrier in the 20th century that had restrained significant progress for more than 4,000 years?

The writer of the New Testament book of Jude offers some intriguing insight regarding the angels (the Watchers) who committed themselves to the task of proliferating their own seed.

Jude Verse 6

> *"And the angels which kept not their first estate,*
> *but left their own habitation,*
> *he hath reserved in everlasting chains under darkness*
> *unto the judgment of the great day."*

This passage makes it clear that not all of the Watchers were judged. Only the select few who were following the lead of Semjaza were punished, and two things about this select group are emphasized by Jude:

1. They did not retain their first estate.

2. They left their own habitation.

The word used for "first estate" is the Greek word, *"archē"* (är-khā'). The word is used 58 times in the New Testament text and most often it's translated as "beginning" (40 times).[8] The word is used by Christ in his teaching, appearing 13 times in the gospels. Each time Christ is referring to something's point of origin.

He used it to refer to the origin of Adam and Eve as being *"at the beginning"* (Matthew 19:4) and he also used it when talking about signs that would point to the beginning of a time of coming great tribulation or sorrow (Matthew 24:3-8).

The Apostle Paul uses the term in his writings a number of times to refer to a place of origin (Philippians 4:15), but he also uses it as a way of indicating a position of rank or station (Romans 8:38, Ephesians 1:21, 3:10 and 6:12, Colossians 2:10 and Col. 2:15). We might have a similar meaning in mind when referring to children "knowing their place" or maybe someone in the workplace "overstepping their bounds."

The word not only refers to a fixed or an assigned point of time (origin), but also an understood order, position or level of status. Jude does not say that this small group of Watchers lost that or had it taken from them, but rather that they made the decision to sacrifice it for their chosen cause – to propagate their own seed or father children (Jude vs. 6).

Jude says that they also left their own habitation. This is also a willful act on the part of this small group. The word that has been translated "habitation" is a very interesting Greek word that is used only one other time in the entire New Testament text. It is the word *"oikētērion"* (oi-kā-tā'-rē-on).[9] Here, in Jude verse 6, it is translated as "habitation." The other usage is by the Apostle Paul in Second Corinthians 5:1-2,

(1) "For we know that if our earthly house of this tabernacle
were dissolved, we have a building of God,
an house not made with hands, eternal in the heavens.

(2) "For in this we groan, earnestly desiring
to be clothed upon with our house which is from heaven:"

The word translated "house"[10] in verse 2 is different than the word that is twice translated "house"[11] in verse 1. The "house which is from heaven," spoken of by Paul in verse 2, is the same word used by Jude. Paul indicates that this house is a physical transformation that will be a part of a future existence.

He illustrates the temporal nature of the first "house" by using the word "dissolved" in verse 1. This is the Greek word *"katalyō"* (kä-tä-lü'-ō), which describes the act of putting something aside that was designed for the journey, not the destination.[12] It was used to reference the act of taking the straps and packs off of a beast of burden once the travelers had arrived, or the traveler taking off his outer garments that he had tied up to protect himself from the elements along the way. Today, we might remove our winter coat once we get inside or kick off our shoes before we sit down to relax.

The first body is a physical, but temporary, dwelling place of the soul/spirit in the earthly flesh and it will be put aside at the end of the journey. The soul/spirit will then be "housed" in a supernatural and everlasting dwelling place – a heavenly body (verse 2).

Paul uses similar terms to paint the picture in First Corinthians 15:53-54,

> *(53) "For this corruptible must put on incorruption,*
> *and this mortal must put on immortality.*

> *(54) "So when this corruptible shall have put on incorruption,*
> *and this mortal shall have put on immortality,*
> *then shall be brought to pass the saying that is written,*
> *Death is swallowed up in victory."*

The interplay of the terms "corruptible"[13] and "incorruption"[14] and the terms "mortal"[15] and "immortality"[16] define a conversion from something that is perishable to something that is both perpetual and eternal. Paul asserts that this is a physical transformation from a temporal physical body to an eternally enduring physical body. This is the type of body that was originally possessed by the Watchers. This is the "habitation" that, according to Jude, was forfeited.

This is the same type of transformed eternal body in which the resurrected Jesus was seen for 40 days on Earth before his ascension into the heavens (Acts 1:3). The last chapters of Matthew, Mark, Luke and John also have details of recorded appearances of Christ following his resurrection. It's this same supernatural, eternal body that he willingly set aside to take on human physicality (John 1:14).

When Jude states that the Watchers "left their own habitation," he does so in an effort to clearly identify this same type of physical transformation. In order to father their own children and produce their own physical lineage, the Watchers exchanged their supernatural, eternally enduring, physical presence, which had no need for reproduction capabilities, for a temporal physical presence, which was designed to reproduce (Gen. 1:28), because it was not physically everlasting. The Watchers, who conspired to abandon their original mission, became flesh so that they might incorporate their physical existence into the realm of flesh-and-blood mankind.

According to Jude, they left their point of origin – that place or position where they were originally ordained to dwell from the beginning – and they surrendered their supernatural body or housing (not their inherent powers, abilities or knowledge). Thus, they were no longer "as the angels of God in heaven"[17] but were as men. As such, they became capable of reproduction.

The Times, They Are a-Changin'

As previously mentioned, Genesis 6:2 uses a term that implies force when it speaks of the Watchers "taking" wives. We earlier equated the action with that of kidnapping or abduction.

Genesis 6:2 also states that the Watchers took "of all which they chose." Did they take one wife each? Maybe, as Cain's descendant Lamech, the Watchers took two wives each (Gen. 4:19). The actual number is not listed, but it does say that they took as they wanted to take and that they took all that pleased them.

With the goal in mind being to produce their own heritage of offspring, it would be easy to imagine that multiple females were taken by each Watcher. The writings of Enoch note that each Watcher took at least one female; making it clear that they did not grab a small collection of females to use as a group. This was the personal choice of each Watcher and to that end each Watcher selected at least one human female as a wife (Enoch 7:1).

That the females in question are referenced as the wife counterparts for the Watchers speaks also to the personal nature of this quest. The Watchers were attempting to breed a new race that would contend with the descendants of Adam and Eve for the dominion of the earth. This was new ground. This was forbidden ground and two unknown aspects were in play.

1. How well would their plans work on a physical level?

2. How much time would they have to procreate before being judged?

The Biblical record, the Book of Enoch and the Book of

Jubilees all refer to the offspring of the Watchers as giants. The description of beings that were physically enormous in stature is the natural visual image when we read the details. Post-flood Biblical references describe the existence of men who were much larger than the norm. Goliath is perhaps the most widely known, but he is by no means the only giant in the post-flood Biblical text.[18]

But, this particular time period is *before* the flood and if the Biblical record is correct, none of these giants would have survived such a catastrophic event. As we piece together the details, we'll see that they actually died off long before the time of the flood.

Genesis 6:4

"There were giants in the earth in those days; and also after that, when the sons of God came in unto the daughters of men, and they bare children to them, the same became mighty men which were of old, men of renown."

Two separate time periods are mentioned: *"in those days"* and *"after that."* We also see a reference to a developing progression: *"the same became mighty men which were of old, men of renown."* The content of this passage actually covers a huge span of time from the arrival of the Watchers (around year 460) to the day that the flood begins (the 17th day of the second month of the 600th year of Noah's life, or Year of the World 1657).

Again, Jubilees 4:15 serves as the pivotal reference to clarify the timeline,

> *"And in the second week of the tenth jubilee*
> *[years 449-455 A.M.] Mahalalel took unto him to wife*
> *Dinah, the daughter of Barakiel the daughter of his father's*
> *brother, and she bare him a son in the third week*
> *in the sixth year, [year 461 A.M.] and he called his name Jared,*
> **for in his days the angels of the Lord descended on the earth,**
> **those who are named the Watchers, that they should instruct**
> **the children of men, and that they should do judgment and**
> **uprightness on the earth."**

According to the Book of Jubilees, Jared is born in year 461. This timeline is substantiated by the Biblical text (Genesis 5:1-15). We noted in the previous chapter that his name means "descending,"[19] and that his father may have given him this name in connection with the initial arrival of the Watchers.

Jared has a son 162 years later and names him Enoch, which means "dedicated"[20] or "set to training."[21] He is the one who documents much of the interaction between the Watchers and mankind. He is not born until year 623, but it appears that everything is going smoothly when he arrives. The Watchers were sent to train and teach mankind and, at this point, there are no red flags or concerns.

At some point in his life, presumably early on, Enoch begins his role as special envoy to the Watchers. In this role, he begins to document the teachings of the Watchers and preserve them, presumably for the purpose of faithfully and accurately passing the knowledge down to future generations. According to his own testimony, Enoch is given a tremendous amount of private revelation regarding all manner of things about the world and universe that were previously unknown or forgotten.

SIDE NOTE: It's possible that many of these things were being personally shown to Adam during his walks with God in the garden. However, with the fall of man and the expulsion from the Garden of Eden, the teaching and revelation of knowledge was cut short and the insight and wisdom were sacrificed. Could it be that man was left to "work it out" on his own, so to speak, and lost the benefit of personal insight from the creator until the days of Enos, when men began to call upon the name of the Lord and the Watchers were eventually sent as a response to mankind's cry for help?

At age 65, Enoch has a son and names him Methuselah. His name comes from a pair of Hebrew words: "*math*," meaning "men" or "males,"[22] and "*sheh'•lakh*," meaning "shooting weapon" or "missile."[23] Put them together and it means "men of shooting weapons." *What?!?* What kind of name is that for a kid, Enoch? Clearly, by the time Methuselah is born in year 688, something had changed.

Even in our day, people don't name their children haphazardly. Whether the newborn is named in honor of a relative or after another person or event, usually the name has significance for the parents. Usually, there was some inspiration that resulted in that particular name being chosen.

Even more so, in ancient times, names were also chosen with care and often carried additional meanings or pointed to noteworthy happenings. Adam and Eve had two very important sons, Cain and Abel. Cain takes Abel's life and is banished. The parents mourn the loss for decades, and then another son is born. Eve names him Seth. Seth is the Hebrew word, *"shāth,"* which means "compensation."[24]

We've seen the meaning in the names of three of Seth's descendants: Jared, Enoch and Methuselah. Now let's look at the documented names in Cain's family tree. Cain names his first son Enoch, which as we've already seen means "dedicated" or "set to training." This is years before the Enoch in Seth's family lineage is born. Perhaps Cain, being separated from all that he had previously known, realizes that it is now up to him to teach and train his children in everything they would learn about the world in which they lived. So, he names his son after the task ahead.

The Book of Jubilees tells us that Cain takes his sister, Awan, as his wife sometime between year 190 and year 196 (Jub. 4:9). This is nearly 100 years after Cain killed his brother, Abel. Much time has passed and either Cain came back home to steal away his sister, or Awan had developed some type of relationship with the banished brother over the years.

The same Jubilee passage records that Cain and Awan give birth to a son that they name Enoch just a few years later. There is no confirmation that Enoch was Cain's firstborn son, only that he was a son born during that period of time and Cain's life apparently changed. Genesis 4:17 says that after Enoch is born, Cain begins building a city that would be known by the name of this son. Maybe this is the place or central hub where the descendants of Cain would be taught and trained. The naming of the son and building of the city indicate that Cain's wandering has finally come to an end (Gen. 4:14).

Cain's son, Enoch, fathers a son and names him Irad (E-rawd), meaning "fleet."[25] We are not told that Irad is Enoch's firstborn son and, unlike the listing of the Seth lineage in Genesis 5, no timetable is given for his birth. While the Book of Jubilees had documented the time frame of Cain's marriage and the birth of his son, Enoch, in Genesis we're only given a list of important names from Cain's expanding family tree. Nothing indicates that they are the firstborn and there are no time markers for the births.

Could Irad have been born much later in Enoch's life? Perhaps some 250 years later? Could "fleet" (the meaning of Irad's name) be intended to mark the arrival of the Watchers, which we have noted was shortly before year 461, the year that Seth's descendant, Jared, is born?

Irad gives birth to a son that he names Mehujael (mekh-oo-yaw-ale'). This name is derived from a pair of Hebrew words: *"mä•khä"* (maw-khaw') and *"'el"* (ale'). The first word means "wiped out" or "obliterated"[26] and the second means "mighty" or "god-like ones."[27] You've probably already composed this phrase in your mind: "Wiped out by mighty, godlike ones."

J.B. Jackson's book, *A Dictionary of Scripture Proper Names*, says the meaning of the name includes: "Blot ye out that Jah is God."[28] Could this name mark the time when things began to change for a small band of Watchers, when those led by Semjaza began to take human wives?

The lineage of Cain goes on to list the name of Mehujael's son. He is named Methusael (meth-oo-shaw-ale'). His name is quite similar to that of Enoch's son, Methuselah, from the lineage of Seth. The Hebrew word is *"meth•ü•shä•āl'"* (meth•ü•shä•āl'). Both names begin with the Hebrew word *"math,"* which, as we found with Methuselah, means "men" or "males."[29] The second portion of the name is different, however. In this case it means the "mighty" or "godlike ones,"[30] very much like what we found in the name of his father, Mehujael.

We now have two contemporaries: Methuselah, through the lineage of Seth, and Methusael, through the lineage of Cain. Both names speak of a mighty race of beings who may have resembled mortal men, but were absolutely godlike in their abilities and characteristics. J.B. Jackson's book adds this definition to the name Methusael: "They died enquiring" or "they died who are of God."[31] Could the name somehow allude to mortal men, who were seeking knowledge and ended up losing their lives as a result?

Welcome to the new world. Welcome to a world in which the Watchers have produced children through the daughters of men known as *"nĕphiyl"* (nef•ēl')... the *Nephilim*.[32] Welcome to the world of the fallen.[33]

Both Methuselah and Methusael have sons. Both sons are given the same name, Lamech (leh'-mek). According to *Strong's Hebrew Lexicon*, the name means "powerful."[34] *Easton's Bible Dictionary* adds the definition "striker down,"[35] and Jackson asserts that the name implies one who "brings low."[36] Putting the definitions together suggests the idea of a powerful person or group with the ability to strike something down with a disastrous or fatal blow and bring it to an end.

These names indicate that something very serious is going on in the earth. The culture and environment is going through significant change and that change has within its power and designs the ability to produce permanent results. A rogue group of Watchers are working to wrest the dominion of the earth from the ones to whom it was given by God, and quite possibly the descendants of Adam and Eve have begun to fight back.

Lamech, from the line of Cain, takes a pair of wives, Adah and Zillah. They're identified in the Book of Jasher as the daughters of Cainan, from the lineage of Seth (Jas. 2:16-17). Lamech fathers two children with each wife. Lamech, from the line of Seth, fathers the builder of the ark – Noah.

Adah's name means "ornament" or "adornment."[37] She gives birth to a pair of boys, Jabal and Jubal. Jabal's name means "streams of water," as in irrigation.[38] Genesis 4:20 tells us that he was the father (point of origin, not physical father) of those who lived in tents and raised cattle. If we envisioned him as the "father of agriculture," then irrigation would make sense. His brother's name means "to lead away, carry away or conduct."[39] He is noted as the "father of musical instruments" (Gen. 4:21) and we get the picture of people congregating to listen to music or being led by music much as a trumpeter might call the troops to arms.

Zillah's name means "provider of shade" or "caster of shadows."[40] She gives birth to a son, Tubal-cain, who becomes known for his work in the field of metallurgy (Gen. 4:22) and a daughter, Naamah, who some regard as the "mother of reading."

Of all the descendants of Cain who must have been living at the time, the names of these specific people are given. The meanings of the names and the distinguishing attributes that are associated with each of the four children of Lamech provide even greater insight as to how their world was changing.

While Cain had built a city, a place of permanence for his family, just a few generations later Jabal is teaching people to live in tents and become more mobile. That seems to be a step backward, unless there is suddenly an urgent reason to become migratory. Jubal is creating instruments that bring people together or perhaps the various sounds also had the purpose of sending a message over greater distances. Associating the sound of a trumpet or horn with a large group of people on the move would not be difficult to envision for any generation.

Tubal-cain, a master of metallurgy, is also said to be the father of sword, shield and armor. Usually, the initial motive for building an army is defense and security. Could this be why Josephus referred to them as warlike?[41] Naamah is traditionally associated with teaching communication through reading. And, what do we read more than anything? Signs, signs... everywhere, there's signs. Perhaps some of the signs were for the purpose of leading people to safety or for helping people find each other as they migrate in temporary encampments to distant lands.

In a little over 100 years, the ancient world has evolved into a distinctively different cultural environment. In the first few decades after their arrival, the Watchers had provided a great deal of knowledge to mankind. But suddenly hundreds of women are abducted as a small group of Watchers begin to pursue their own agenda, and the fallout of their corrupt objectives gives birth to a world that mortal men never envisioned. The Book of Enoch describes the world as a place filled with horrific violence and bloodshed (Enoch 9:9-10).

Are we reading a lot of details into the spaces between the lines? Maybe we are. But the names and their meanings are a part of the ancient record, so maybe, just maybe, we're not.

It's A Boy!!! Well, Sort of...

A small group of the Watchers took unto themselves human women as wives and successfully fathered children through them. Mission accomplished! End of story! Not quite; mission underway would be a better assessment. The objective was to bring about their own race of descendants for the express purpose of competing with mankind for the ownership of the planet. Their firstborn children are referred to as *"nĕphiyl"* (nef•ēl') in Genesis 6:4. This is the only time this Hebrew word is used in the pre-flood Biblical text and it's almost always translated as "giants" in the various translations.[42] Some translations, however, do not translate the word at all, choosing rather to leave it as "Nephilim."[43]

The root of the word itself means "to fall" or to be "cast down" (cause to fall).[44] It's where we get the implication of fallen angels, but the descriptive name doesn't apply to the angels themselves. It applies strictly to the product of their breeding.

The first-generation Nephilim were powerful, aggressive and ruthlessly ambitious. They may have been both male and female in gender, but the majority of ancient texts refer to them as sons, not sons and daughters. Their fathers, the Watchers, were a godlike presence on the earth and had unquestionably made it their mission to become the self-imposed rulers of the planet.

As such, their offspring, the Nephilim assumed a self-appointed right to rule and forced mortal men into a subservient or perhaps even a slave-like existence. Enoch says that they *"consumed all the acquisitions of men"* and *"when men could no longer sustain them, the giants [Nephilim] turned against them and devoured mankind."* (Enoch 7:3-4).

Apparently they had an insatiable appetite for excess, which seems to carry over into a variety of areas. Enoch notes that they ate meat. This was a direct dishonoring of the heretofore sacred animal kingdom. Enoch notes that they ate meat of all kinds, including *human flesh*!

Enoch goes on to document that the violence extended beyond just a war on man. Every part of God's original creation was under siege.

Enoch 7:5

> *"And they* [the giants or Nephilim] *began to sin against birds, and beasts, and reptiles, and fish, and to devour one another's flesh, and drink the blood."*

SIDE NOTE: Nothing that was a part of God's original creation was a carnivore. Humans and animals consumed only herbs, vegetables, fruit and grains as food (Gen. 1:29-30). Even after the fall and Adam and Eve's realization that they were naked, they still did not take the life of an animal for clothing, but chose fig leaves instead (Gen. 3:7). It was God who first clothed them in the skin of an animal, thus making it acceptable to construct clothing and shoes from animals (Gen. 3:21). In

125

Genesis 3:17-19 Adam is once again told that he is to eat only that which grows from the ground: herbs, vegetables, fruit and grains. Animals were only to be used for the atonement sacrifice (Gen. 4:4) and the making of clothing, which may have been a part of the atonement sacrifice. Animals were never taken for food! (I cover this topic in greater detail in *My End of the Circle*, a companion book to this volume.)

Enoch also states that the sexual desires of the Nephilim were insatiable and could not be gratified. Thus, they continued forcefully taking the daughters of men as they desired and fathered numerous children by them as a result. Also, they apparently never reached a point of physical maturity or adulthood. The descriptions of Enoch seem to indicate that the first generation of Nephilim never stopped growing (Enoch 7:2).

Enoch speaks of their height as being 3,000 *ells* (Enoch 7:2). The ell was an ancient measurement from the fingertip to the *el*-bow that was approximately 18 to 20 of our modern-day inches, similar to the cubit. The description of 3,000 ells may be a hyperbole to indicate that the Nephilim grew beyond that which was measurable and that even after they had reached an immense size, they continued to grow. It may also be a mistranslation of the original text, as Hebrew numbers are given to such errors. There's more on these known translation issues in the next chapter.

The Nephilim were an abhorrent abomination in the earth. The Watchers had produced a hybrid race that was never intended to exist on the planet, and this race was internally driven to destroy everything that was directly descendent from God's original creation.

Live... and Let Die

Although the first-generation Nephilim were directly fathered by supernatural beings, they were still subject to the fate and constraints of flesh and blood humans. As with humans, their lifespan was limited both by longevity and by the inescapable fact that they could be physically killed. It's entirely possible that the mortal offspring of Adam and Eve were able to bring down a few, but for the most part, humans were no match for the giants.

Enoch 10:9-12

> *(9) "And to Gabriel said the Lord: 'Proceed against the bastards and the reprobates, and against the children of fornication: and destroy* [the children of fornication and] *the children of the Watchers from amongst men [and cause them to go forth]: send them one against the other that they may destroy each other in battle: for length of days shall they not have.*

> *(10) "'And no request that they* (i.e. their fathers) *make of thee shall be granted unto their fathers on their behalf; for they hope to live an eternal life, and that each one of them will live five hundred years.'*

> *(11) "And the Lord said unto Michael: 'Go, bind Semjaza and his associates who have united themselves with women so as to have defiled themselves with them in all their uncleanness.*

> *(12) "'And when their sons have slain one another, and they have seen the destruction of their beloved ones, bind them fast for seventy generations in the valleys of the earth, till the day of their judgment and of their consummation, till the judgment that is forever and ever is consummated.'"*

In this Book of Enoch passage, God speaks to Gabriel about the Watchers' hope that their sons will produce an eternal existence and that their days will be equivalent to 500 years (verse 10). However, verse 9 indicates that God had set in motion different plans, which included his intervention on behalf of mankind so that the seed of the Watchers would meet an earlier than expected demise.

As a result, the fate of the first-generation Nephilim is sealed. Ultimately, they will be destroyed through war with their own kind, and their parents, the Watchers, will be bound as prisoners and made to watch helplessly as it all unfolds.

Apparently this happened well within the 500-year time frame referenced by Enoch. Although the Watchers pled for leniency, none of their cries for mercy were granted. After the death of the first generation of Nephilim, the Watchers are imprisoned in the depths of the earth for 70 generations where they await a final judgment. There's more on the Seventy Generations Prophecy in Appendix 2.

The current timeline puts the initial arrival of the Watchers sometime just before the birth of Jared in Year of the World 461. Things are rocking along pretty smoothly and mankind continues making significant advances under the tutorage of the Watchers for about 160 years or so. At some point between year 623, when Enoch is born, and year 688, when Enoch's son, Methuselah, is born, the Peaceful Progress Train jumps the rails. We take this from the allusion to violence in the meaning of Methuselah's name: "the men of shooting weapons or missiles."

If the writings of Enoch regarding the lifespan of the first-generation Nephilim can be taken accurately, we can add 500 years to their beginning point (sometime between year 623 and year 688) and come to a calendar date of around 1150. The reference in Enoch chapter 10 says that they had hoped to live 500 years, but Gabriel is told by God that their violent rampage will come to an earlier end. Thus, it would seem that the direct descendants of the rebel Watchers have been completely exterminated sometime before year 1150.

Who Knew the Grandkids Would Be Such Fun?

June 25, 1348 – A trade ship docks in a port known today as Weymouth, Dorset, in England, to unload its cargo and replenish its supplies. The ship's cargo includes rats. This is not entirely uncommon, but the rats on this trade ship bring with them a flea infestation. The fleas carry the *Yersinia Pestis* virus. It will later become known as the Black Death. By December of 1349, nearly half of England's population had become infected and died.[45] It's said that there's a commemorative plaque attached to the wall of the Ship Inn in the Port of Weymouth to this day.

The first squadron of flea-infested rats most likely never left the port, but there's little doubt that the disease they carried certainly did. The lifespan of the fleas that spawned the outbreak was less than a year, but the disease ravaged England for nearly 18 months and returned 20 years later for a second round. Eventually, it spread throughout all of Europe. It's been estimated that more than 100 million people died due to the Black Death.[46, 47]

It would be presumptuous to say that the eradication of the first-generation Nephilim solved all the world's troubles and things got back to normal. Much like the spread of the Black Death throughout Europe, the initial outbreak resulted in a fast-moving, widespread infestation. Their sons and their daughters were now running rampant in the earth and, as the family tree expanded, so did the diversity of corruption.

Genesis 6:5

> *"And GOD saw that the wickedness of man was great in the earth, and that every imagination of the thoughts of his heart was only evil continually."*

We use the word imagination to express things that we mentally visualize, but that's not the intended meaning the word that is translated "imagination" in this passage. The word that is translated as "thoughts" could be used in that way, as it's the Hebrew word for "plan" or "devise."[48] However, the word translated as "imagination" denotes the end product of someone's thoughts or plans. It means "to form, to frame" or "to fashion"[49] and it's from the root word that is used in Genesis 2:7-8 where *"the LORD God formed man of the dust of the ground."*[50]

The rampaging, out-of-control violence of the giants (the first-generation Nephilim) was gone, but the meticulous scheming of their offspring (second, third and possibly fourth generation) was in full swing. They looked like men. They walked like men. They talked like men. But their intention was the same as their fathers: to confiscate complete control of the planet from the descendants of Adam and Eve, *and rule!*

Jubilees 5:1

"And it came to pass when the children of men began to multiply
on the face of the earth and daughters were born unto them,
that the angels of God saw them on a certain year of this jubilee
[this is an unspecified year and an unspecified jubilee],
that they were beautiful to look upon; and they took themselves
wives of all whom they chose, and they bare unto them
sons and they [the sons] *were giants."*

Enoch 9:8-9

(8) "And they [the Watchers] *have gone to the daughters of men*
upon the earth, and have slept with the women, and have
defiled themselves, and revealed to them all kinds of sins.

(9) "And the women have borne giants, and the whole earth
has thereby been filled with blood and unrighteousness."

These passages from the Book of Jubilees and the Book of Enoch refer to the time period identified in Genesis 6:4 as *"in those days."* These events transpired during the days of Jared, kicking off with the arrival of the Watchers shortly before his birth in Year of the World 461 and eventually giving way to the days of the giants at some point before the birth of Enoch's son, Methuselah, in year 688. The total lifespan of Jared is 962 years, according to Genesis 5:20, which means that he lived over 360 years into the lifetime of Noah or Year of the World 1423, to be exact.

This is meaningful because, when Christ is asked by his disciples about the end of the world, he refers to events unfolding on the earth during the days of Noah (sometimes spelled Noe), not the days of Jared (Matthew 24:37). Something horribly violent happened during the days of Jared, but something remarkably different is going on during the days of Noah. This is a second period of corruption that is identified in Genesis 6:4. It's set apart as an event all of its own by the phrase *"and also after that."*

Many interpret the phrase to be a reference to a second infestation of giants after the flood. Although the post-flood Old Testament text clearly speaks of giants, Genesis 6:4 is not referring to post-flood events. Everything in Genesis chapter 6 is in reference to things that transpire *before* the flood.

Genesis 6:4

*"There were giants in the earth **in those days; and also after that,** when the sons of God came in unto the daughters of men, and they bare children to them, the same became mighty men which were of old, men of renown."*

The word that has been translated "when" is also a key element to this particular verse. Traditionally we see the word as indicating a frame of time. It tells us "when" something happened. In this case, the word is more source-oriented, telling us "why" something happened. It's the Hebrew word *"asher"* and it's repeatedly translated as because, wherein, wherefore, whereas, etc., in other passages throughout the Old Testament text.[51]

We might more easily comprehend the intention of the word in this passage if we substituted the word "because" and arranged the phrases in a slightly different order. If we insert the word "because" (another accepted translation of the original Hebrew word) in place of the word "when" and move the phrase up front as a qualifying statement of cause, the passage would read like this: *"Because the sons of God came in unto the daughters of men and they bare children to them, there were giants in the earth in those days **and** also after that...."*

The last portion of the passage calls attention to a continuation or progression of what began **in those days**:

> *"and also after that... **the same became**
> mighty men which were of old, men of renown."*

The term "mighty men" refers simply to those of position or stature in the sense of forceful show of strength. The same term is used throughout the Old Testament text to refer to warriors or those who were considered to be elite or valiant soldiers in an army.[52] The same term might be used for a ruler or leader. There's really nothing supernatural or mystical about the term.

The same word is used in Judges 6:12 to refer to Gideon, who considered himself a servant, but would become a great leader of an army of specialists.

> *"And the angel of the LORD appeared unto him,
> and said unto him, The LORD is with thee,
> thou mighty man of valour."*

The phrase "men of renown" associates them with great fame and glory. The word is translated in the Old Testament text as "fame" four times, "famous" three times and even once as "infamous."[53] Again, there's nothing particularly magical or mystical about the term. They're simply being identified as those who are or will be accredited with great fame.

The phrase "which were of old" has some sticking power though. It is used 439 times in the Old Testament text and almost without exception it identifies something as being eternal, everlasting, perpetual, continuous, or ancient beyond time (prior to the creation of Adam),[54] or in this sense – *Godlike!*

Hence, the children or descendants of this union between the Watchers and the daughters of men became famous, or perhaps infamous, as valiant warriors and leaders who could *rightfully* claim ancestry that predated Adam and were hence Godlike in their existence.

Sure, the first-generation Nephilim were rampaging, beastly creatures that threatened the very existence of mankind before eventually killing themselves off out of their unquenchable thirst for violence. But the grandkids, now, *they* were special and they became more than just a little famous.

Giving Birth to Legends

The presence of the word "became" in the last phrase of Genesis 6:4 provides the opportunity for the phrase to be taken both literally and prophetically (an allusion to their legendary fame in the years after the flood):

> *"....the same became mighty men
> which were of old, men of renown."*

Although pre-flood records are scarce, it's fairly easy to project how the offspring of the Nephilim became something incredible during their own time period. But did they become

134

something more? Did they also become legendary gods, revered and worshipped by many of the ever-expanding post-flood civilizations?

Keep in mind that the phrase "the same became" refers back to those identified by the "and after that" distinction. It does not refer to new living, breathing beings that were born after the flood. It calls attention to the offspring of the first generation Nephilim and clearly indicates that they carved out a lasting legacy.

Probably the best known of all the ancient gods is Zeus. Perhaps the popularity and notoriety of the Greek pantheon in modern day is due to the expansion and indoctrination of Greek culture throughout the world following the conquests of Alexander the Great. The story of the Olympians was recorded by Homer in his poetic works *The Iliad* and *The Odyssey*, circa 760-710 BC.

As brilliant as Homer was, he most assuredly didn't build the stories of the gods and titans out of his own imagination. His writings, although poetry, were the documentation of the ancient history and the legacy of the Greek gods. He recorded and preserved the stories that had been commonly told of the centuries-old exploits of the gods and historical events in which they were directly involved. As we'll see, many of these same stories were told by cultures that preceded the Greeks by several centuries.

As any person's imagination begins to piece together the details of a storyline, it does so by using things that are either common knowledge or personal knowledge. Homer was no different. While Tolkien built the backdrop of *Lord of the Rings* from the basics of ancient lore and presented it as a highly stylized work of fiction, Homer worked with tales that were handed down from generation to generation as highly regarded fact and presented his work as historically accurate.

Although the most ardent *Lord of the Rings* enthusiasts may see parallels between some of the saga's characters and settings with that of ancient lore, no one would ever mistake any of the characters for something other than fiction. A thousand years from now, no one will be worshipping Sauron or leading archeological quests for the ring.

That was not the case with Homer's works. *The Iliad* and *The Odyssey* may have been poetry, but they were never considered fiction.

Although Enoch doesn't give us any names of the Nephilim, he does explicitly describe the first-generation children of the Watchers as extreme in every aspect. He tells us that they were violent and, as such, they fought with each other uncontrollably. It wouldn't be a stretch to propose that, as they fathered their own children, they fought with them as well. Enoch even tells us that they not only ate human flesh, but also devoured their own kind (Enoch 7:3-6).

Homer tells us that Zeus was the son of a titan named Cronus. The Romans knew Cronus as Saturn and celebrated an annual festival known as Saturnalia, which is the origin of our modern-day Christmas. Sorry, Jesus may be the modern-day "Reason for the Season" but originally, it was Cronus or Saturn. Credit the Roman Catholic Church with doing an excellent job of repackaging and marketing of this pagan festival, which was previously scorned and openly banned by the Catholic hierarchy.[55]

I reference Saturnalia to illustrate the widespread acceptance and popularity of the ancient gods. These stories were not myths and fables to the ancient Greeks and Romans any more than the story of Christ would be to modern-day Christians. The story of Zeus was commonly accepted as factual, and he was the primary god that was worshipped by most of the civilized world from the time of Alexander until well after the death of Christ in the first century.

Acts 17:22-23

> (22) *"Then Paul stood in the midst of Mars' hill, and said,*
> *Ye men of Athens, I perceive that in all things*
> *ye are too superstitious.*
>
> (23) *"For as I passed by, and beheld your devotions,*
> *I found an altar with this inscription, TO THE UNKNOWN GOD.*
> *Whom therefore ye ignorantly worship, him declare I unto you."*

The Greeks worshipped a plethora of gods in the first century. In an attempt to communicate to his listeners in a way that they clearly understood, Paul begins with an acknowledgement of the temples and images of the many gods to whom the Greeks paid homage, even their altar to the one who may have existed without their knowledge – The Unknown God. Although they were consciously trying to "cover all bases" in their worship, all roads led back to Zeus. For the Greeks, Zeus reigned supreme over all.

In the story of Zeus, his father fears being dethroned at the hands of his own children. Because of this fear, it is said that

Cronus ate his own children as they were born. This had happened five times prior to Zeus' mother, Rhea, making the decision to hide the newborn Zeus in a cave on Mount Ida in Crete. When Zeus is born, Rhea gives Cronus a large rock that is wrapped in a blanket in the place of his newly born son. Cronus promptly swallows the stone, blanket and all, thinking that his future is once again preserved. With regard to the question of who actually took care of the baby Zeus in the cave, there are a number of different versions to the tale.

> SIDE NOTE: This is the same plan of action taken by the mother of Moses when the Pharaoh was killing off the firstborn sons of the Jews during their captivity in Egypt. King Herod, likewise, demanded the death of all newly born sons around the time of Christ's birth in an effort to preserve his throne. Christ survived the death decree because he was born in the manger of secluded stables of a somewhat remote location. Did Moses' mother and King Herod find inspiration for their desperate acts from the ancient tale of Zeus, or another similar legend?

Once Zeus matures into adulthood, he takes a woman named Metis, the daughter of Ocean and Thetys (who were the brother and sister of Cronus) to be his wife and begins to devise a plan to dethrone his father. Knowing that he can't do it alone and having been made aware of his five siblings who, according to the tale, are still alive and well inside of the stomach of Cronus, Zeus decides that his first step should be to free his brothers and sisters.

Zeus prepares a poisonous mixture and slips it into the nightly drink of Cronus. Some versions of the tale have the mixture being served up to Cronos by Metis. In either case, the potion results in Cronus becoming severely ill and vomiting violently, thus coughing up the stone, which was given to him as if it were Zeus. He also coughs up Hestia, Demeter, Hera, Hades, and Poseidon, the brothers and sisters of Zeus.

According to tradition, the egg-shaped stone that is said to be the very one coughed up by Cronus is set down as the cornerstone of ancient Greece's most sacred site – the Temple of Delphi. Located along the slopes of Mount Parnassus, the site is the home of the renowned Oracle of Delphi, and some of the oldest structures on the site date back to 1600 BC. Most of the ruins of the Temple of Delphi that are visible today date back to the fourth century BC. No date is given for the original placement of the legendary stone, but it's still there to this day and the locals still revere it as the actual stone that was once in the belly of Cronus.

The Greeks also have their version of the great flood story. In the Grecian account, the flood is poured out upon mankind because Zeus has observed their horrific decline into all manner of debauchery, even to the point of cannibalism. Enough is enough. Zeus destroys the world. Only Deucalion, the son of Prometheus, and Pyrrha, the wife of Deucalion, survive the nine-day watery judgment from the great Zeus. They do so by hiding themselves in a wooden box and waiting out the storm.

The Romans' pantheon of deities follows that of the Greeks in such lockstep that it can hardly be separated as its own religious concept. But the time period of the Greeks far predates that of Rome, going as far back as 2800 BC in the estimation of some. As previously mentioned, the time period of the oldest verified civilizations, according to Historyworld.net, dates back to around 3100 to 3200 BC. These two predominant empires are known as Egypt and Sumer.

Each of these civilizations had its own pantheon of deities, and Zecharia Sitchen devotes nearly 70 pages of his book, *The 12th Planet*, to detailing the various commonalities that each culture's hierarchy of gods shared. A case could be made that the origins of the gods of Olympus can be found in the earliest cultures of ancient Mesopotamia.

> SIDE NOTE: There is a proposed theory that the birth of the ancient gods of mythology can be directly tied to the practice of ancestor worship. In short, ancient ancestors were seen as godlike beings due to their lengthy lifespans. While the theory is built around some interesting reasoning, there's not a lot of evidence to suggest that Adam, Seth, Jared, Methusaleh or Noah, all of whom lived in excess of 900 years, were ever revered as gods or worshipped. Those beings of the ancient world that were regarded as godlike beings and worshipped were the domineering descendants of the Nephilim, not the flesh-and-blood descendants of Adam and Eve. However, there's at least one reference indicating that the Sumerian worship of Nin.ti may have actually had ties to Eve as the "Lady of Life" or "Lady of the Rib."[56, 57]

Two Parts Bob and One Part Fido

Another peculiar commonality that many ancient cultures share is a collection of monstrous beings that were comprised of an animal/human combination. Here are a few from the Greeks that you will no doubt recognize:

- A centaur – the head and torso of a man, combined with the legs and torso of a horse.

- A chimera – a three-headed creature that was part lion, part goat and had a snake for a tail.

- A gorgon – a female with snakes for hair. Medusa might be the most well-known, but she was not the only one of these.

- An ichthyocentaur – very similar to the centaur, but with the tail of a fish in place of the back pair of legs.

- A minotaur – the head and shoulders of a bull and the chest-to-feet torso of a human.

- Pegasus – a winged horse, sired by Poseidon and foaled by Medusa.

- A satyr – a human upper torso that was combined with the hind legs of a goat.

- A siren – a mermaid-like female whose irresistible song lured sailors to their deaths.

Egypt is famed for quite a few animal/human hybrids as well:

- Anubis – human body mixed with the head of a jackal.

- Horus – human body mixed with the head of a falcon.

- Sobek – human body mixed with the head of a crocodile.

- Thoth – human body mixed with the head of an ibis.

- Taweret – female human body mixed with the head of a hippopotamus.

Each of these was regarded as and worshipped as a god in ancient Egypt, and there are a number of others. But the question remains, where did the idea of mixing humans and animals together to form one creature come from? It certainly can't be seen in anything that was a part of God's original creation. In fact, God was very emphatic that everything was to reproduce only *after its kind*.

The phrase is used no less than 10 times in the first chapter of Genesis. It's used with regard to the creatures that lived in the seas. It's used with regard to the birds that flew through the air. It's used with regard to the animals that lived on the land. It's even used with regard to the plants and trees. All, every single one of them, were said to be created *after their kind* and every indication is that they were designed to reproduce in the same manner.

Genesis 6:11-12

> *(11) "The earth also was corrupt before God,
> and the earth was filled with violence.*

> *(12) "And God looked upon the earth, and, behold, it was corrupt;
> for all flesh had corrupted his way upon the earth."*

In these two verses, the word "corrupt" is used three times. It is the same Hebrew word in each case and it means to destroy, to ruin, to pervert or to spoil.[58] Verse 12 specifies that this corruption had spread to all flesh. The word used for flesh can be used to denote the physical bodies of both humans and animals.[59] It speaks to the primary fleshly existence of all living things. Question: How much is all?

Where would ancient cultures from around the world get the idea of mixing, splicing or combining the human form with that of an animal? Could it be that the idea began with and has been passed down from the corruption of all flesh in the "Days of Noah," shortly before the flood? Would this have been something that Noah and his sons, Ham, Shem and Japheth, related to their children and grandchildren after the flood?

Jubilees 5:1-3

> *(1) "And it came to pass when the children of men began to multiply on the face of the earth and daughters were born unto them, that the angels of God saw them on a certain year of this jubilee, that they were beautiful to look upon; and they took themselves wives of all whom they chose, and they bare unto them sons and they were giants.*

> *(2) "And lawlessness increased on the earth and **all flesh corrupted its way,** alike men and cattle and beasts and birds and everything that walks on the earth - **all of them corrupted their ways and their orders,** and they began to devour each other, and lawlessness increased on the earth and every imagination of the thoughts of all men (was) thus evil continually.*

> *(3) "And God looked upon the earth, and behold it was corrupt, and **all flesh had corrupted its orders,** and all that were upon the earth had wrought all manner of evil before His eyes."*

Enoch 7:5-6

*(5) "And they began to sin **against birds, and beasts, and reptiles, and fish**, and to devour one another's flesh, and drink the blood.*

(6) "Then the earth laid accusation against the lawless ones."

A picture begins to clearly emerge from these two passages: the corruption that began with offspring of the Watchers and the daughters of men expanded into the animal kingdom. Nothing on the earth that had been originally created by God was exempt from Nephilim defilement.

In the first chapter of Genesis we find that everything is after its kind. In Jubilees we find that "all flesh had corrupted its orders." Again, it seems appropriate to ask the question: How much is all?

In the first chapter of Genesis, Adam is told that both he and the animal kingdom have been given all manner of plants (fruit, vegetables, grains and seeds) as food. They're never told that it is acceptable to eat meat of any kind. The Enoch passage clearly states that all manner of flesh was being devoured (including human flesh) and that blood was being consumed as a beverage.

The unique wording of verse 6 of the Enoch passage declares that it is the earth itself that "laid accusation against the lawless ones." That's very interesting wording and eerily reminiscent of what God had said to Cain in Genesis regarding the death of Abel – *"the voice of thy brother's blood crieth unto me from the ground,"* (Gen. 4:10). This is the first mention of blood in the Biblical text.

Enoch 9:1-3

> (1) "And then Michael, Uriel, Raphael, and Gabriel
> looked down from heaven and saw much blood
> being shed upon the earth, and all lawlessness
> being wrought upon the earth.

> (2) "And they said one to another: The earth **made without
> inhabitant** cries the voice of their crying up
> to the gates of heaven.

> (3) "And now to you, the holy ones of heaven,
> the souls of men make their suit, saying,
> 'Bring our cause before the Most High.'"

Verse 2 says that it is indeed the voice of the earth that is crying up to the gates of heaven. The use of the word in reference to the blood of Abel "crying out from the ground" (Gen. 4:10) carries with it the connotation of a loud outcry for help or uproarious clamor and screams.[60]

Enoch 9:1 states that when the four angels looked down, they saw much blood. At this point violence is rampaging without restraint. It may be fitting to pause and wonder if nearly the entire remnant of God's original creation has either died or been corrupted at the hands of the Nephilim? The Watchers' primary objective was to conquer the earth and wrest control of it from those who were made in the very image of God (Gen. 1:26). It's Year of the World 1657. Has the mission been accomplished?

We Have A Winner!

In 1961, The New York Museum of Modern Art hosted an exhibit entitled "The Last Works of Henri Matisse." Matisse was a French artist, known for his fluid, original paintings and his use of color. French-born stockbroker and Matisse admirer, Genevieve Habert, attended the exhibit and questioned the hanging of a piece known as "Le Bateau" (The Sailboat).

In Habert's view, the artist wouldn't feature the less detailed portion of the work on the top and place the more detailed features to the bottom.

After some discussion and careful consideration, everyone agreed. The painting was hanging upside down. With some 100,000 people attending, the mistake had gone undetected by anyone for 47 days, including Habert on two previous visits.[1]

In Genesis 6:12 we discovered that the way, or order, of all flesh had been corrupted throughout the earth, and we posed the hypothetical question: How much is all?

We also noted that this corruption of species unfolded over a period of nearly 1,200 years. On one hand, the landscape changed drastically and abruptly with the arrival of the first generation Nephilim. On the other hand, we found a slower infiltration of species perversion that was orchestrated by their descendants.

This perversion continued to the point of all flesh becoming corrupted and the existence of God's original creation, both man and animal, being threatened with extinction. In essence, who could really tell which paintings hung right-side up and which were hanging upside down?

Genesis 5:28-29a

> *(28) "And Lamech lived an hundred eighty and two years, and begat a son:*
>
> *(29a) "And he called his name Noah,"*

It's Year of the World 1057. A son is born to Lamech and his wife, Betenos (Jubilees 4:28). The newborn is so unusual that Lamech openly questions whether the child is even his. Enoch offers personal insight regarding the birth.

Enoch 106:2-5a

> *(2) "And his body was white as snow and red as the blooming of a rose, and the hair of his head and his long locks were white as wool, and his eyes beautiful. And when he opened his eyes, he lighted up the whole house like the sun, and the whole house was very bright.*
>
> *(3) "And thereupon he arose in the hands of the midwife, opened his mouth, and conversed with the Lord of righteousness.*
>
> *(4) "And his father Lamech was afraid of him and fled, and came to his father Methuselah.*
>
> *(5a) "And he said unto him: 'I have begotten a strange son, diverse from and unlike man,'"*

The next few verses tell the story of Lamech's conversation with his father, Methuselah, and how his newborn son has many of the physical attributes of the Watchers. Lamech is afraid because his initial thoughts are that the child can't possibly be his flesh-and-blood son, but must be a product of the angels or Watchers.

> SIDE NOTE: The 200 Watchers who produced the first-generation Nephilim were judged, bound and imprisoned prior to the birth of Lamech, during the days of Enoch (Lamech's grandfather). Lamech had no doubt heard the stories of their judgment and the thought of his son being born with such amazing features could have invoked a terrifying flashback.

Lamech is so convinced that his son is a product of the Watchers that he refuses to take any consolation from his wife's testimony that she had been with no one other than him and that the child was indeed his son. He also is not satisfied with the counsel of his father, Methuselah. Lamech wants first-hand information from the one who knows everything there is to know about the Watchers – Enoch.

We noted earlier that Enoch was born in Year of the World 623 and that he fathers Methuselah at age 65, in the year 688. We're told in Genesis 5:22-24 that Enoch lived 300 years after the birth of Methuselah and then he was no longer around because "God took him."

Something very unusual happened in the life of Enoch at age 365, and it doesn't take a math wizard to determine that it transpired in the year 988, a full

Event	Date
Birth of Noah	Year 1057
Enoch "taken"	Year 988
Length of Time	69 Yrs

Chart #7

149

69 years before this birth of Lamech's extraordinary son (See Chart #7.) How then is Methuselah going to ask anything of his father, Enoch? According to the Genesis passage, Enoch is clearly not around.

Enoch 106:7-8

> *(7) "'And now, my father, I am here to petition thee and implore thee that thou mayest go to Enoch, our father, and learn from him the truth, **for his dwelling-place is amongst the angels.**'*
>
> *(8) "And when Methuselah heard the words of his son, he came to me to the ends of the earth; for he had heard that I was there, and he cried aloud, and I heard his voice and I came to him. And said unto him: 'Behold, here am I, my son, wherefore hast thou come to me?'"*

God had taken Enoch to a secluded location and people no longer saw him on a daily basis, but apparently he wasn't removed from the earth to the point of being no longer accessible. Methuselah knew where to go if he wanted to search for Enoch and apparently, he found him. (I cover this topic in greater detail in *My End of the Circle,* a companion book to this volume.)

Methuselah relates to Enoch the circumstances of his visit: a child had been born to his son Lamech and the child was very unusual. He talks of Lamech's great fear and worry about the origins of the child, and it would appear that Methuselah shares in Lamech's anxiety. He then asks for Enoch to provide insight as to the truth regarding the child.

Enoch responds by assuring Methuselah that he need not worry, for he has seen the birth and the life of the child in a vision. He then proceeds to give the details of the prophetic vision:

- Lamech is indeed the father of the child (Enoch 106:18).

- The child is to be named Noah (Enoch 106:18).

- Lamech will die before Methuselah, and Methuselah will be a direct part of Noah's life during an important period of time (Enoch 106:18).

- Noah would father three sons (Enoch 106:16).

- A great flood would come upon the earth (Enoch 106:15).

- The flood would last for one year (Enoch 106:15).

- Noah's sons would have post-flood descendants (Enoch 106:17).

- Some of their descendants would be giants (Enoch 106:17).

- These giants would be born of flesh, not of Watchers (Enoch 106:17).

- The earth would be cleansed of all species' impurity (Enoch 106:17).

- The flood is a judgment for the sin and unrighteousness that transpires during the days of Noah (Enoch 106:18).

- There will be a continuation of unrighteousness after the flood judgment (Enoch 106:19).

- The post-flood continuation of unrighteousness will extend for generation upon generation (Enoch 107:1).

- A generation of righteousness will eventually come

and sin would finally be destroyed forever from the face of the earth (Enoch 107:1).

That's probably a little more information than Methuselah was anticipating.

Methuselah: *"Hey, Dad, is this boy really Lamech's son?"*

Enoch: *"Well, yeah. But, as long as you're here..."*

The Trail Runs Cold

Finding written information about the world before and during the time of Noah is fairly easy. Finding information about the post-flood world isn't too difficult either. But recorded documents that talk about the early life of Noah himself aren't all that abundant.

What then? Shall we just fabricate a few things that sound good in an effort to string together enough paragraphs to qualify as a standalone chapter?

Actually, I want to make every effort to avoid even the slightest perception of creative license at work in this section. We'll attempt to pull together the information that we do have and use it to piece together our mosaic. In the end, the various texts will tell the story and a trustworthy portrait should emerge.

To this point we've used passages from the Biblical text, while mixing in additional details from the Book of Jubilees, the

Book of Enoch, the Book of Jasher and *The Antiquities of the Jews*, by Flavius Josephus.

Like the Book of Enoch and the Book of Jubilees, the Book of Jasher also dates back to antiquity. It's referenced at least twice by name in the Old Testament, Joshua 10:13 and 2nd Samuel 1:18. The Apostle Paul refers to a pair of magicians from the old world in 2nd Timothy 3:8, calling them by name: Jannes and Jambres. The only known ancient text that mentions the two by name is the Book of Jasher, verifying that Paul had at least a working knowledge of the ancient text.

The document was originally written in the Hebrew language and apparently never translated into Greek. Thus it was not found present among the Dead Sea Scrolls (even though other portions of the Old Testament text and additional Hebrew documents were). The earliest translation of the book from the original Hebrew into English dates to the J.H. Parry publication of 1840 with ties to the Mormon Church.[2]

There are strong arguments to its validity, as well as fervent opinions to its lack of legitimacy. In either case, Jasher is not considered an inspired or error-free manuscript, and it was never intended to be considered as a portion of the Old Testament scriptures. It's an ancient record of Jewish history that by all accounts dates back more than 3,500 years.

There's a section in the Book of Jasher that provides some insight into Noah's life where the Old Testament text remains silent. Although it contradicts the Book of Jubilees, it does so with respect to names primarily, and it does not contradict the Old Testament text.

Just Say, "No." It's the End of the World

The introduction of Noah in Genesis leaves the reader with a "jump-to-the-middle-of-the-story" feeling. We're told that he is born when his father, Lamech, is 182 years old (Gen. 5:28-29), and the first recorded incident about Noah himself is that he's 500 years old when he begins to father his sons. What?!? Half of a millennia and nothing noteworthy has happened?

In fairness, the Genesis passage is a historical genealogy that most readers mumble through as the pages turn. It's a critically important record of lineage with time stamps of noteworthy births, but on the surface, it seems like pretty boring stuff with an all-capital B-O-R-E.

Beginning with Adam, the same repetitious pattern plays out for nine consecutive generations. So-and-so lived a number of years and "begat" (fathered) so and so. The angels rejoiced! Then, he lived another number of years while fathering additional children. The angels rejoiced repeatedly! And, after a number of years, he died. The angels wept. Change the names. Change the numbers. It's pretty much the same bland wording for 31 verses. Oh... let's leave out the rejoicing and weeping part. The text doesn't document any rejoicing or weeping of angels. Cough, cough, throat clear.

As previously noted, the name that is listed isn't always the firstborn son, and by simply adding together the ages at which each succeeding son is said to be born, we can track the number of years from the creation of Adam to the time that Noah is born. (See Chart #8.)

The world is 1,057 years removed from creation when Noah

is born, and 500 years later not a single significant thing about his life has been written down. Yet, it was noted by Enoch at the time of Noah's birth that Noah would be the one to build the ark, ride out the flood and thus preserve the life of everything that God had fashioned on days five and six of creation.

Name of Son	Age of Father	Year of Birth	Verse in Genesis 5
Adam	Eternal	Day 6	Gen. 1:26-31
Seth	130	130	3
Enos	105	235	6
Cainan	90	325	9
Mahalaleel	70	395	12
Jared	65	*461	15
Enoch	162	623	18
Methuselah	65	688	21
Lamech	187	875	25
Noah	182	1057	28-29

* The Book of Jubilees states that Jared was born in 6th year of the 3rd week of the 10th Jubilee. This is year 461. No months are given as a part of dates of birth in Genesis Ch. 5. We have noted year 461 thereby acknowledging the count of years in the Book of Jubilees. A difference of a year does not make one account right and the other account wrong. Both can be right and there is no conflict in the count.

Chart #8

According to Enoch's prophetic vision, Noah would also be the father of three sons, who would survive the flood with him and end up jump-starting civilization after the flood waters had subsided. Surely Noah didn't sit on a cliff for five centuries and watch mountain goats run by. There must be some backstory as to what he did in those 500 years and why he was the one chosen to build the ark.

It is here that the Book of Jasher adds some much needed texture to the landscape. Jasher chapter 5 begins with a listing of deaths in the lineage of Seth, the son of Adam. Adam had already passed away in Year of the World 930 and Seth, his son, had died in year 1042.

The Book of Jasher picks up the roll call of significant deaths with the passing of Enos, the son of Seth, who died in year 1140 (Jas. 5:1). The Book of Jasher notes that Noah was 84 at this time. The hint is that Noah either knew Enos or was at least aware of his passing. Jasher continues with the death of Enos' son, Cainan, in year 1235 and notes that Noah is 179

(Jas. 5:2). Again, the hint is that Noah either personally knew Cainan or at least was aware of his passing.

Earlier in Jasher it's noted that a great ceremony and mourning was convened to commemorate the death of Adam (Jas. 3:14-15). How could that event not have been one of the most significant events in the life of those living? Possibly this same type of significance followed with the passing of Adam's son, Seth; Seth's son, Enos; Enos' son, Cainan; and so on.

Mahalaleel, the son of Cainan, passes away at age 895. The year is 1290. Noah is 234 years old at this point (Jas. 5:3). Jared, the son of Mahalaleel, is the next to die, at the ripe old age of 962. This is year 1423 and Noah is 366 (Jas. 5:4). The Book of Jasher calls attention to this because all of these patriarchs are considered to be the leaders of a godly line, the lineage of Seth.

We tracked the descendants of the seed of the serpent for the better part of two complete chapters. Let's not forget the importance of the seed line of Eve, which, according to her own declaration, passed through Seth. This is the lineage that's documented so carefully in Genesis chapter 5. This is the line we saw tracked by the Book of Jubilees. Here again is the same genealogy embedded in the pages of the Book of Jasher. As Noah ages, the entire bloodline is dying, and Noah to this point has not fathered a son, nor even taken a wife.

By year 1423 everyone in the prophetic bloodline from Adam to Jared has died. (See chart #9.) Enoch is off in private isolation at this point because at age 365 something unusual transpired in his life.

The only ones left of Seth's all-important lineage are Methuselah, Lamech and Noah. Methuselah is 735 years old at this point and Lamech is 548. While it's possible that Lamech may father additional children, he's already been told specifically by his father, Methuselah, through Enoch himself,

Name of Son	Age at Death	Year of World	Verse in Genesis 5
Adam	930	Year 930	5:5
Seth	912	Year 1042	5:8
Enos	905	Year 1140	5:11
Cainan	910	Year 1235	5:14
Mahalaleel	895	Year 1290	5:17
Jared	962	Year 1423	5:20
Enoch	Taken by God	Year 988	5:23-24
Methuselah	969	Year 1657	5:27
Lamech	777	Year 1652	5:31
Noah	950	Year 2007	9:29

Chart #9

that Noah is the one who will preserve the bloodline. Noah may not have a wife at this point or any prospects of children on the horizon, but he's only 366, so there's plenty of time. No worries.

At this stage, an interesting question sits on the table waiting to be mulled over: Why is Noah the only option? All of the patriarchs in Seth's lineage fathered multiple children over the course of their long lifetimes. Aren't there plenty of options besides Noah who can propagate the lineage and keep it alive?

Seemingly, valid arguments could be made for other options. After all, Genesis 5:30 does say that Lamech lived nearly 600 years after the birth of Noah and had a number of sons and daughters. Surely, one of Lamech's other sons was married with children, right?

Two things direct the discussion back to Noah as the only option. First, he was the one who was identified as the fulfillment of the prophecy as told by Enoch to Methuselah. The prophecy clearly stated that everything rested on the life of Noah and his three sons. Even though it was getting late in the game and he still had not married, it was Noah, according to Enoch, who was destined to fulfill the prophecy.

The second aspect is the twofold quandary of qualification. The seed of the woman had to stay within the lineage of Seth and, as Genesis chapter 5 records in detail, Noah met that qualification. The seed or bloodline also had to remain unquestionably pure.

Keep in mind, the ultimate goal of the conquest being carried out by the Nephilim was to completely corrupt the entire seed of creation, thereby leaving no heir in the bloodline of Seth, who was the replacement for Abel and divinely appointed to be the cornerstone of the lineage of Christ. And, as we discovered in the previous chapter, they were certainly closing in on this prime objective.

Genesis 6:8-10

> *(8) "But Noah found grace in the eyes of the Lord.*
>
> *(9) "These are the generations of Noah:*
> *Noah was a just man and perfect in his generations,*
> *and Noah walked with God.*
>
> *(10) "And Noah begat three sons, Shem, Ham, and Japheth."*

These verses fall on the heels of God's decision to destroy the earth due to the corruption of every living thing on the planet (Gen. 6:7). Out of all that corruption, God sees Noah and notes that he was a just man and that he was perfect in his generations.

In the midst of God's commitment to complete and utter

destruction, Noah finds grace or acceptance in his sight. The word generation is used twice in verse 9, and it's two completely different Hebrew words. The first mention is a word that means exactly what you might expect when you see and read the word generation. This is the Hebrew word *"towlĕdah"* (tō•led•ä') and it's used to refer to a genealogical list of descendants:[3] "These are the generations of Noah:"

The second use of the word is the Hebrew word *"dowr"* (dōre). This word refers to a group of people who live during a particular period of time.[4] They may or may not be related. Think of the popular 1960s song by The Who, because in this case we're "talkin' 'bout my generation," well... Noah's actually.

We're also told that Noah was a "just man," implying that he was lawful and righteous. Keep in mind that this is in stark contrast to everything else we've read thus far about "Noah's Generation." The Biblical text pronounces that generation corrupt, not only in behavior, but also in reproductive order. The Book of Enoch gives multiple statements regarding the wickedness and violence. The world was a brutal, deceitful place, but Noah was "just."

Verse 9 also tells us that Noah was "perfect" in his generation. This is the Hebrew word *"tamiym"* (tä•mēm'), which is most often used to convey the idea of something that is complete, whole, sound, or unimpaired.[5] It is translated 44 times in the Old Testament text as "without blemish" and six additional times as "without spot." It's derived from a root word that was used to indicate something that was completely consumed or finished.[6] In essence, there was no spot, defect, or blemish in Noah. He was complete, without any corruption.

There's no question that the Nephilim had corrupted bloodlines far and wide, but Noah, the son of Lamech and Betenos, born 1,057 years after the creation of the world is singled out as being free from contamination. Not only is he of direct lineage that can be traced back to Adam and Eve without bloodline corruption, but his behavior is also righteous and just. And, most importantly, Noah serves the same God that formed Adam from the dust and Eve from Adam's rib – *The Creator*.

The last phrase of verse 9 makes this clear: *"and Noah walked with God."*

In the Book of Jubilees, there is an indication that the sons of Noah also were divinely accepted (Jub. 5:19). With respect to the purity of the bloodline that would eventually trail all the way to the birth of Christ, the heritage of Noah's sons would be of supreme importance. If this is the case, it would seem that their mother, the wife of Noah, must have been a part of the uncorrupted bloodline as well.

Name of Son	Name of Wife	Related By:	Point of Reference
Adam	Eve	From his own Rib	Gen. 2:22
Seth	Azura	His own Sister	Jub. 4:11
Enos	Noam	His own Sister	Jub. 4:13
Cainan	Mualeleth	His own Sister	Jub. 4:14
Mahalaleel	Dinah	Daughter of Father's Brother	Jub. 4:15
Jared	Baraka	Daughter of Father's Brother	Jub. 4:16
Enoch	Edna	Daughter of Father's Brother	Jub. 4:20
Methuselah	Also named Edna	Daughter of Father's Brother	Jub. 4:27
Lamech	Betenos	Daughter of Father's Brother	Jub. 4:28
Noah	Emzara	Daughter of Father's Brother	Jub. 4:33

Chart #10

Knowing that the bloodline of Seth was of critical importance, the family lineage is kept closely protected from the possibility of alteration and infiltration. While many of the sons and daughters married those who were not directly from the trunk of their family tree, those mentioned in the genealogy of Genesis chapter 5 did not marry outside of the bloodline. Chart #10 lists the wives of each person in the genealogy and shows how each wife was related to her husband prior to marriage.

All references in the chart are from the Book of Jubilees, which as we have previously stated has some issues with accuracy when it comes to dates and names. Most likely this is due to language translation, as the Book of Jubilees was translated from Ancient Hebrew into Greek and then into English. The Septuagint, a Greek translation of the Hebrew Old Testament, also displays some inaccurate information when it comes to dates.

The Septuagint adds an additional 100 years to some references of time and, in some instances, the Book of Jubilees has dropped 100 years from the count. For instance, the Book of Jubilees has Enoch being born to Jared at age 62 (Jub. 4:16), whereas the Old Testament text has Enoch being born when Jared is 162 (Gen. 5:18). Apparently, translating Hebrew numbers can lead to oversights.

We find a similar dating issue in the writings of Josephus. In his *Antiquities of the Jews*, Josephus states that Arphaxad, the son of Shem, is born 12 years after the flood.[7] Genesis 11:10 makes it clear that Arphaxad was born two years after the flood. Josephus also adds 100 years to the life of Arphaxad prior to the birth of his son, Salah, listing Arphaxad at 135 years of age, as opposed to the 35 years of age given in Genesis 11:12. Josephus is most likely working from the Septuagint as a reference.

In all cases of question, we take the Old Testament text as the final word of authority. The Hebrew scribes took month upon month of extreme care when copying the holy text and would have been diligent in preserving accuracy by eliminating even the slightest errant quill stroke. The Greek translators were never so meticulous.

Unfortunately, the Old Testament text only lists the wife of Adam, and not the wives of succeeding generations, so we're left to work through what we can find recorded in other esteemed ancient Hebrew texts in our efforts to fill in the blanks. When it comes to the disparity of names listed in ancient texts, the question of accuracy can be one of minor concern or a major point of contention. The choice is up to the individual reader.

The Book of Jasher gives us a slightly different history regarding the lineage of Noah's wife and gives her name as Naamah.

Jasher 5:14-16

> (14) "And the Lord said unto Noah, Take unto thee a wife, and beget children, for I have seen thee righteous before me in this generation.
>
> (15) "And thou shalt raise up seed, and thy children with thee, in the midst of the earth; and Noah went and took a wife, and he chose Naamah the daughter of Enoch, and she was five hundred and eighty years old.
>
> (16) "And Noah was four hundred and ninety-eight years old, when he took Naamah for a wife."

We noted earlier that Noah lived for quite a while before taking a wife, and Jasher tells us that he was still single at age 498. By that point, it would seem that Noah was committed to living life unmarried and never fathering children.

When we consider the social state of the world in which Noah lived, it becomes quite easy to understand why someone might choose that path. We might even resign ourselves to Just Say, "No," because, from the looks of things, it very well may be The End of the World.

One Little, Two Little, Three Little Baby Boys

Late in life, Noah is instructed by God to take a wife. Having been thus directed, it would seem plausible that the person Noah was to choose would be someone who was divinely selected and of pure lineage. According to the Book of Jasher, Naamah is the daughter of Enoch and the sister of Noah's grandfather, Methuselah.

This actually makes a lot of sense. As we will soon see, Methuselah will be a key figure in Noah's life in the final years that lead up to the flood. The ages of Noah and Naamah are given, so let's do a little math to test whether or not the timeline is conceivable. Noah is 498, so:

- It was Year of the World 1555. (1057, year Noah was born + 498, Noah's age at marriage = 1555)

- Naamah was 82 years older than Noah. (580, Naamah's age – 498, Noah's age = 82)

- Naamah would have been born in year 975. (1057, year Noah was born – 82, Naamah's birth year = 975)

- Enoch was born in year 623 and "taken" at age 365, which was year 988. (623 + 365 = 988)

- Naamah is born 13 years before Enoch is "taken." (988 – 975 = 13)

Giving birth to children around age 600 may not have been a common happening before the flood, but presumably it was possible. Almost all of those listed in the Genesis 5 genealogy lived in excess of 900 years. As such, it would be realistic to envision an extended period in which they were in peak health and fully capable of reproduction.

The Hebrew text tells us that Noah's three sons were all born after Noah was 500 years of age (Gen. 5:32). The verse does not indicate that the three were born as triplets, but merely that Noah was 500 prior to the first son being born. Genesis 9:24 indicates that Ham was the youngest of the three, and Genesis 10:21 reveals that Japheth was older than Shem. So the order of their listing, Shem, Ham, and Japheth, is not a relative statement of ages, but rather a listing by order of historical significance.

Jasher 5:17

> "And Naamah conceived and bare a son,
> and he [Noah] called his name **Japheth**,
> saying, God has enlarged me in the earth;
> and she conceived again and bare a son,
> and he [Noah] called his name **Shem**, saying, God has
> made me a remnant, to raise up seed in the midst of the earth."

There is no mention in the Book of Jasher of Noah's third son, Ham, being born. Although Jasher 5:32 and 5:35 specify that three maidens were chosen by Noah to be the wives of his sons, Ham is not mentioned by name until after the flood (Jasher 7:1).

Could the absence of Ham be an inference that Japheth and Shem were the children of Naamah and that Noah's youngest son, Ham, was born to a different mother? The verse clearly indicates that *Naamah conceived* and gave birth to children that Noah named Japheth and Shem.

Fathering a child, particularly a son, through a handmaiden or servant girl would not have been an uncommon or forbidden practice in that time period. The Genesis 5 genealogy highlights the name of the son whose descendants would preserve the holy bloodline of Seth. It also states that each person also fathered sons and daughters afterward, and nowhere declares that each child was born to the same mother as the named progenitor of the bloodline.

Before you start ripping pages out and burning them ceremoniously, consider the post-flood account of Abraham. Although he is revered as the father of the nation of Israel and rightly so, he's also the father of Ishmael through his handmaiden, Hagar (Gen. 16).

Sarah, Abraham's chosen wife, was identified by Abraham himself as his half-sister (Gen. 20:12). Thus, she was of closely guarded family lineage and bloodline. Hagar, on the other hand, was Sarah's personal handmaiden and a servant from Egyptian lineage (Gen. 16:1). At Sarah's bequest, Abraham fathers a son through Hagar and names him Ishmael (Gen. 16:15).

Now, before you're ready to toss baby Ishmael out with the bath water, be mindful of the fact that out of respect for Abraham, God promised to bless him, prosper him and make of him a great nation (Gen. 17:20). This all transpires prior to the birth of Isaac and apparently does not interfere with the overall divine plan to continue the holy bloodline through Isaac.

This little detour through the documented life and lineage of Abraham opens the door to the possibility that Noah's son, Ham, may have been fathered by Noah through a woman who was not the mother of Japheth and Shem. She also would not have been aboard the ark (as she would not have been Noah's wife) and would not have entered into the post-flood world. And, most importantly, fathering a child through someone other than Naamah would not have corrupted Noah, thus jeopardizing his standing as just in the eyes of the almighty.

> **SIDE NOTE:** As stated earlier, the order of the sons listed in Genesis 5 is an indication of historical significance, *not* the order of birth. Japheth was born first, but is listed last. Shem is listed first, because the sacred bloodline follows his line of descendants through Abraham to Isaac and through Isaac's son, Jacob, leading ultimately to the birth of the nation of Israel and eventually Christ. Ham is most likely listed second because his bloodline follows the firstborn son of Abraham, Ishmael, through the mother of Ishmael. Ishmael's line of descendants follows to the establishment of numerous Arab nations.

The Book of Jubilees indicates that all three of Noah's sons are born from the same mother, but it also lists Shem as the oldest, Ham as the middle child, and Japheth as the youngest (Jub. 4:33). It also specifies that Shem is born in Noah's 500th year, that Ham is born two years later, and that Japheth is born a couple years after that. It's possible that this was an injected interpretation of the Hebrew text on the part of the Greek transcriptionists. The order follows that which is given in the Hebrew text. The first son is born when Noah is 500, not before, and the other two sons are born at appropriate intervals in the order as given by the Hebrew text.

The four ancient records that we have cited, the Old Testament, and the books of Enoch, Jubilees, and Jasher, agree upon two things – Noah fathered three sons who joined him on the ark and all four men brought their wives. Thus, the human occupants of the ark consisted of these eight people, no more and no less.

The four documents also agree on one other tidbit that can be deduced by its collective absence in each record: Noah fathered three sons prior to the flood, but fathered no additional children once the family finally left the ark. All peoples and future generations were direct descendants of Shem, Ham or Japheth.

Everybody Wants to Rule the World

It's getting late in the game and time is starting to wind down. At this point most of the great patriarchs who were followers and worshippers of the Creator God, who walked with Adam in the Garden of Eden, have passed away. There are still a few who worship and serve the Creator God, but most of the descendants of Adam have turned their attention to other beliefs and these beliefs were sealing their fate.

We all believe in something. We are programmed to believe.

It's engineered deep within our being to have faith, to have hope in something. We think in terms of individual beliefs, but believing is a group dynamic. The overall popularity of what an individual believes makes it easier for that individual to have faith in what he or she believes, regardless of the nature of that belief.

As such, our beliefs change over a period of time. Many children collectively believe in Santa Claus, perhaps the Easter Bunny and even the Tooth Fairy. As children mature, each in their own stage of development slowly disassociates from the belief in the jolly old elf. Thus, the belief that once was, is replaced with another belief. Santa, the fantasy figure, then becomes the embodiment of the collective goodwill of mankind, or a more rational representation of reality. In essence, the child becomes a part of the universal Santa.

> SIDE NOTE: It is my sincere hope that there are no seven-year-olds reading this. If there are, *Spoiler Alert.* Sorry... I didn't intend to bring you up to speed before you were emotionally ready to make the leap.

The prevailing belief of Noah's Day was built upon the "Doctrine of Emanations," which teaches that all of creation is, in reality, a small part of God. In essence, at the point of creation, the Creator God poured bits and pieces of himself into the very fabric of creation. Thus, the overall composite of creation (nature) becomes the equivalent representation of the Creator, and the Creator ceases to exist as an individual entity.[8] God is evident in all things he created (nature), therefore nature is God.

Genesis 2:7

"And the Lord God formed man of the dust of the ground,
and breathed into his nostrils the breath of life;
and man became a living soul."

As a living soul, man was the preeminent resident of all creation. God himself decreed that man should have dominion over the fish of the sea, the fowl of the air and every creeping thing on the earth (Gen. 1:26). Having dominion supremely granted, what more could man want? The only thing left was to "become" God, and this is the dangling string in the sweater that the serpent (the garden manifestation of Satan) chose to pull.

Genesis 3:1-5

(1) "Now the serpent was more subtil than any beast of the field
which the LORD God had made. And he said unto the woman,
Yea, hath God said, Ye shall not eat of every tree of the garden?

(2) "And the woman said unto the serpent,
We may eat of the fruit of the trees of the garden:

(3) "But of the fruit of the tree which is in the midst
of the garden, God hath said, Ye shall not eat of it,
neither shall ye touch it, lest ye die.

(4) "And the serpent said unto the woman,
Ye shall not surely die:

(5) "For God doth know that in the day ye eat thereof,
then your eyes shall be opened, and ye shall be as gods,
knowing good and evil."

The serpent's crafty reasoning was the very thing that Eve wanted to hear and believe: you will have complete knowledge and understanding and as such, you will become more intimately connected to everything in creation. You'll be a part of creation on the same level and to the same extent as God. *Ye shall be as gods!*

This is the primary belief that resulted in Satan's initial fall from his own position as the preeminent centerpiece among the entire host of angels.

Isaiah 14:12-14

> *(12) "How art thou fallen from heaven,*
> *O Lucifer, son of the morning!*
> *How art thou cut down to the ground,*
> *which didst weaken the nations!*
>
> *(13) "For thou hast said in thine heart, I will ascend into heaven,*
> *I will exalt my throne above the stars of God: I will sit also upon*
> *the mount of the congregation, in the sides of the north:*
>
> *(14) "I will ascend above the heights of the clouds;*
> *I will be like the most High."*

Satan's initial goal was to be as God. His premise and belief was the birth of the Doctrine of Emanations. Because God poured bits and pieces of himself into the very things that he was creating, those things had the power to exist. *"And he is before all things, and by him all things consist."* (Colossians 1:17). If all of creation is made up of little parts of God, then the more God creates, the more of his essence is poured into the creation, and God is consequently lessened as a result of the process.

If this belief is true, then by simply combining the collective forces of a large enough portion of creation, Satan would have sufficient power to overthrow God and claim the throne (verse 13) and once he has a throne, Satan could declare himself as a God (verse 14).

Dear Eve,

Why would you possibly want to continue being an insignificant part of creation when you can enter into a realm of transcendent knowledge and become one of the gods? Come. Let us become fully aware and grow spiritually together.

Your friend in the pursuit of spiritual awareness,

The Serpent

Please to Meet You, Can You Guess My Name?

The post-flood, post-Exodus Israelites participated in a very mysterious annual sacrificial offering that held a direct link to the prevailing apostasy of Noah's day. Leviticus, chapter 16, describes in detail a ritual that the Israelites were to perform once each year. It occurred during the festival of Yom Kippur and became known as the Day of Atonement.

It was personally orchestrated by the High Priest. In the Leviticus account, this was Aaron. He was to first offer a sacrifice for himself and his family. This was a bullock or young bull that had been specifically selected because it was perfectly healthy and without flaw.

After Aaron's sacrifice was accepted, he then moved on to the special ceremonial sacrifice for the nation of Israel. This sacrifice involved an identical pair of goats that were also judged to be completely healthy and without blemish. It was important that the goats selected for this sacrifice were identical in every way, so as to not be able to tell one from the other without marking them.

Aaron presented the "twin" goats to the people of Israel and then cast lots to divide one from the other in a selection process. One lot was marked as being for the Lord's sacrifice and the other lot was marked as being "for the scapegoat." (Leviticus 16:8).

The Hebrew word used in this passage is *"azazel"* (az•ä•zāl').[9] It's translated as "for the scapegoat" in association with the actual goat that was used in the sacrificial ceremony. However, the Book of Enoch chapter 10 informs us that *Azazel* is the proper name of one of the fallen angels that is judged with the Watchers (Enoch 10:4-8).

A long wool cord that had been dyed red was tied around one of the horns of the goat that the lots had identified as "for Azazel." The Azazel goat was then kept near the altar to "witness" the sacrifice of the goat that was reserved for the Lord. *After* that sacrifice had been offered and accepted, the fate of the Azazel goat (the scapegoat) was sealed. It was then led to a specific place in the wilderness and cast into a ravine.

The Mishnah, written about 200 AD, contains additional details on this sacrifice. In it, we find that the journey of the scapegoat into the wilderness was actually a passing of the goat from priest to priest at each of 10 different stations.[10] Since the ritual was performed on a High Holy Day, there was a limit as to the amount of work that one person could do. Thus, 10 different stations were needed to see the task through to its completion.

> SIDE NOTE: Noah was the 10th person born in the sacred bloodline from Adam, and it was through his obedience that the holy bloodline was preserved through the flood. Does this directly correlate to the 10 different stations in the scapegoat ritual? We can't tell for sure, but it's an interesting parallel.

Once the last priest made it to the ravine with the goat, he would tie the loose end of the red wool cord to a large rock on the edge of the ravine. He would then ceremoniously throw the scapegoat into the ravine. With one end of the cord tied to a boulder and the other end tied firmly to one of the horns of the goat, the horn would be ripped off of the head of the goat as it fell into the abyss.

If the ritual was done correctly, the red cord would turn white. At that point, the priest would return to the 10th station and report to the priest who was waiting for his return. That priest would then return to his station and report. This reporting would continue until news reached the High Priest that the scapegoat had been cast into the ravine and the red cord had turned white. At that point, the High Priest would read Isaiah 1:18 and the entire camp would erupt in celebration, for the ceremony was complete and the sacrifice had been accepted.[11]

Isaiah 1:18

> *"Come now, and let us reason together, saith the LORD:*
> *though your sins be as scarlet, they shall be as white as snow;*
> *though they be red like crimson, they shall be as wool."*

> **SIDE NOTE:** The Babylonian Talmud records the miracle of the red cord turning to white in Yoma 40a, but it also includes two other mysterious happenings at the conclusion of the ceremonial sacrifice. At the end of the day, the gates of the temple would close by themselves and an angel would "trouble the waters" of a certain pool in Jerusalem. According to John chapter 5, this pool was known as the Pool of Bethesda, and many sick and afflicted waited around the pool for the waters to be stirred (John 5:1-4).

The Talmud also indicates that these miracles stopped happening about 40 years prior to the destruction of the temple in 70 AD. This would have been in fulfillment of the sacrificial death of the messiah, Jesus Christ, in 32 AD.[12]

John 1:29

> *"The next day John seeth Jesus coming unto him,*
> *and saith, Behold the Lamb of God,*
> *which taketh away the sin of the world."*

According to the genealogy of Christ in Luke chapter 3, Jesus was the 70th generation from Enoch and as such, he fulfilled the prophecy recorded in Enoch 10:12 that the Fallen Angels (the Watchers who sought to corrupt the sacred bloodline) would be held bound for 70 generations prior to their fate being finally sealed once and for all. There's more on this prophecy in Appendix 2.

So, how do we connect the dots between the serpent's "ye shall be as gods" conversation with Eve and a Watcher named Azazel, who's been completely ignored in the overall storyline to this point?

Enoch 10:8

> *"And the whole earth has been corrupted through the works that were taught by Azazel: to him ascribe all sin."*

We've discussed at length the Watchers and their actions among mankind. The focal point centered on the violence and horror they brought into the world with their stealing of women and fathering of hybrid creatures, whose brutal and sadistic behavior nearly destroyed all human flesh.

What we didn't cover in great detail was the very thing that the Watchers were sent to do: teach mankind about their Creator and their Creator's desire to have an interactive relationship with them.

Adam was placed in the Garden to care for it, and he was specifically given dominion over all other living creatures. It was intended for Adam's descendants to continue fulfilling this role as the chosen stewards of God's creation. Nature, as it was created, was a paradise. Man was to nurture it, *not worship it!*

Many of the Watchers apparently stayed true to their original commission, but a rebellious number abandoned their mission and forged their own agenda. It was this small, self-serving group that produced a race of descendants who were innately bent on wrestling dominion of the earth from the very ones to whom it was gifted.

Those 200 spawned violent acts and deviant teachings, but the one to whom primary accountability is ultimately assigned is Azazel. Charged to instruct mankind in the mysteries and wonders of the Creator, he chose to divert man's education towards the mysteries and wonders of creation. The focal point was redirected toward mysteries and secrets. A deceitful training emerged featuring the godlike magic of nature. This was the cornerstone of Emanations – creation contains the magic of God. Thereby, creation is worthy of worship.

Just as the entirety of a nation's sins was transferred to the scapegoat in the Day of Atonement Sacrifice, so the entirety of the pre-flood deception of mankind was ascribed to Azazel. He was the scapegoat and he was cast into the ravine.

Enoch 10:4-5

> *(4) "And again the Lord said to Raphael:*
> *'Bind Azazel hand and foot,*
> *and cast him into the darkness:*
> *and make an opening in the desert,*
> *which is in Dudael, and cast him therein.*
>
> *(5) "'And place upon him rough and jagged rocks,*
> *and cover him with darkness, and let him abide there forever,*
> *and cover his face that he may not see light.'"*

You Think Ya Know, But Ya Just Don't Know!

The act of belief is a group dynamic. When the overwhelming majority shares a common belief the dynamic is strengthened. When that belief is openly embraced and heralded as acceptable, it then becomes easier to believe than to *not* believe. When the aspects of that belief are publicly practiced, then immersion into the principles of that belief can be assumed.

How then is a belief that has been accepted and proclaimed by a society ever uprooted and replaced by an opposing belief? It's because belief is a group dynamic and it doesn't stand the test of individualism. Move outside the believing group, and the power of the belief is subject to decline.

Noah and Methuselah had more than belief. They had conviction. They worshipped the God of Adam – the God of Creation. While belief is a group dynamic, conviction, on the other hand, is an individual dynamic.

If we believe in something so strongly that it transcends belief, faith or hope and enters into the realm of accepted factual reality, it becomes a conviction. As a conviction, it begins to transform our actions and we're more likely to hold to the conviction steadfastly, even if others do not share the belief. Thus it's our convictions, and not our beliefs, that ultimately determine the choices we make when choices are presented.

The conviction of Noah and Methuselah was that God was separate from the things that he created and as a result, the things created were not at that time, nor would they ever become a part of God. God was God and worthy of worship because of who he is. Creation was the direct handiwork of God and, although marvelous, it was never intended to be worshipped.

After the death of Noah's father, the Book of Jasher tells us that Methuselah and Noah became inseparable. Noah is 595 years old. He is married with three sons. Methuselah was 964. He still has children and grandchildren living on the earth. The flood is just five years away.

Jasher 5:22-25

> (22) "In that time, the Lord said to Noah and Methuselah,
> Stand forth and proclaim to the sons of men
> all the words that I spoke to you in those days,
> peradventure they may turn from their evil ways,
> and I will then repent of the evil and will not bring it.
>
> (23) "And Noah and Methuselah stood forth,
> and said in the ears of the sons of men,
> all that God had spoken concerning them.
>
> (24) "But the sons of men would not hearken,
> neither would they incline their ears to all their declarations.
>
> (25) "And it was after this that the Lord said to Noah,
> The end of all flesh is come before me, on account of their evil
> deeds, and behold I will destroy the earth."

This passage seems to indicate that in spite of everything that had previously transpired, there was still the opportunity for people to turn away from the prevalent belief that creation was worthy of worship and return to worshipping the Creator God.

The passage does not indentify how many people would need

to return to the true worship of the Creator God for the earth to be spared. It simply indicates that five years before the flood, there was still an open door.

Verse 24 makes it quite clear that not only were men unwilling to redirect their worship to the Creator God, they weren't even willing to listen to Noah or Methuselah and contemplate their appeal. Thus, God's decision is made resolute: *"The end of all flesh is come before me, on account of their evil deeds, and behold I will destroy the earth."*

Finally, the grand question that has troubled so many is definitively answered: If man had become so wicked that God was moved to pronounce a drastic measure of judgment, why did he have to destroy the entire world in the process? Why violently destroy the earth, when He could have used any number of methods to bring about the death of those who were unrepentantly wicked?

It was the very nature of their wickedness that made the destruction of all creation mandatory. By annihilating every living thing on the earth, the question of whether God was a part of creation or separate from creation was eternally answered. If the Doctrine of Emanations was indeed true, the destruction of creation would be in essence the destruction of God himself. The Great Flood would forever settle the argument.

Romans 1:20-25

> (20) *"For the invisible things of him from the creation of the world are clearly seen, being understood by the things that are made, even his eternal power and Godhead; so that they are without excuse:*

(21) "Because that, when they knew God,
they glorified him not as God, neither were thankful;
but became vain in their imaginations,
and their foolish heart was darkened.

(22) "Professing themselves to be wise,
they became fools,

(23) "And changed the glory of the uncorruptible God
into an image made like to corruptible man,
and to birds, and fourfooted beasts, and creeping things.

(24) "Wherefore God also gave them up to uncleanness
through the lusts of their own hearts,
to dishonour their own bodies between themselves:

(25) "Who changed the truth of God into a lie,
and worshipped and served the creature
more than the Creator, who is blessed forever. Amen."

It is not clear how long Methuselah and Noah pleaded with the sons of men to heed their warnings and turn from their pagan worship. Was it a matter of hours? Days? Weeks? Or months? Whatever the case, business really starts to pick up once the time for reasoning has passed.

My Three Sons (and Their Wives)

Noah is told to separate himself from civilization and go to a specific place. Once there, construction of the ark was to be his sole task. By this time Shem and Japheth were more than 90 years of age, having been born shortly after Noah reached age 500.

Knowing that Shem gives birth to a son at age 100, just two years after the flood (Gen. 11:10), we can surmise that he was at least 97 at the start of the flood and 92 when the construction of the ark begins (97 years of age + 1 year on the ark + 2 years after the flood = 100). We could also make a case for Shem being 98 years of age when the flood begins, and the date of the birth of his son as being marked from the beginning of the flood. We also know that Japheth was older than Shem (Gen. 10:21).

The question regarding the approximate age of Ham is really one that can't be answered with certainty. It's entirely possible that he was born to someone other than the mother of Shem and Japheth and quite possibly much later in Noah's life. We only know that he was the youngest of the three and that he was old enough to be married by the time the ark was finished. Whether he was 20 or 90 at the time of the flood is something about which we can only speculate.

Once the ark comes to rest, we will see some behavior attributed to Ham that seems to support the thought that he might be considerably younger than Shem and Japheth and that they were indeed his step-brothers.

It's Year of the World 1657. The ark is complete and Methuselah is now 969 years old. It's nearly time to begin store-housing supplies and collecting the animal occupants. Noah, his wife and their sons are approaching the final stages of preparation for what has to be a most unnerving event – the destruction of the entire world.

Noah knows what lies ahead and, by now, it would seem that many long hours of discussion and speculation have transpired. As things have unfolded, it would be easy to envision Methuselah as being actively involved or periodically checking on the progress and offering encouragement.

We are now just days away from the utter and complete devastation of the planet and Noah's year-long struggle for survival, which prompts me to once again ask the question: How in the world did this ever become a happy little children's story?

I don't know about you, but at this point the gravity of the situation is beginning to weigh heavily on me. Conspiracy theories pop up and get shot down with such frequency in our day that they hardly carry any significant impact. Even the supposed final countdown of the Mayan calendar in December of 2012 was a mere whimper on the world's collective anxiety meter.

Cataclysmic dates for the out-of-the-blue arrival of Nibiru are set and moved almost week by week; and yes, I know that the infamous search for the destructive 10th planet has been in full swing since the *New York Times* article, "Clues Get Warm in the Search for Planet X," hit the newsstands in early '80s.[13] There's never a shortage of stories and pseudo-stories on the topic.

End of the World proclamations come from all corners in our day. Be it newly discovered comets, rogue asteroids or even the wild speculation of alien invasion, there's no shortage of "Chicken Littles" or "Boys Cryin' Wolf" on the internet. It's almost as if some are attached at the hip to the quest of being the first to predict the inevitable doomsday event that actually will happen. Surely, they must know that there's not an award to be won once the proverbial dust settles.

Noah knew the time was drawing near and it would appear

that Methuselah knew it as well. How sobering a feeling that must have been!

Jasher 5:35-36

> (35) "Then Noah took the three daughters of Eliakim,
> son of Methuselah, for wives for his sons,
> as the Lord had commanded Noah.
>
> (36) "And it was at that time Methuselah the son of Enoch died,
> nine hundred and sixty years old was he, at his death."[11]

Noah goes to his father's brother, Eliakim, and brings back three daughters of Eliakim to be wives for his three sons. They were the first cousins of Shem, Ham and Japheth. Thus, the marital union between cousins in the bloodline of Seth continued.

The Book of Jasher does not give the names of the three women, neither does it explain how it was determined which son was matched with which daughter. The marriages take place just before the passing of Methuselah, and it would be reasonable to presume that Methuselah was personally involved in the process. In this case, there are three weddings and then a funeral.

The first verse of the next chapter reports that after the death of Methuselah, Noah is instructed by God to gather his family into the ark and make final preparations. It is now seven days before the flood.

Genesis 7:10-11

> (10) "And it came to pass after seven days,
> that the waters of the flood were upon the earth.

(11) "In the six hundredth year of Noah's life, in the second month, the seventeenth day of the month, the same day were all the fountains of the great deep broken up, and the windows of heaven were opened."

Lions and Tigers and Bears? Seriously?

"Canst thou draw out leviathan with a hook?"

It's the opening salvo in a series of proposed quandaries that God presents to a man named Job in the 41st chapter of the Old Testament book of Job. There's some speculation that the beastly animal described in the verses following was a mythological sea monster or an ocean-roaming urban legend passed down by sailors in ancient times.

The lengthy description of the creature is quite imposing, to say the least. While there's no shortage in early literature of nefarious sea monster tales, I have to wonder why God would choose a scarcely known creature of the shadows that might even be fictitious, if he wanted to engage Job in somber conversation.

Although Job answers not a single question that God poses, if the animal was indeed unknown to him, a logical reply would be: "How should I know? And what's the point of this whole conversation?" In essence, the entire Q&A would be quite silly.

However, if Job had a personal knowledge of the beast, the questions would tend to have a far greater resonance with him. In that scenario, a more serious reaction and response from Job on the matter would be anticipated.

With that in mind, let's take a quick look at the questions as they are asked:

Verse 1: *Canst thou draw out leviathan with a hook? Or his tongue with a cord which thou lettest down?* (Is it possible to go fishing for him?)

Verse 2: *Canst thou put a hook into his nose? Or bore his jaw through with a thorn?* (Can you put him on a leash or have him pull your cart like an ox?)

Verse 3: *Will he make supplications unto thee? Will he speak soft words unto thee?* (Can you envision him ever being at your mercy?)

Verse 4: *Will he make a covenant with thee? Wilt thou take him for a servant forever?* (Is it possible to negotiate terms with him or make him abide by your rules?)

Verse 5: *Wilt thou play with him as with a bird? Or wilt thou bind him for thy maidens?* (Could you make him into your pet or cage him for display?)

Verse 6: *Shall the companions make a banquet of him? Shall they part him among the merchants?* (Is there any chance you might serve him up as dinner or sell parts of him as merchandise?)

Verse 7: *Canst thou fill his skin with barbed irons? Or his head with fish spears?* (Do people hunt for him as they might other animals? Would normal hunting methods work against leviathan?)

Verse 8: *Lay thine hand upon him, remember the battle, do no more.* (Pick a fight with him and it's quite possibly the last thing you will ever do.)

Verse 9: *Behold, the hope of him is in vain: shall not one be cast down even at the sight of him?* (You might come up with a brave plan to go nose to nose with him, but once eye to eye, men are paralyzed with fear.)

Verse 10a: *None is so fierce that dare stir him up:* (Everyone and everything has enough sense to leave leviathans alone! Nobody picks a fight with these things.)

Verse 10b: *Who then is able to stand before me?* (I, the Creator God, designed leviathan way back on day 5 of creation. If people are terrified of leviathan, shouldn't they also have a humbling respect for the God who created him?)

Verse 12: *"I will not conceal his parts, nor his power...."* (In essence, God is saying: "I created this thing for a reason and I put him on display.")

Verse 13: *Who can discover the face of his garment? Or who can come to him with his double bridle?* (Who can tell the front from the back? And who would attempt to put him in a double bridle? A "double bridle" is the harness that is used by those who ride horses. It's designed to wrap around the face of the horse in a way so that the rider can easily govern the direction of the animal while riding. That's just not possible with leviathan because he has a long neck and he can quickly whip his head/face around in any direction he chooses.)

> **SIDE NOTE:** Some have suggested that leviathan may have been a T-Rex. This verse indicates that leviathan had a long neck. That attribute certainly doesn't fit with what we know about T-Rex.

Verse 14: *Who can open the doors of his face? His teeth are terrible round about.* (Leviathan had powerfully strong jaws and fierce teeth.)

Verse 15-17: *(15)His scales are his pride, shut up together as with a close seal. (16)One is so near to another, that no air can come between them. (17)They are joined one to another, they stick together, that they cannot be sundered.* (Leviathan was covered with scales. The scales were beautiful and they were so tightly woven together that he could not be scaled as a fish. Thus, his scales were more like the scales of a snake.)

Verse 18-21: *(18)By his neesings a light doth shine, and his eyes are like the eyelids of the morning. (19)Out of his mouth go burning lamps, and sparks of fire leap out. (20)Out of his nostrils goeth smoke, as out of a seething pot or caldron. (21)His breath kindleth coals, and a flame goeth out of his mouth.* (As you may have guessed, the word translated "neesings" means to blow air out through the nose. There's no question that leviathan had the ability to breathe fire through its nostrils and mouth.)

By now, we can most confidently conclude that the description of leviathan in Job chapter 41 is that of a fire-breathing dragon. The description continues for another dozen verses: He is incredibly strong. He does not fear man, nor does he fear any of man's weapons. Verse 29 says that he laughs at the shaking of a spear. Verse 33 says that he is unlike any other creature on the face of the earth, which brings us face to face with a daunting dilemma:

How in the world did Noah get a pair
of these things on the ark?

Making a List & Checking It Twice

The commonly accepted notion is that once the ark was built, Noah and his sons began a monumental task of collecting animals. The mantra is two of every kind, which would undoubtedly be a mating pair that would be capable of producing offspring once the ark came to rest and it was time to jump-start the world. The loosely constructed concept leaves us with an assortment of questions and a whole basketful of chaos.

1. Was Noah familiar with every animal that existed?
2. Did Noah know where they lived and how to catch them?
3. How did he know when he had them all?
4. What about spiders and snakes and rodents?
5. What about poisonous creatures?
6. What about predators? Even if you catch them, how do you keep them from eating the rest of the occupants?
7. How do you keep the penguins cool?
8. How do you keep the iguanas from freezing?
9. How do you keep the beavers from chewing?
10. How do you keep the woodpeckers from pecking?
11. Don't amphibians need water at least part of the time?
12. What do you do with all these animals once you've got 'em?
13. What do you do with all the poop?

14. Did he keep nocturnal creatures away from the rooster?

15. How do you balance the payload and stabilize the weight?

16. How do you keep the animals at peace throughout the trip?

17. Do monkeys get seasick?

18. How do you feed this herd?

19. What about sea life?

20. What about things that live in the ground?

21. Did the buffalo have an onboard home in which to roam?

22. Why didn't he save unicorns?

23. What about dinosaurs?

24. What about Bigfoot and the Yeti?

There are so many animals from all over the world, and so many different environments and climates. We're still discovering new species to this day. There's just no way that he had the ability or the time to catch two of everything and, even if he did, he'd run out of room for them. This is where the whole story just crumbles under its own weight, right?

The World I Know

It's fairly easy to see that this section is going to open a pretty large can of worms. Ah.... worms. They fall into the "creatures that live in the ground" category, and the question of whether or not they were on the ark is just one of the many things that have to be given a reasonable amount of consideration somewhere in the next few pages.

Before venturing too deeply into The Great Hall of Animals (or maybe that should be haul of animals), it would probably be a good idea to evaluate the world in which they existed. Did it have polar ice caps and blistering dry deserts? Were the continental land masses separated by miles of oceans? Did some animals thrive in one particular environment, but not exist at all in a different part of the world? Was the flood itself indeed global, or is this the point where we determine that it simply couldn't have been?

There's a lot of ground to cover here, and perhaps the most difficult thing will be to keep speculation at a safe distance as we work primarily with sound reasoning and interpretation of information from commonly trusted sources. Although we'll take a closer look at the overall differences in composition of the pre-flood earth versus the post-flood earth in the next chapter, some general visual images have to be put into place if we are to make any realistic attempt at resolving the legitimate improbability issues that are inherent with Noah's animal conservation project.

There's more than enough evidence to indicate that any large-scale natural disaster changes the overall landscape in which it occurs. A sizable earthquake not only levels manmade buildings, but also alters the natural surroundings to a measurable degree.

February 27, 2010 – An earthquake, measuring at 8.8 on the Richter Scale, shook the Chilean coastline of South America.

According to the US Geological Survey (USGS), the epicenter was about 1.9 miles off the coast of Pelluhue. NASA records state that the quake shifted Earth's "figure axis" by about three inches and shortened the length of our day by 1.26 microseconds.[1] These are measurable and recorded lasting effects of the earthquake.

NASA defines Earth's figure axis as "the axis about which Earth's mass is balanced." Their report explains that "a shift in Earth's figure axis will cause Earth to wobble a bit differently as it rotates, but it will not cause a shift of Earth's axial tilt in space – only external forces such as the gravitational attraction of the sun, moon and planets can do that."[2]

March 11, 2011 – A magnitude 9.0 earthquake shook Japan. The Japan earthquake was memorable because of the densely populated island nation and the graphic recorded visuals of the tsunami that accompanied the quake. The devastation and loss of life were massive. Aside from the physical damage to manmade structures, NASA reports that this quake resulted in a six-and-a-half-inch shift in Earth's figure axis and shortened our days by an additional 1.8 microseconds.[3] The Japan quake, which was measurably stronger than the Chilean quake, was only the fifth largest recorded quake since 1900, according to NASA.[4]

> SIDE NOTE: For the curious, the four quakes with a higher magnitude reading than the 2011 quake off the coast of Japan are:

1. May 22, 1960 – 9.5 magnitude quake near Chile

2. March 28, 1964 – 9.2 magnitude quake near Prince William Sound, Alaska

3. December 26, 2004 – 9.1 magnitude quake near Northern Sumatra

4. November 4, 1952 – 9.0 magnitude quake near Kamchatka, Russia

It's not all that difficult to see the superficial effects and measure the lasting behind-the-scenes impact that a sizable earthquake has on our world. Volcanoes are another shape-shifting tool at nature's disposal. History records a number of massive eruptions that forced their way through the crust and rained down varying degrees of devastation on huge regions of the world.

Mount Vesuvius, located in Naples, Italy, gives us perhaps the most widely known volcanic eruption in history. In August of 79 AD, Vesuvius went through a series of consecutive eruptions. It started with a plume of ash that blanketed nearby cities. Shortly after, the first of up to six separate destructive pyroclastic surges wreaked devastation beyond comprehension. We associate the story of Vesuvius with Pompeii, because much of the city's ruin was preserved in the lava flow. It is believed that it was the fourth of the six surges that buried Pompeii. [5]

In more modern times, we're familiar with the massive eruption of Mount St. Helens in 1980. May 18th began with an early morning earthquake around 8:30 that registered 5.1 on the Richter Scale.[6] The earthquake signaled a series of explosions that increased in intensity as the day unfolded. Finally, around 3:50 p.m. the mountain exploded with such force that nearly 1,300 feet of its peak was blown away, leaving a large, horseshoe-shaped crater.[7] The massive melting of surrounding snow and glaciers triggered large mudflows that caused Spirit Lake to flood and later overflow, resulting in additional damage to the surrounding landscape.[8] Aerial photos of the region before and after the eruption reveal a substantial degree of geographic makeover.

History tells us that nature reshapes our world. What we see today is not what once was, nor is it a trustworthy representation of what will be in the far-reaching future. Shorelines have been redefined by time. Sandstorms have buried once proud civilizations and earthquakes have leveled them. The world we know is not the world that Noah knew, and we would be foolish to presume that it was.

Come Together, Right Now... Over Me

January 6, 1912 – Alfred Wegener, a German geophysicist and meteorologist, presented his concept of continental drift for the first time. It was something he had been contemplating for a number of years after being a part of an expedition to Denmark and Greenland. During the expedition, Wegener had the opportunity to analyze rock types, geological structures and fossils from both sides of the Atlantic Ocean. His examination led him to conclude that there was a noteworthy connection between the coastal areas of the two opposing continents.

Wegener's theory was that there once had been a giant super-continent, which he named *Urkontinent* (German for primal continent). In 1915, he published *The Origin of Continents and Oceans,* which documented his research and officially proposed his theory. Expanded editions of his continuing research were published in the 1920s.

In 1925, his work was finally published in English. The translation presented Wegener's theories in dogmatic, assertive tones that were common with German-to-English translations. As a result, it was received so poorly by American geologists that the American Association of Petroleum Geologists organized a conference to directly refute Wegener's theories.[9] Radical ideas are seldom embraced without opposition by the established authorities in any field of study.

By the early 1950s the newly emerging geological science of paleomagnetism was gaining traction. Pioneered by S.K. Runcorn at Cambridge and P.M.S. Blackett at Imperial College, the early data was producing evidence in support of Wegener's super-continent theory.[10] Independent studies of rock and fossil samples from all around the world were slowly changing minds and opening up the established scientific community to the idea that Wegener's proposals had merit. The theory of Pangaea was born.

Australian geologist Samuel Warren Carey built upon Wegener's theories and became a key figure in the developing concept of Plate Tectonics.[11] The concept is a scientific theory that attempts to explain the large-scale motions of Earth's lithosphere. Lithosphere is Greek for "rocky sphere" and is the scientific name for what we most commonly think of as Earth's crust and upper mantle.

Plate Tectonics identifies the lithosphere as having been broken up into seven or eight major plates and several minor plates. It's commonly accepted that these plates move, some as much as 100 millimeters each year.[12] There's another measurable process in the works, primarily along the Atlantic and Pacific trenches, in which the ocean floor is spreading.[13] This quantifiable fact presents a problem. If the ocean floor is spreading (or growing as some like to term it), then the planet, as a whole, must be expanding or growing.

The idea of an Expanding Earth isn't too well received by most Tectonic Plate proponents, as they see a need to keep the size of the planet constant. They've attempted to accomplish this by proposing that there are two types of lithospheres. In their model, the earth is composed of an oceanic lithosphere and thicker continental lithosphere. Each of these lithospheres is topped by its own type of crust.[14]

Along the great ocean trenches, the oceanic lithosphere maintains an open crack, which allows molten magma from the core to seep up through the trench. As the molten magma meets waters of the surrounding ocean, it cools. This process results in newly deposited ocean floor, the growth of which has been measured by geologists.

Measuring the varying ages of ocean floor deposits tends to substantiate the theory even further. The ocean floor that is closer to the trench is substantially younger than the ocean floor that is closer to the continental shelf.[15] If this process is happening along all ocean trenches, and the evidence verifies that it is, the ocean floor must be growing.

Geologists who opposed the idea of an Expanding Earth introduced the idea of plate subduction.[16] Put simply, it's more or less a conveyor belt principle; as one inch of new ocean floor emerges, a corresponding inch must disappear. If you're going to gain lithosphere (crust) in one area (this appears to be undeniable), then we have to lose lithosphere (crust) in another area (in an effort to maintain the size of the earth as stable and unchanging).

For most geologists, keeping the size of the earth constant is crucial and the thought of a smaller Earth presents a number of problems.[17] As *Science Daily* explained in a 2011 article, "Any significant change in Earth's radius will alter our understanding of our planet's physical processes and is fundamental to the branch of science called geodesy, which seeks to measure Earth's shape and gravity field, and how they change over time."[18]

There are really two major points of contention:

1. Change the size of Earth and account for the distribution of mass.

2. Change the size of Earth and account for the regulation of gravity.

It's actually a head-throbbing conundrum. Either Earth's mass has remained constant, and thus the gravitational pull at the surface has decreased over time, or Earth's mass has grown with the volume in such a way that the surface gravity has remained constant, or, Earth's gravity at its surface has increased over time, in line with its hypothesized growing mass and volume.[19] Take your pick. Each option provides its own heart-pounding episode of mind checkers.

Some geologists, however, are open to the idea that the earth was indeed much smaller than it is currently and, citing evidence of continued ocean floor growth, a few even propose that it's continuing to expand or grow. Samuel Warren Carey was actually a staunch proponent of the Expanding Earth Theory. After nearly 30 years of research, he finally published a 448-page book detailing his theory in 1976.[20]

So thorough was Carey that he even weighed in on the gravity dilemma as it related to the size and weight of dinosaurs. His belief was that Earth's current gravity equivalent would have crushed the dinosaurs or at the very least severely restricted their overall growth.[21]

Independent of Carey, German geologist Ott Christoph Hilgenberg published a work entitled *Vom wachsenden Erdball (The Expanding Earth)* in 1933. Although the two were apparently unaware of each other's work, they produced remarkably similar findings. Both men's research led them to envision a 50% smaller Earth with one primary land mass and much smaller bodies of water.

A Little On The Creative Side

Though the idea of a much smaller planet contradicts current perception, the early verses of the Creation account recorded in Genesis appear to support this solitary land mass with smaller bodies of water proposal.

Genesis 1:1-2

(1) "In the beginning God created the heaven and the earth.

(2) "And the earth was without form, and void;
and darkness was upon the face of the deep.
And the Spirit of God moved upon the face of the waters."

We are guilty of reading past those initial ten words (verse 1) as if they're commonplace, but they contain an amazingly profound declaration — THE BIRTH MOMENT OF THE UNIVERSE.

Those ten words most plainly declare that in that instantaneous moment, three vital components, which previously did not exist, were brought into being by a presumed but unknown entity that possessed the power and the desire to do it.

This verse, in and of itself, proposes the origin of three crucial elements that are necessary for anything that has ever existed to have life.

TIME – *"In the beginning..."* To the best of our current understanding, nothing can exist without having a time period in which to exist. The statement, "In the beginning," establishes a period of time in which something can exist. It establishes the reality of "when."

SPACE – *"...God created the heaven..."* This is the establishment of location. To the best of our current understanding, nothing can exist without having a place in which to exist. This statement establishes the reality of "where."

MATTER – *"...and the earth."* This portion is commonly interpreted as a reference to the planet we call home, Earth. But the following verses make much more sense if we exercise a measure of patience here. In verse 1, the reference to "the

199

earth" is an indication of the establishment of what we have come to know as the base elements that form all discernible matter and, more explicitly, the atomic structural elements that ultimately comprise the base elements that we recognize.

Whether these elements exist in a solitary or a combined state is immaterial, as we know that they maintain the unique quality of being capable of existence either in combination with other elements or in complete isolation. This is the establishment of "what," and from this "what," everything that we know to exist can be produced.

The second verse of the Genesis account declares that what was created in verse 1 exhibited no recognizable markings or definition. We are told that it was without form and void. The word translated "without form" is the Hebrew word "tohuw" (tō'•hü), meaning chaos or unreality.[22] The word "void" is the Hebrew word "bohuw" (bō'•hü), signifying emptiness.[23] There was no composition, configuration or order and there was no life or life form of any kind. In essence, all that existed at that time, existed in a state of disorder.

Verse 2 also states that darkness presided across the face of the deep. The phrase, "face of the deep" indicates that, whatever this is, it has a surface and it has volume. It is four-dimensional in nature (length, breadth, depth, and height – Ephesians 3:18). It is also referenced as the "face of the waters" in the very next sentence. Altogether, these statements paint an image of an unstructured conglomeration of matter that was present within an unrepressed body of water with undefined dimensions. It has a surface, which gives it a beginning and an end. Therefore, it is an *enclosed system*. This indication in the record is immensely important. (More details about the four dimensions and enclosed system universe are presented in the book *My End of the Circle*, a companion book to this volume.)

To visualize individual planets, solar systems, or even galaxies such as the Milky Way at this point is to leap several stages ahead in the process of development or creation. Let's continue working our way through the Genesis account.

Genesis 1:3-5

> *(3) "And God said, Let there be light: and there was light.*

> *(4) "And God saw the light, that it was good:*
> *and God divided the light from the darkness.*

> *(5) "And God called the light Day,*
> *and the darkness he called Night.*
> *And the evening and the morning were the first day."*

If you've just put the Sun in your mental image, you've jumped ahead once again; several days ahead, actually. What we know as the Sun is not mentioned until verses 14 through 19 and at that point it is attributed as a Day 4 happening. Be patient in your mental image. There's no indication that there are any planets or stars established at this stage. There is time, space, and elements or matter, which appear to exist within a four-dimensional expanse of water. The only combination of elements that are confirmed to exist at this point would be hydrogen and oxygen, thus producing the existence of water, which science tells us is primary to the existence of life.

Verse 2 also mentions darkness: *"and darkness was upon the face of the deep."* There's no further declaration as to what "darkness" actually is, but it has an established presence that is more than just the absence of light, and it's on the "face" or the outside of the expanse of water. In verse 3 we see the establishment of light and, as we'll see in verse 4, the light is also clearly positioned on the outside of the expanse of water.

> **SIDE NOTE:** Could the introduction of light be the creation of angelic beings? We're told that they were a part of creation (Psalms 148:1-5), that they *"sang for joy"* when the foundations of the earth were laid (Job 38:4-7), that they are essentially beings of light (Daniel 10:4-6, Luke 2:9, Acts 12:7, and 2nd Corinthians 11:14), and that they are an innumerable host (Hebrews 12:22). Also, Christ often referred to those around him as children of the light or children of the darkness. Clearly there's much more to light and darkness than our basic comprehension of luminescence and the lack thereof.

Keep in mind, there is no Sun to this point, which means that the light which is introduced in verse 3 is not confined or restricted in any way. It's not tied to a stationary source. It simply exists. It isn't gernerated from a specified point of origin. Light, along with darkness (which was identified in verse 2), is everywhere across the face of the watery expanse. This dual presence of light and darkness raises a conflict that must be resolved. Verse 4: *"and God divided the light from the darkness."*

Because we've always known light to have a point of origin, this is a very difficult concept to visualize. For us, light starts in the bulb and bounces off the walls and desktop. For us, light starts with the rising of the Sun and reflects off the surface of the ocean or pierces its way through the trees. That's how we experience light today, but that's not the portrait that is painted in Genesis 1:4.

In Job 38:19, Job is asked, *"Where is the way where light dwelleth? and as for darkness, where is the place thereof?"* Needless to say, he has no answer to the question.

The last part of verse 4 clearly states that light and darkness are divided. Before this, both existed, but neither had boundaries. There is a glow and there is blackness thick enough to be felt. Once boundaries are assigned to each, things can then exist in the light and be illuminated. Light can also be pushed aside, leaving something in the night. *"And God called the light Day, and the darkness he called Night"* (Gen. 1:5).

Moving past verses 4 and 5 where light is introduced, we come to a very perplexing declaration in verse 6. Something very unique is established for the purpose of separating water from water.

Genesis 1:6

"And God said, Let there be a firmament in the midst of the waters, and let it divide the waters from the waters."

The firmament, mentioned in verse 6, has long been thought of as the establishment of an atmosphere, but again, it seems we're jumping ahead of the methodical progress. Instead of the firmament being a defined atmosphere, could it possibly be the establishment of a different type of measurable field?

At this point the water is divided into sections above and below the newly introduced element, referred to as a "firmament," but it remains otherwise unconfined. Water, which to this point has not been designated into areas where it does and does not exist, is simply divided from itself in the same way several acres of open land might be divided by a fence. The fence may serve as a marker of sorts, but it does not cause land to exist on one side, while ceasing to exist on the other.

To this point we have time, space and matter. We also have light, darkness and water. Light and darkness were given distinctive boundaries in verse 4 and now, water is divided into water that is above and water that is below. The question is, above and below what? If we envision "the firmament" as being a dividing line or fence, then we can more easily see the methodical progression as we continue. Things seem to get a little more defined in verse 9.

Genesis 1:9-10

> (9) "And God said, Let the waters under the heaven
> be gathered together unto one place,
> and let the dry land appear: and it was so.

> (10) "And God called the dry land Earth;
> and the gathering together of the waters called He Seas:
> and God saw that it was good."

This is the first activity that might appear to be confined to a more specific location, as opposed to the previous descriptions of universal actions and results. However, it may still be a little premature to jump to that conclusion and envision this as an event that is solely restricted to the planet we know as Earth.

It could be easily argued that the establishment of the force that separates water from water took place throughout what we have come to know as the universe. If bodies of water are separated from other expanses of water throughout the universe, then we are still a step or two away from any indication of creation activity being isolated to a particular location.

Picture if you will a child blowing a breath of air through a bubble wand. As bubbles begin to fill the room, the illustration takes shape. Each bubble is comprised of an enclosed field of soapy liquid, which serves to separate air that is trapped inside of the bubble from the air that is present on the outside of the bubble. In the Genesis creation account, the element on the inside and outside of these bubbles is defined as water, and we are not given any indication as to how many of these bubbles emerge when the water separation takes place. We'll take a closer look at this force that separates water in the next chapter.

Verse 9 draws the reader's attention to the water on the inside of a bubble. This water is "gathered together" into one place so that dry land can emerge or appear. Did this take place solely on the planet we call home? Or did this gathering of water take place inside of bubbles throughout the universe, thus causing the formation of planetary bodies, solar systems, galaxies, etc.?

In either case, verse 9 serves as the first reference to the appearance of anything that could be recognized as an inhabitable surface area by today's understanding. The land mass appears when the vast majority of water is assigned to a new location, most of which is apparently beneath the surface.

From this point forward, the water beneath the firmament (inside of a bubble) is confined into restricted basins that are called seas (verse 10) and massive caverns beneath the surface that are later identified as fountains of the great deep (Gen. 7:11). The Hebrew word for "great" carries the meaning of abundant or exceedingly sufficient.[24] There is also reference to flowing water called rivers in Genesis chapter 2. From this point, water flows freely throughout the planet, and it seems to do so as one globally connected body of water.

It is inconceivable that what we recognize today as continents, oceans, seas and rivers are even slightly representative of the original geography that was revealed when the waters were "gathered together unto one place" and the dry land appeared.

Reconstructing Construction

If we were to go back through the last few passages and remove the word Genesis, along with the verse notations, and any mention of an outside force that negotiates the overall step-by-step development, we'd end up with something that reads very similar to a description of the popularly accepted Big Bang Theory.

Replace light with heat. Allow water to be your cooling agent and plug in gravity as your driving force of stabilization that causes individual heavenly bodies to take shape and settle into their orbits. It's quite obvious where this is leading. It's not a perfect model by any means, but it does sound like the Creationists and the Big Bang Theorists are driving their convertibles in the same neighborhood.

The problems grow out of their behavioral nature as rival gangs. They both want the same construct, but neither wants the truth to fall outside of their basic bonding tenant: Creationists must have their concept of a personal God, and Big Bang Theorists absolutely don't want anything resembling an intelligent designer, unless the designer can be identified as nature. There doesn't appear to be any middle ground.

However, there actually are proponents of a third option and these theorists, although blatantly dismissed out of hand by both parties, seem to be gaining traction in some corners of the discussion. Their developing doctrine is based on evolution to a point, with an intercessory intervention from a much more highly developed (evolved) race of beings. The folks who propose this are known in pop-culture as Ancient Astronaut Theorists.

The basis of their theory asserts that all things in the universe were born out of the Big Bang. From that point, evolution ran its course in all corners of the universe, but not everything evolved at the same measured pace. A race of beings, alien to this planet, evolved at a faster pace than life on this planet and attained the capability of space travel along with highly advanced science and medicine. These extraterrestrial life forms accomplished this while the evolving life on Earth was still trying to figure out the process of hunting and gathering.

These advanced beings then traveled here as a part of their exploration of the cosmos, and modern man developed on this planet with the outside help of bio-engineering experiments performed by these ancient space voyagers. In short, life everywhere evolved, but modern man exists because of the intervention of super-intelligent beings that traveled here from another point of origin.

Although some of their methods, documentation and theories may sound as if they came from a couple of steps beyond the fringe, attention must be paid to this concept as a systematic belief construct that is growing in popularity.

Even though they do not proclaim belief in a creator, they openly embrace the Bible as a historical record that provides some level of validity to their doctrine. Insert the concept of alien beings in place of the Watchers, which they openly do,[25] and many of their proposed possibilities would also run parallel to things we discussed earlier in this book. Be aware, that their presentation of evidence is often couched in terms of a "what if" scenario in an effort to proliferate their doctrine.

To Be or Not To Be Is Still the Primary Question

Three proposals may be on the table, but the primary question is yet to be answered: Is that all ya got?

It is a fundamental premise of science that energy can neither be created nor destroyed. If that's the case, then everything that exists (whether known or yet to be discovered) existed at the moment of the Big Bang or the moment of Genesis 1:1.

Einstein's Theory of Relativity was built around the premise that "Energy cannot be created or destroyed; it can only be changed from one form to another." This principle is known as the Law of the Conservation of Energy or the First Law of Thermodynamics.[26] If Einstein is right, and no one has successfully proven him wrong, it would seem that we do not possess the ability to create new energy or matter, although we've no doubt tried in the past and are still making every effort to forge previously nonexistent energy today.

So the creation of energy and matter seems definitively outside of our capability, but does that mean that no new matter or new energy is coming into existence by other means? The question and distinction is important, because without the development of new matter, the idea of an Expanding Earth simply can't be supported. Neither, by the way, can support be given to the concept of an Expanding Universe.

Enter Hubble's Law and the theory of an Expanding Universe. Although principally attributed to Edwin Hubble, the idea was derived from a published article on the topic of general relativity by Georges Lemaître in a 1927 paper.[27] The article proposed that the universe was indeed expanding and suggested an estimated value for the rate of expansion, which is now recognized as the Hubble Constant.[28]

The law is built from the observation that objects in deep space and objects in near space are moving away from the earth at a noticeable rate. This is commonly accepted as a direct, physical observation of the expansion of the spatial volume of the observable universe.[29]

Hubble's Law has two possible explanations. Either the earth is at the center of an explosion of galaxies (which Copernicus disproved in the 15th century) or the universe is uniformly expanding everywhere. This universal expansion was predicted from general relativity by Alexander Friedmann in 1922[30] and by Lemaître in 1927,[31] well before Hubble made his 1929 analysis and observations, and it remains as a cornerstone component of the Big Bang Theory.

So, energy cannot be created nor destroyed, but everything is expanding. How can that be? If one object moves further away from another object, what substantive something has filled in the additional space between the two?

That's easy to resolve on a personal level. Two people move away from each other and matter simply realigns to fill in the gaps. But how do you solve the issue in space? Where does the gap-filling matter come from? How do you expand the balloon without pumping more air into the balloon?

It would seem that the Universe is the ultimate perpetual motion machine, but science tells us that it, in fact, is not.[32, 33] Science also asserts that perpetual motion machines can't exist at all without an outside force providing additional energy to keep them going. [34, 35] But having an outside source of energy would invalidate the whole perpetual motion notion. If you're developing a headache right about now, rest assured... you're not alone.

Nanna-Nanna-Nanna-Nanna... BAT---!

This seems like the perfect place to reach out for help from a cape-wearing crusader. Okay, so we're not actually lighting up the night sky with the outline of a bat insignia in hopes of luring the fictional crime-fighting vigilante into our conversation, but we are going to call attention to an animated illustration that was produced by the graphics wizard who's best known for putting ink on storyboards.

In 2006 Neal Adams produced a 10-minute video that's drawn nearly 2 million YouTube viewings. The well-crafted simulation takes the earth, as we know it today, back through a series of changes wherein ocean floor growth is systematically removed. The result, after all sections have been taken away bit by bit, is a smaller version of Earth with a single collective land mass.

Although it's very well put together and produces quite the riveting watch, the short video is not without its detractors. Those who discredit the illustration call into observance some of the following issues:

- The video doesn't represent the actual known size of the continents, especially Africa. This is primarily true and is directly connected to the overlooked discrepancies of modern world maps. The continental illustrations just aren't accurately portrayed. Common knowledge. Commonly disregarded.

- The video doesn't take into account the extending continental shelf that surrounds each land mass. This is also primarily true. In an effort to completely connect each continent, the video continues ocean floor retraction until everything has nowhere left to go.

- The video doesn't even attempt to explain where the lost ocean water is hiding or to what location the retracted ocean floor has been reassigned. The assumption is that both are absorbed into Earth's core, but the viewer is left to draw that conclusion on their own.

On the surface, there are clearly some questions to be raised and answers to be sought, but many of those who project opposition to the video clip have done so with venom and disdain, attempting to discredit Adams as entirely unqualified when it comes to interpreting the data of geological science and projecting ideas that are worthy of consideration.

Being no stranger to scorn, the historically esteemed Galileo is credited with proposing that "In questions of science, the authority of a thousand is not worth the humble reasoning of a single individual." Personally, I find Adams' work to be quite impressive and thought-provoking.

Plain and simple, the video presents an interesting concept, but not without leaving room for a number of legitimate issues to be raised:

- Adams' source for the size, shape and configuration of continents seems to come from the National Oceanic and Atmospheric Administration website, better known as NOAA.gov.[36] It can also be found as part of Geology 101 at Cornell University.[37] If the illustration presents an inaccurate size, shape, or proportion, it really doesn't seem logical to blame Adams.

- For those screaming that Adams' animation goes too far and fails to respect the boundaries of continental shelf geography, ummm… press pause at any point you'd like. You've still got a massive amount of ocean floor that has been retracted, which results in a much smaller globe.

- What about all the water? Where did it go? Genesis 1:9 seems to indicate that it covered the entire surface of the earth, prior to being gathered together into one place, which was later described as seas, rivers and fountains of the great deep (massive subterranean caves that are found all over the globe and show ample evidence that they were once filled with water).

For the detractors who wish to scream, "We work with facts, not conjecture or supposition," please understand that for the most part, we do not work with facts. We never have and we never will. We work with what we perceive as factual and find, as we go, that facts have a way of undergoing perpetual alteration as additional knowledge and insight becomes available.

In every age, knowledgeable men have made the false assumption that we know all there is to know, and self-bravado has inspired a virtual pounding of the chest and a blanket challenge to those who "know less" to prove wrong those who "know more." It's really no big surprise that the know-it-all cycle continues today.

Making use of the map imagery provided by NASA through NOAA, which appears to be commonly accepted and endorsed by institutions of higher learning, and working with the systematic conjecture of geologists such as Wegener, Carey, Hilgenberg, and others, of the knowledge we have, we're left with an old world that's vastly different than the world we know today. It is smaller, perhaps up to 50% smaller. It is primarily one globally connected land mass, where man and animals have few limitations to their ability to roam. And there is sufficient water beneath the crust to flood it entirely.

Here Kitty, Kitty...

There's an old joke that starts with the proposed question, "What do you call a cat with three ears?" The quickly agreed upon response is, "It doesn't much matter, because the cat is not going to come to you anyway."

The general pretentious nature of cats aside, there's an elephant of a question in the room and it's still waiting for us to pull up a chair at the discussion roundtable. The question of Noah's animal collection can be divided into several proposed discussions that include a general head count, a method of gathering, and a plan for caretaking. Again, we'll attempt to take a systematic approach to compiling data from the sources that are available and endeavor to leave speculation out on the fringe of the discussion to collect dust.

With all the different kinds of animals roaming the planet, the idea of sorting out who had reservations on the ark may seem a little intimidating. The blanket approach would be to include any and every different type of animal that we find in the world today, but the numbers would quickly grow to a point several notches beyond capacity overload. The "save everybody" approach just isn't a viable option.

The Interagency Taxonomic Information System (ITIS),[38] a U.S. Government-sponsored database designed to provide reliable information on species names and their hierarchical classification, lists just a little over 5,300 families of known animals. That number balloons exponentially when we move to classification of genus and species. It would probably be easier to funnel 15 pounds of sugar into a 5-pound bag than to logically argue for the presence of every known animal on the ark.

Deep breath. Step back. One more deep breath. The task appears daunting at first, but a little bit of research shows that the animal kingdom is surprisingly easy to breakdown. Through the helpful assistance of A-Z Animals dot-com, we find that all living organisms belong to one of five different *kingdoms*: animals, plants, fungi, bacteria, and protists or single-celled organisms. [39]

Each kingdom is further broken down into *phylums*. Our interest is in only one of the five – the *animal* kingdom. It contains only nine major *phylums*:

1. *Mollusca:* Primarily invertebrates such as snails and slugs, and water-dwelling invertebrates including clams, oysters, octopus and squid

2. *Porifera:* Primarily sponges

3. *Cnidaria:* Primarily anemones, corals, and jellyfish

4. *Platyhelminthes:* Primarily flatworms and flukes

5. *Nematoda:* Primarily nematodes and parasitic worms

6. *Annelida:* Primarily earthworms, night crawlers, leeches and ragworms

7. *Arthropoda:* Primarily flies, shrimp, spiders, crabs, ants and cockroaches (It has been estimated that more than 80% of all living creatures fall into this phylum.)[40]

8. *Echinodermata:* Primarily starfish, sea urchins, sea cucumbers and sand dollars

9. *Chordata:* Primarily vertebrates (All ark occupants fall into this phylum.)

Our interest is in only one of the nine – the *Chordata* phylum. The phylums are broken down into more specific categories called *classes* and the *Chordata* phylum splits neatly into these six classes:

1. *Mammalia* (mammals)

2. *Actinopterygii* (bony fish)

3. *Chondrichthyes* (cartilaginous fish)

4. *Aves* (birds)

5. *Amphibia* (amphibians)

6. *Reptilia* (reptiles)

There's no need for Noah to go fishing. So we can eliminate two of the six defining classes. Now we're getting somewhere. We need to keep an eye out for land-dwelling mammals, birds, amphibians and reptiles.

The classes break down by *orders*. The *Mammalia* class is divided into several easily recognized orders, such as: *Carnivora* (carnivores), *Primates* (apes), *Proboscidea* (elephants), *Artiodactyla* (hoofed animals of the field), and *Rodentia* (rodents), along with many others that aren't so commonly known. There are 29 orders in all, two of which are composed of aquatic mammals who most likely won't be in need of a boat.

The following list was pulled from the Interagency Taxonomic Information System (ITIS) website under the class: *Mammalia*.

1. The order of *Afrosoricida* includes moles.

2. The order of *Artiodactyla* includes cloven-hoofed animals of the fields (sheep, goats, camels, pigs, cows, deer, giraffes, and antelopes).

3. The order of *Carnivora* includes flesh-eating mammals (lions, tigers, bears, wolves, jackals, and even seals).

4. The order of *Cetacea* is primarily aquatic mammals such as whales and porpoises.

5. The order of *Chiroptera* includes bats.

6. The order of *Cingulata* includes armadillos.

7. The order of *Dermoptera* includes flying lemurs.

8. The order of *Erinaceomorpha* includes gymnures and hedgehogs.

9. The order of *Hyracoidea* includes hyraxes.

10. The order of *Lagomorpha* includes rabbits, hares and pikas.

11. The order of *Macroscelidea* includes elephant shrews.

12. The order of *Monotremata* includes egg-laying mammals, such as the spiny anteater.

13. The order of *Perissodactyla* includes horses, zebras, donkeys, rhinoceroses and tapirs.

14. The order of *Pholidota* includes pangolins and scaly anteaters.

15. The order of *Pilosa* includes anteaters and sloths.

16. The order of *Primates* includes all apes, monkeys and humans.

17. The order of *Proboscidea* is primarily elephants. It would have also included mammoths.

18. The order of *Rodentia* makes up approximately 43% of the *Mammalia* class and includes: rats, mice, porcupines, hamsters, beavers, squirrels, chipmunks, lemmings, muskrats, and guinea pigs. (Rabbits are not rodents.)

19. The order of *Scandentia* includes tree shrews.

20. The order of *Sirenia* includes aquatic mammals such as sea cows, manatees and dugongs.

21. The order of *Soricomorpha* includes desmans, moles and shrew moles.

22. The order of *Tubulidentata* includes aardvarks.

23. The order of *Dasyuromorphia* is primarily Australian marsupials.

24. The order of *Didelphimorphia* includes opossums.

25. The order of *Diprotodontia* includes kangaroos and wallabies.

26. The order of *Microbiotheria* includes very small South American marsupials. Most of this order is thought to be extinct.[41]

27. The order of *Notoryctemorphia* includes marsupial moles.

28. The order of *Paucituberculata* includes shrew opossums.

29. The order of *Peramelemorphia* includes bandicoots and bilbies.

The list of *Aves* (birds) includes forty different orders, the list of *Amphibia* (amphibians) includes three, and *Reptilia* (reptiles) includes only four.

The most defining question is: How far back towards the trunk of each family tree do you feel the need to go before you're comfortable that all bases have been covered and no species or potential species has been left behind?

We've covered a few hundred animals so far and there seems to be a lot of room for crossover, as moles and shrews kept popping up from time to time and, no, I won't be making any Whack-A-Mole jokes. This is serious stuff. Focus. Focus. Focus!

At the next level the individual *orders* are divided into more distinct *family* groups, and those are afterwards divided into categories of *genus*. As you move from *kingdom* to *phylum* to *class* to *order* to *family* to *genus* and eventually to *species*, there's a greater definition of characteristics at work, which decreases the number of animals that are included in each category. Moving in reverse from *species* towards *kingdom*, the defining characteristics are more general than specific, and the number of animals included in each category increases.

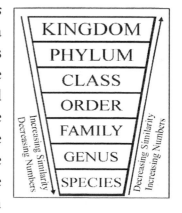

For instance: the animal kingdom includes the *Chordata* phylum, which encompasses the *Mammalia* class, which houses the *Carnivora* order, which contains **all cats.** If we move forward into the family divisions of the *Carnivora* order, we come to the *Felidae* family (cats only). If we move into the genus of the *Felidae* family, we find a division into small cats (bobcats and domestics), medium cats (panthers and cougars), and large cats (lions and tigers).

Parisian artist Alice Bouchardon designed an infographic entitled "Dogs Evolution" that was featured in an article on the Fast Company Design website about the evolution of dogs in January of 2014. The graphic attempts to make sense of the "Darwinian" and "Not-So-Darwinian" developments that have produced the vast array of dog breeds that are commonly known today.

Midway through the article, a 2010 study from UCLA is cited: "According to a genetic analysis by UCLA in 2010, what we call dogs today likely originated as gray wolves about 33,000 years ago in the Middle East, the same area where both domestic cats and many livestock animals originated." [42]

Again, the question of origin surfaces: How far back towards the trunk of each family tree do you feel the need to go before you're comfortable that all bases have been covered and no species or potential species has been left behind?

If research indicates that all dog breeds known today (domestic and wild) can be traced back to a breed of gray wolf that lived somewhere in the Middle East several thousand years ago, then how many "dogs" did Noah need to preserve so that Westminster could produce an annual dog show and give out ribbons?

So, what about our cats? *National Geographic* tells us that,

"Scientists have identified the house cat's maternal ancestors and traced them back to the Fertile Crescent. The Near Eastern wildcat still roams the deserts of Israel, Saudi Arabia, and other Middle Eastern countries. Between 70,000 and 100,000 years ago the animal gave rise to the genetic lineage that eventually produced all domesticated cats." [43]

What about larger cats? Testing by Warren Johnson and Stephen O'Brien of the U.S. National Cancer Institute used mitochondrial and nuclear DNA to show that ancient cats evolved into eight main lineages of cats that moved from continent to continent via the Bering land bridge and Isthmus of Panama. Johnson and O'Brien project that about 60% of the cats we know today developed within the last million years. [44]

We could continue to find mountains of research data, all of which points steadfastly to a common theme: the diversity in the animal kingdom that we see and know today was not nearly as varied in ancient history. The perplexing problem on the table isn't where all the animals we know today came from, but how long did it take them to get here?

See & Say, Round One

There's an interesting contrast between the Biblical text of Genesis chapter 1 and Genesis chapter 2 with regard to the creation account. In Genesis chapter 1, all sea life and bird life is brought forth from the water on Day 5 (Gen. 1:20-23). Land animals are formed out of the dust of the ground on Day 6 (Gen. 1:24-25). The land animals are spoken of in three distinct categories: beasts of the field, cattle, and creeping things.

- *Beasts of the field* are animals that have paws for feet. They reproduce by live birth and by laying eggs. This includes all land-dwelling mammals and reptiles.

- *Cattle* are also beasts of the field, but they're designated as beasts that have hooves rather than paws. In this category you also have a distinction between animals with cloven hooves and animals with a single primary hoof.

- *Creeping things* are things that are born in the water, but primarily live on the land. They creep from a water-based environment to a land-based existence. Although the term is used in a broader sense at times to encompass every living thing that moves, in this case "creeping things" is a specific reference to amphibians.

So far we have birds (Day 5) and land-dwelling mammals, reptiles and amphibians (Day 6). We also have all creatures of the sea, but as previously mentioned, they most likely won't need a boat to survive.

The distinctions are important, because later God tells Noah specifically what will be destroyed by the flood so that Noah knows exactly what needs to be saved.

Genesis 2:19

> *"And out of the ground the LORD God formed every beast of the field, and every fowl of the air; and brought them unto Adam to see what he would call them: and whatsoever Adam called every living creature, that was the name thereof."*

Close attention to the wording of Genesis chapter 2 presents a bit of a perplexing problem. Genesis 1:20-23 clearly states that birds are made out of the water, but Genesis 2:19 says that they're made out of the ground. We're not even two full chapters into the Bible and we've got a glaring contradiction. How can this be? *How can this be!!!*

Perhaps we should back up a little bit and look at the context of what was happening. All of what we are about to read in Genesis chapter 2 transpires as a part of the 6th Day of Creation, shortly after Adam takes his initial breath.

Genesis 2:7-8 is our lead in,

(7) "And the LORD God formed man of the dust of the ground,
and breathed into his nostrils the breath of life;
and man became a living soul.

(8) "And the LORD God planted a garden eastward in Eden;
and there he put the man whom he had formed."

Chapter 2 is providing additional details regarding ongoing activity that taking place as a part of Day 6. A garden is planted in a land identified as Eden and Adam is introduced to the garden. The wording identifies a bit of a timeline for us, revealing that Adam, along with every other creature that had been created, was formed from the dust (or water in the case of birds) and took their first collective breath outside of the Garden of Eden. From this point forward, all activity is taking place within the Garden of Eden.

Genesis 2:9

"And out of the ground made the LORD God to grow every tree
that is pleasant to the sight, and good for food;

223

the tree of life also in the midst of the garden,
and the tree of knowledge of good and evil."

If our timeline is correct, it would certainly appear that Adam is present and watching as these things take place. This is a teaching moment. Adam is being shown the origin of how things came into being and he's also being instructed as to everything's purpose for existing. There is no question for Adam as to the nature of God. God is the Creator and everything else is God's Creation. Adam clearly knows and understands that *the two are not the same.*

Genesis 2:10-14

(10) "And a river went out of Eden to water the garden;
and from thence it was parted, and became into four heads.

(11) "The name of the first is Pison:
that is it which compasseth the whole land of Havilah,
where there is gold;

(12) "And the gold of that land is good:
there is bdellium and the onyx stone.

(13) "And the name of the second river is Gihon:
the same is it that compasseth the whole land of Ethiopia.

(14) "And the name of the third river is Hiddekel:
that is it which goeth toward the east of Assyria.
And the fourth river is Euphrates."

The description of the location of Eden is quite interesting, as names for lands and rivers that emerge in the post-flood world are given. The four rivers are said to spring from a single flowing river; once again underlining the concept of water being one globally connected body that flows freely throughout the world. It is also noteworthy that the rivers are said to compass or encircle[45] "whole lands" as opposed to just running several hundred miles through a territory.

The indication is that these are the four main rivers which maintain the flow of water from the fountains of the deep and reach throughout the entire planet.

Genesis 2:15-17

> *(15) "And the LORD God took the man, and put him into the garden of Eden to dress it and to keep it.*
>
> *(16) "And the LORD God commanded the man, saying, Of every tree of the garden thou mayest freely eat:*
>
> *(17) "But of the tree of the knowledge of good and evil, thou shalt not eat of it: for in the day that thou eatest thereof thou shalt surely die."*

Verse 8 informs the reader where God put the man that he had created: God planted a Garden in Eden and there he put the man that he had created, Adam. Verse 15 confirms once again that Adam was created outside of the garden and goes on to tell us why Adam was put in the garden, "to dress and to keep it." From this point, it's quite clear that man was intended to have stewardship over everything that was created.

Verses 15 and 16 directly state that Adam was not left to his own discovery. On the contrary, God introduced Adam to the existence and properties of every tree; presumably this included all vegetation. Adam is also made aware of a very unique tree that he is to leave alone: the Tree of Knowledge of Good and Evil.

Genesis 2:18-20

*(18) "And the LORD God said,
It is not good that the man should be alone;
I will make him an help meet for him.*

*(19) "And out of the ground the LORD God formed
every beast of the field, and every fowl of the air;
and brought them unto Adam to see what he would call them:
and whatsoever Adam called every living creature,
that was the name thereof.*

*(20) "And Adam gave names to all cattle,
and to the fowl of the air, and to every beast of the field;
but for Adam there was not found an help meet for him."*

Having introduced Adam to all plant life and given specific direction as to how to care for the Garden, it's determined that man is alone. He is the only creature of his kind and this is not long-term beneficial. Adam needs a companion. Keep in mind that Day 6 of the creation record does not close until Eve is created and God proclaims that everything is very good. At this point, things aren't *very* good yet and Adam still has all his ribs.

In verse 19 we see a second fashioning of animals. These animals are exact duplicates of animals that were formed out of the water on Day 5 and out of the earth or ground earlier on Day 6. Currently, those animals are living outside of the garden and there are no animals inside the garden.

Something very unique and special happens in verse 19 that's often casually overlooked. Adam is personally shown that every living thing is brought into being and given life by God. Adam had not yet been formed when fish and birds were fashioned out of the water on Day 5 (Gen. 1:21-22). Adam was yet to be molded from clay when God formed all the beasts of the field (mammals, reptiles and amphibians) out of the earth on Day 6 (Gen. 1:24-25). But Adam is present and personally involved as God fashions each animal, one by one, out of the ground in the Garden of Eden in Genesis 2:19.

The passage makes it clear that every single animal was formed from the ground in the presence of Adam and that Adam named them one by one. This would include every animal in existence: all birds, all beasts of the field, all reptiles, all amphibians. Don't miss the fact that verse 19 says, "every living creature."

Amphibians were formed by God, named by Adam, and then released into the wetlands around the rivers. Birds were formed by God, named by Adam, and then released to fly. Reptiles and beasts of the field were formed by God, named by Adam, and then released to roam. Verse 19 says that Adam named "every living creature." These are referred to in Genesis as "kinds."

> **SIDE NOTE:** A question could be raised regarding fish and creatures of the sea. A distinction can be made that Adam only witnessed the making of creatures that breathed air. This defining characteristic could be tied to the qualification of "wherein is the breath of life" that is found the instructions to Noah in Genesis 6:17 and the checklist of ark occupants in Genesis 7:15. It would seem, however, that if the Creator fashioned air-breathing animals and fowl for the purpose of Adam knowing their origin, that Adam saw all of creation fashioned by the hands of the Creator and

named every animal, including things that lived in the rivers and seas.

Adam watched as God formed each kind of animal out of the ground and Adam gave it a name; but when everything was complete, when every kind of animal had been formed in the sight of Adam, when every kind of animal had been given a name by Adam, there was nothing like Adam. Not one kind of animal was found to be a suitable lifelong companion and mate for Adam. He was different.... *a different kind!*

Genesis 2:21-23

(21) "And the LORD God caused a deep sleep to fall upon Adam, and he slept: and he took one of his ribs, and closed up the flesh instead thereof;

(22) "And the rib, which the LORD God had taken from man, made he a woman, and brought her unto the man.

(23) "And Adam said, This is now bone of my bones, and flesh of my flesh: she shall be called Woman, because she was taken out of Man."

Previously Adam had watched as God formed every living creature out of the ground. Adam named each of them as they were formed. As a result of being involved in this process, Adam had no question about where animals, or plants for that matter, came from. They came from God. God formed them by his power and might. Adam clearly understood that God was "The Creator" and that God was very much *separate from* and *different than* creation.

Now, Adam comes face to face with someone who is vastly

different from anything that he watched God form from the ground. She is not formed from the ground like the other animals. She is unique. Adam recognizes that she is formed from him and declares her to be "bone of my bones, and flesh of my flesh." She is Adam's *kind*.

There are still some instructions to be given and we will take the time to review them in a later chapter; but from this point, we can move back to Genesis chapter 1 and draw Creation, Day 6, to a close.

Genesis 1:31

> "And God saw every thing that he had made,
> and, behold, it was very good.
> And the evening and the morning were the sixth day."

He's Got Your Nose & She's Got Your Eyes

Throughout the first chapter of Genesis we see the phrase "and it was good" being used as a final assessment of that which had been created, molded or made on that particular day. Day 6 closes with the phrase "and it was very good." It would seem that the Creator was pleased with the end result.

In the late 1700s a school of thought began to emerge in Europe that introduced the concept of Theistic Evolution. Propelled by the ideas and writings of Swedish botanist Carl Linnaeus, the concept blending Divine Creation and the progression of species by the process of evolution began to gain popularity. Being a self-proclaimed Christian, Linnaeus held to a foundational belief that God had created everything, but saw a diversification within species to the point of projecting additional development of the species into the various life forms that were present in his lifetime.[46]

As the theory generated discussion and gained acceptance, the debate ceased as to whether or not the teaching was heresy and turned to where in the sand a line should be drawn. In essence, what exactly did God create? And what did he leave up to the course of individual species development?

This is a pivotal question for discussion, as it has a direct bearing on what Noah would have been instructed to preserve and what would have been left to perish. If all variations within a species can in fact be traced to an ancient ancestral representative of the species, then how many representatives within the species are needed for the eventual variety to emerge?

The previously discussed theory of a smaller Earth, consisting primarily of a single large land mass and a globally connected, flowing body of water, would greatly reduce the ranges of extreme variation in climate and environment that we experience today. In short, it would be irresponsible to presume that the environment and climate that is experienced in our present-day world would be an accurate representation of the environment and climate that would have existed prior to an extinction-level event such as a global flood.

If the before-and-after impressions of Earth's environment and climate are pointing towards a radical variation, then it's reasonable to anticipate the same degree of radical variation throughout the five defined kingdoms of life forms: animals, plants, fungi, bacteria, and protists or single-celled organisms.

Prior to the flood, deviations in the various life forms that were named by Adam in Genesis 2 and the life forms that were included as ark occupants would have been minimal, not drastic. They would have also lived in less varied environments and climates. As such, the preservation of all such life forms would have been a much more clearly defined task.

Genesis 7:13-16

> (13) "In the selfsame day entered Noah, and Shem, and Ham, and Japheth, the sons of Noah, and Noah's wife, and the three wives of his sons with them, into the ark;

> (14) "They, and every beast after his kind, and all the cattle after their kind, and every creeping thing that creepeth upon the earth after his kind, and every fowl after his kind, every bird of every sort.

> (15) "And they went in unto Noah into the ark, two and two of all flesh, wherein is the breath of life.

> (16) "And they that went in, went in male and female of all flesh, as God had commanded him: and the LORD shut him in."

The defining phrase, "after their kind" or "after his kind," is used four times in verse 14. Being so often repeated, it would seem that it carries significance. This is the final "All aboard!" call prior to the door of the ark being sealed. Let's compare it with the initial instructions for gathering the animal occupants.

Genesis 6:19-20

> (19) "And of every living thing of all flesh, two of every [sort] shalt thou bring into the ark, to keep them alive with thee; they shall be male and female.

(20) "Of fowls after their kind, and of cattle after their kind,
of every creeping thing of the earth after his kind,
two of every [sort] shall come unto thee, to keep them alive."

We see "after their kind" repeated in verse 20. Verse 19 makes use of the phrase "of every sort." In the reproduction of the above text, we have placed the word "sort" in brackets. There is no Hebrew word in the original text that is translated as "sort" in the English printing. It was added for reading clarity. The same principle is repeated, as the word "sort" is added to the text in verse 20. I mention this for those who may be curious as to a difference between the original Hebrew words that were translated as "sort" and "kind."

The directive of verse 19 makes it clear that Noah was instructed to bring two of every sort and more specifically "they shall be male and female," or by sets of two, as in a mating pair.

How Did 7 Get So Lucky?

Collecting in pairs of males and females was the defining base minimum. There were some animals that were specifically designated to be gathered by sevens. We instinctively comprehend that to mean seven pairs. Luckily for us, it's spelled out this way because it really sheds light on another prevailing misread of the text.

Genesis 7:1-3

(1) "And the LORD said unto Noah,
Come thou and all thy house into the ark;
for thee have I seen righteous before me in this generation.

(2) "Of every clean beast thou shalt take to thee by sevens,
the male and his female:
and of beasts that are not clean by two,
the male and his female.

(3) "Of fowls also of the air by sevens,
the male and the female;
to keep seed alive upon the face of all the earth."

Let's take time to carefully review something obvious here, because at first glance, it's anything but obvious. Seven is an odd number. Therefore when we read, "Of every clean beast thou shalt take to thee by sevens, the male and his female," we visualize a certain number. Because we know that seven is an odd number and that complete sets of male and female pairs cannot be made out of a group of seven animals without having one left over with no mate, we subconsciously interpret the final number as a total of 14. The number given, being an odd number in this case, is only realistic if it refers to the number of pairs, as opposed the actual number of animals.

The very next phrase speaks to the "unclean" animals, "and of beasts that are not clean by two, the male and his female." It's the same exact wording as the head count specification that is given for the clean animals. But because two is an even number, we subconsciously calculate the final number as a total of two. If the wording is the same (and it clearly is), then the number also refers to the number of pairs and should be calculated to a final total of four – two males and two females.

The overall breakdown of the ark's passenger list should read:

- Humans – 4 pairs (male & female)
  Total = 8

- Clean mammals – 7 pairs (male & female)
  Total = 14 of each kind

- Unclean mammals – 2 pairs (male & female)
  Total = 4 of each kind

- Reptiles (unclean) – 2 pairs (male & female)
  Total = 4 of each kind

- Amphibians (unclean) – 2 pairs (male & female)
  Total = 4 of each kind

- All birds – 7 pairs (male & female)
  Total = 14 of each kind

This is a pretty sizable adjustment to the traditional head count. Conventional interpretation identifies the clean animals as being those set aside for sacrificial purposes. According to Leviticus, chapter 1, sacrificial animals were limited to young bullocks, rams and lambs (cows, goats and sheep). It also specifies that only the males were to be offered up in sacrifice.

If Noah were taking extras in this category specifically for the purpose of sacrificial offerings, he would have been instructed to gather a certain number of newly born males only. Once a sacrificial animal was old enough to reproduce, it was no longer considered suitable for sacrifice.[47] First-born males were required to be older than seven days (Leviticus 22:27) and to be used within the first year from birth (Deuteronomy 15:19-23).

There is a small assortment of birds that are also considered suitable as sacrificial offerings. No age designations are given for sacrificial birds.[48] Doves and pigeons are identified as a part of the sacrificial animals group (Lev. 1:14). Ravens, vultures, hawks, etc. were not a part of that grouping. Genesis 7, verse 3 clearly states that all birds were to be taken in groups of seven pairs, not just the birds that were suitable for sacrifice.

A closer look at Leviticus chapter 11 reveals that the general scope of "clean animals" extended beyond the identification of sacrificial animals. In this post-flood setting, during the lifetime of Moses and Aaron, the term "clean" was used to identify what animals were suitable as food. With Noah being given the post-flood directive to eat meat (Gen. 9:3), it would seem appropriate that the edible animals that he and his descendants were to consume would be preserved in higher numbers – seven mating pairs, a group of 14.

With regard to Noah's post-flood sacrifices, we must remember that Noah was instructed to take pairs for the express purpose of preserving the living things that were created by God. These were to be preserved, not sacrificed. Noah would have only used newly born juvenile males in his post-flood sacrifices (Gen. 8:20).

The delineation between animals considered clean and those identified as unclean was actually pretty simple. Leviticus 11 gives us the details:

- CLEAN ANIMALS – (verse 3) Animals that have parted hooves and chew their cud, such as cows, goats, sheep, antelope, deer and yaks

- UNCLEAN ANIMALS – (verse 4) Animals that chew their cud, but don't have parted hooves, such as the camel or horse

- UNCLEAN ANIMALS – (verse 7) Animals that have parted hooves, but don't chew their cud, such as swine

- UNCLEAN ANIMALS – (verse 6) Animals that chew their cud, but have paws instead of hooves, like the hare or rabbit

- CLEAN ANIMALS from the water – (verse 9) Things that have both fins and scales, such as any fish that can be scaled

- UNCLEAN ANIMALS from the water – (verse 10) Whatever doesn't have both fins and scales, such as shrimp, crabs, oysters, catfish, eels, and *all* mammals, such as whales, seals, manatees, porpoise

- UNCLEAN BIRDS – (verses 13-19) 20 different species of winged creatures are listed that are not to be eaten: the eagle, the ossifrage, the osprey, the vulture, the kite, the raven, the owl, the nighthawk, the cuckow (seagull), the hawk, the little owl, the cormorant, the great owl, the swan, the pelican, the gier eagle, the stork, the heron, the lapwing, and the bat (We do not commonly recognize the bat as a member of the bird family, but this reference is to winged creatures, not specifically birds.)

- ADDITIONAL UNCLEAN BIRDS – (verse 20) Any bird that creeps upon "all fours" or birds that do not fly, such as an ostrich, an emu or a penguin. Chickens and turkeys can fly and roost off of the ground.

- CLEAN INSECTS – (verses 21-22) Any insects that fly and also *"have legs above their feet, to leap withal upon the earth;"* the locust, the beetle and the grasshopper are listed.

- UNCLEAN INSECTS – (verses 23-24) All other insects that fly and have four feet, as well as insects that would feed on a dead carcass, such as flies, roaches and ants

- ADDITIONAL UNCLEAN ANIMALS – (verse 27) Any animal that *"goeth upon his paws;"* this would be any animal that has paws instead of hooves, and includes all reptiles and amphibians.

- SPECIFICALLY MENTIONED UNCLEAN ANIMALS – (verse 29-30) The weasel, the mouse, the tortoise, the ferret, the chameleon, the lizard, the snail, and the mole

Further instructions are given regarding touching an animal that has died, as opposed to being killed for food or for sacrifice. The body of an animal that was found dead was identified as unclean, even though it might otherwise be considered a clean animal that was suitable for food.

Leviticus 11:46-47

(46) "This is the law of the beasts, and of the fowl, and of every living creature that moveth in the waters, and of every creature that creepeth upon the earth:

(47) "To make a difference between the unclean and the clean, and between the beast that may be eaten and the beast that may not be eaten."

How many animals were present on the ark? The evidence suggests that the numbers with regard to variation of species can be significantly reduced, but the commonly accepted head count with regard to how many of each type of animal needs to be significantly increased.

The easy response is: Noah had a boat load. The practical assessment is: If it roams the earth in our present day, then some prominent relative close to the trunk of family tree survived the flood with Noah's assistance. This would include all known animals, as well as those that are yet to be discovered.

With regard to animals that are currently classified as being extinct, it seems apparent that they existed in Noah's day either as a part of God's original creation that was individually named by Adam (Gen. 2:18-20) and thus designated to be preserved through the flood, or they existed as a part of the animal kingdom that had been corrupted through genetic engineering by the Nephilim.[49] In the latter case, they were condemned as a part of the corruption of God's original creation that was left to perish in the flood.

What's Causin' All This?

There's a crack in the crust of the earth. Actually, there are several. All around our globe, huge cracks in the crust run for hundreds and in some cases thousands of miles across all types of terrain. They stretch across the ocean floor and along majestic mountain ranges. They run unopposed in their journey, stopping at nothing until they intersect with another similar crack.[1]

They're known as fault lines and if you were to plot them out on a globe, the world would look like a giant boiled egg that has been tapped several times against a countertop, but not yet peeled. These cracks in the crust provide definitive boundary markers for the tectonic plates.

Scientific studies indicate that these cracks play important roles in earthquakes and volcanic activity. It's thought that movement within these cracks also impacts the growth and development of mountain ranges.[2] The San Andres Fault, in California, is perhaps one of the most widely studied cracks because of its open exposure along the California coastline.

There's no denying it. The crustal layer of our earth is riddled with cracks and these cracks penetrate deep into the heart of the earth. But why? At what point in time did Earth's crust begin to crack? It has been observed that when stress, caused by rising magma, overwhelms the strength of the foundational rock in the crust, fault lines often develop within a tectonic plate far from its natural boundary.[3] Evidence shows that it takes a monumental force to initiate these cracks and though it may take some time for the pressure to build up, the movement of a fault line or the development of a new crack can be sudden and devastating.

Earthquakes send waves of motion through the crust in every direction. While the effects of the quake may be seen and felt in all directions, the fault line itself is seldom drastically redefined by the fallout. Fault lines circle the globe, defining permanent boundaries and remaining primarily unchanged by any newly observed activity.

They serve as clear separations between the North American Plate and the Pacific Plate. They also delineate between the African Plate, the South American Plate and the Antarctic Plate. The Arabian Plate has distinct boundaries from the Indian Plate and the Eurasian Plate. Australia has a plate to call its own. And, try as it might to snuggle up to the Antarctic Plate, it's kept at a distance by the Southeast Indian Ocean Ridge.

These centuries-old, well-known cracks divide the globe into the broken pieces that make up our world. But, I wonder, has it always been cracked? And has the activity along these cracks always wreaked such devastation and destruction?

At the close of the creation account recorded in the first chapter of Genesis, God said that everything was not only good, but that it was very good. How good could it be, if there were cracks in the crust all around the world that were just waiting for enough pressure to build up so that they could snap and send rippling waves of unrelenting energy across the surrounding landscape, demolishing everything in their path? How could *that* be good? How could that *possibly* be good?

The Big Chill

May 30, 2013 – The location is identified as a "Remote Island in the Arctic Ocean." Most likely it's the well known New Siberian Islands. An incredibly well preserved specimen of a woolly mammoth has been found. Semyon Grigoryev, the head of the Russian expedition, described the find as being so thoroughly preserved that they were able to extract free-flowing blood. He also described the appearance of the muscle tissue as being still "red, like the color of fresh meat."[4]

The discovery of frozen animal life near the poles is much more ordinary than it might seem. It's been reported from numerous sources that some mammoth finds have been so well preserved that their raw meat could be harvested and sampled as food.[5] The primary reason that the quest for mammoths became so popular was not the scientific community's desire to study their astonishing preservation in ice, but rather for the lucrative value of their sizeable ivory tusks, some as much as 13 feet in length and weighing more than 150 pounds.[6]

The reason this particular story garnered headlines relates more to the resolve of Russian scientists to bring the animal back from extinction so that it might once again populate areas of Siberia, where it's thought the animal once thrived in the frigid environment.[7]

The New Siberian Islands play host to a mixed array of animals preserved in the ice. Documented finds include the aforementioned mammoth, as well as rhinoceros, buffalo, musk ox, a few varieties of deer and even horses. Numerous types of trees, including elm and hazel, which are not currently growing anywhere near the region have also been excavated.[8]

French scientist Bernard Buigues claims to have located a virtual "prehistoric zoo" buried in the Arctic permafrost near the Siberian town of Khatanga. Woolly rhinos, steppe lions, giant deer, foxes and hardy breeds of horses are said to be among the identified residents.[9]

These discoveries and more date back to a period of time that has become known as the Ice Age. During this time the brutally cold climate stretched across the North American continent to regions as far south as the Missouri River,[10] and some glacial effects can be seen as far south as present-day St. Louis. Large portions of northern Europe and Asia were also buffeted with extremely cold temps and layers of snow and ice during this same period of time. Ice also prevailed from the southern polar cap, though not to the same extent.

Discoveries of a wide variety of vegetation, known to thrive in tropical locations, have long been rumored in the polar regions from sources such as explorer Robert Falcon Scott.[11] A few have been documented.

Some animals that are thought to live only in warmer climates, such as hippopotamuses, have reportedly been found buried in ice alongside animals thought to thrive in frigid climates.[12] These finds are apparently more commonplace than rare, as the remains of hippos have been documented in a myriad of sites within England and Wales.[13]

In some instances animals have been found frozen in walking position, suggesting that they may have been buried quite catastrophically. In some cases they are found with food still in their mouths or undigested food in their stomachs.[14] Those who hunt wildlife in frigid temps know the need to dress out fresh kills on site to best preserve the meat. Failure to do so allows for the freezing outer body to trap the heat of the inner body, which triggers an early onset of spoilage.

If an animal has been found frozen in ice with slightly digested food still present in its stomach or fresh strands of recently consumed food present in its mouth, it's a clear indication that their internal organs rapidly froze solid, cutting short the natural process of digestion or spoilage. Finds of this nature undermine the concept of a slow climate change and point instead to a near immediate, cataclysmic freezing process that happened within just a few hours, as opposed to over the course of days, weeks, months or years.

But even thin sheets of frost take a while to develop, right? Certainly, thick sheets of ice capable of burying a large land mass and raging destructive havoc on the world upon which it was intruding would take an incredibly long period of time.

Search "Ice Tsunami" on YouTube for a visual example of how rapidly ice can take over its surroundings and how much damage it can do to otherwise storm-ready structures. Parts of Minnesota and Ottawa were buried within minutes by a freak, small-scale ice intrusion in May of 2013, and a number of astonishing video clips were posted shortly thereafter.

Relics and evidence left behind from the Ice Age serve up an abundance of mysteries, including the question of the cause that initiated the massive freeze and turned much of the planet into a wasteland unfit for man or beast. While scientists continue to differ on the potential cause, one thing is beyond dispute: colossal portions of the earth were at one point in time buried under unforgiving ice. How could this be? How could this possibly be?

At the close of the creation account recorded in the first chapter of Genesis, God said that everything was not only good, but that it was very good. How good could it be, if there were regions of the world where animal and plant life could thrive abundantly for long periods of time, and then be suddenly frozen over in a moment of time by a devastating climate collapse?

Feeling A Bit Parched

The Sahara Desert stretches across the northern portion of the African continent from the Atlantic Ocean to the Red Sea. Although massive, the Sahara is only the third largest desert region in the world in square miles. The next 11 largest desert areas combined don't equal the expanse of the Sahara. When sorted by size, the most widely known desert in the United States, the Mojave, doesn't even score a position in the top 20 list.[15] All in all, there are 61 recognized deserts, large and small, around the globe.

For those who are curious, Antarctica, the South Pole, is by definition a desert and ranks as the largest with a land mass of 5,339,573 square miles. Santa's home turf, the North Pole, with a land mass of approximately 5,300,000 square miles, ranks slightly behind at number 2. The Sahara jumps into the list at number 3 with a land mass that is nearly 2 million square miles smaller than either of the poles.

The combined land masses of the Arabian (Sinai Peninsula),

the Gobi (parts of China and Mongolia), the Kalahari (parts of Southern Africa), the Patagonian (parts of Argentina and Chile), the Great Victorian (parts of south central Australia), the Syrian (parts of Iraq, Jordan and Syria), the Great Basin (Parts of Nevada and Utah), the Chihuahuan (parts of Mexico, New Mexico, Texas), the Great Sandy (parts of Western Australia), the Karakum (Turkmenistan), and the Colorado Plateau (Western United States) would fit inside the expansive Sahara.

By definition, deserts are stretches of land with unforgiving climate conditions that are not conducive to the same types of flourishing plant and animal life that easily thrive in other parts of the world. Deserts are classified as either wintery or subtropical. They're most often characterized as barren areas of land devoid of regular intervals of rainfall, which leads to harsh living conditions.

Approximately 71% of Earth's surface area is covered by water.[16] Of the remaining land mass, approximately one-third of it is considered arid or semi-arid.[17] A widespread lack of vegetation exposes the unprotected top soil, which is then continuously stripped barren by prevailing winds and erosion. Not much is growing there. Therefore, not much can grow there.

Categorizing a third of the remaining 29% as desert is the equivalent to identifying a little over 9.5% of Earth's overall surface area as supremely challenged when it comes to providing suitable living conditions. Combine the desert portions of the world (9.5%) with the portion of Earth's surface that's covered by water (71%), and we're left with a very small world after all. If these numbers are accurate, then less than 20% of the entire globe would be considered capable of providing a thriving environment for plants, land-dwelling animals or humans.

But wait, at the close of the creation account recorded in the first chapter of Genesis, God said that everything was not only good, but that it was very good. How good could it be, if more than 80% of the world that was initially created consisted of turbulent oceans and vast life-disdaining wastelands? Could that really be the world that the Creator God fashioned and asked Adam to dress and keep?

The Sky Is Falling

It is popular belief that some 65 million years ago the dinosaurs had a really bad day. A piece of rock hurtled its way through Earth's atmosphere and left a huge divot in the landscape of the northern Yucatan Peninsula.[18] Named after a nearby Mexican town, the Chicxulub Crater is more than 110 miles wide and 12 miles deep. The predominant theory is that this massive dent in the crust was caused by the impact of a meteor estimated to be more than six miles in diameter.[19]

Needless to say, it left quite the impression. Although it's one of the most widely known meteoric impact sites and thought by many to be the signature impact that brought the age of the dinosaurs to an end, Chicxulub is actually only the third largest known impact crater in the world.[20] The Vredefort Crater, located in Free State, South Africa, is over 185 miles wide and is considered to be a little over 2 billion years old. The Sudbury Crater, in Ontario, Canada, is approximately 155 miles in diameter and dates back 1.849 billion years.

These age estimates are commonly accepted by the scientific community, but cannot be definitively proven.

There's no record that anyone was standing on the corner in Winslow, Arizona, when it happened, but perhaps the most widely known impact crater in the United States can be found there. It's known simply as "The Meteor Crater," getting its name because the United States Board on Geographic Names commonly assigns names of natural features based on the name of the nearest post office, and the nearest post office to this impact crater just happened to be named Meteor.[21] Feel free to sidetrack yourself into your own private chicken vs. egg discussion if you'd like.

Before being officially named, it was known as the Canyon Diablo Crater and the scientific community refers to it as the Barringer Crater, honoring Daniel Barringer as the first person to recognize it as a meteor impact crater. The site is actually owned by the Barringer family and proclaimed as the "best preserved meteorite crater on Earth."[22]

It may indeed be the best preserved and it may be the most widely known, but it's not the largest impact crater in the United States by a long shot. That distinction goes to the Chesapeake Bay Crater in Virginia. The Barringer Crater is a little shy of being three-quarters of a mile wide. By comparison the crater in Chesapeake Bay is nearly 53 miles wide.[23] The Barringer Crater is also dwarfed by the Beaverhead Crater, which dots the earth on the Idaho-Montana border and measures slightly over 37 miles in width.[24]

Oh, and there's that famous 22-mile-wide impact crater in Manson, Iowa. The Manson Crater is significant because it was previously believed to be the evidence divot left behind by the asteroid or comet that wiped out the dinosaurs — until isotopic ages indicated that it was simply too old to be the culprit.[25] Now it's just a 22-mile-long valley surrounded by corn.

The remains of impact craters have been identified and documented all over the world. Not a single land mass is left out. It's as if the planet has literally been showered with space debris, but science has carefully assigned each impact into its own individual time period.

The assigned time stamps of most impact craters are separated from the next one on the list by millions of years. The smallest proposed gap in time is the 500,000-year gap that separates the Gosses Bluff Crater in Northern Territory, Australia, from the hole in the ground named after Thor's hammer, Mjolnir, in Barents Sea, Norway.[26] Just think what a mess this place would be if it experienced multiple impacts on the same day.

At present, there are about 175 documented impact craters around the world.[27] There are also a number of areas that are regarded as being damaged by meteors that exploded prior to impact.

Historically known as the Tunguska Event, the mysterious June 30, 1908, explosion of a small incoming asteroid or comet over what is now known as Krasnoyarsk Krai, Russia, was the subject of discussion, investigation and scientific study for decades.[28] Estimated to have been between 200 and 620 feet wide, the object exploded some three to six miles above Earth's surface and ranks as the largest such event in recorded history.[29]

The force of the explosion has been estimated at a level about 1,000 times greater than that of the atomic bomb dropped on Hiroshima, Japan.[30] The devastation from the blast encompassed over 830 square miles and felled approximately 80 million living trees.[31] The explosion was of such magnitude that it would have been capable of leveling a large metropolitan area and registering a 5.0 shock wave on the Richter Scale.[32]

On February 15, 2013, in Chelyabinsk, Russia, a near-Earth asteroid burned across the sky at an estimated 60 times the speed of sound.[33] Even at a distance of more than 80 miles, the roaring object generated a glow that was more intense in magnitude than the sun.[34] When it exploded, approximately 18 miles above Earth's surface, the object released energy estimated at 20 to 30 times greater than the atomic blast of Hiroshima.[35]

The night sky plays host to a number of meteor showers throughout the year. The Quadrantids can be seen each year in early January. The Lyrids arrive in April. The Eta Aquarids put on a show in early May. The Delta Aquarids follow in late July. The Perseids wrap up the summer months each August. The Draconids open October. The Orionids pass through two weeks later. The South Taurids, North Taurids and Leonids span the month of November. And, December plays host to the Geminids.[36]

These showers burn streaks across the upper atmosphere and thrill stargazers on a regular basis. Each is associated with a constellation or star cluster that is prevalent in the section of the night sky that serves as the stage. But these are just dust particles, small pieces of space rock at best. Seldom do any of them pierce the atmosphere to the point of threatening onlookers. They create streaks, but not craters.

Impact craters and midair explosions of high magnitude are reserved for the truly significant slices of stray rock. Even though thousands of chunks of ice, many the size of a small house, bombard our upper atmosphere on a daily basis, there's no real threat of destruction.[37] But at least 175 objects have left breathtaking, lasting evidence that they fell from the sky. And, regardless of how long ago it might have been or the amount of time between direct hits, the impact craters serve as a reminder that Chicken Little was right, at least every now and then.

Millions of years ago? Thousands of years ago? Since 1908 or 2013? At what point did things — big, dangerous things — start falling from the sky? In reading the last few verses of the creation account from Genesis, chapter 1, we find that God said that everything was not only good, but that it was very good. How good could it be very good, if massive chunks of rock, with the capability of wiping out entire civilizations, were positioned to fall from the sky without warning? Seriously, does that sound like anything that anyone in their right mind would call good?

Seven Rays From Sun Day

The night sky lights up with the twinkle of distant stars, but the day sky is given over to a star that anchors the orbital path of the planets. This star, our Sun, provides the potential for life on Earth to exist. It also showers our planet with continual doses of radiation that slowly kill.

Science commonly recognizes seven main spectrums of radiation that emanate from the sun. They are: radio waves, microwaves, infrared light, visible light, ultraviolet light, X-rays and gamma rays.[38] Identifying their properties and overall effects is fairly simple.

Radio waves are most easily identified as invisible waves of sound that are picked up by radios or stereos. We think of them as sound waves because that's the end result that we associate with their unseen presence in the world around us. But in reality, they are actually electromagnetic radiation and our familiarity with the end product leads to a general oversight of their nature. These same types of waves are naturally produced by stars, pulsars, quasars, and most importantly – the sun. As far as we know, they are harmless.

Microwaves have a little shorter wavelength than radio waves and also fall into the category of a scientific development with which we've become quite familiar. Microwave ovens are a basic staple of technology in most homes and offices and quite possibly fall only slightly behind refrigerators and running water on the checklist of kitchen necessities. The principle of Wi-Fi technology, which provides continual wireless access to internet feeds, also piggybacks on microwave technology.[39] Although considered to be predominantly safe, there is still a theory that suggests that long-term exposure to microwaves (from the sun, not the in-home appliance) may be associated with the development of cataracts.[40]

Infrared light – In the early 1800s, astronomer William Herschel first discovered a level of radiation in the light spectrum that was beyond red light and thus generally invisible to the naked eye. Since then, studies have shown that nearly 50% of the energy from the Sun that is responsible for heating the earth arrives in the form of infrared light.[41] Infrared is primarily the visibility of a heat signature and, as such, it has become the primary instrument for night vision technology.[42]

Visible light – The spectrum of visible light is made up of the wavelengths that can be observed by the naked eye. While infrared light is responsible for nearly half of the Sun's radiated energy that heats the earth, the other half is primarily visible light that is absorbed and then re-radiated back into the atmosphere at longer wavelengths.[43] The spectrum of the rainbow displays the only portions of the electromagnetic spectrum that can be seen by the human eye. This prism of color activates our natural ability to see things that are around us. The invisible spectrums of infrared and ultraviolet illuminate things that we cannot see naturally. They would be positioned adjacent to the red band (at the top of the rainbow) and blue band (at the bottom of the rainbow) if they were visible.

Ultraviolet light – Although Earth's atmosphere filters much of the current ultraviolet light that's emitted by the Sun, it's still thought that as much as 10% of the Sun's Earth-bound radiation falls into the UV spectrum.[44] UV is one of the most powerful and damaging spectrums of light. A little bit of UV causes the skin to release melanin into the outer layers, resulting in a tanning effect. Too much UV in a short period of time results in cellular damage from radiation burn, or sunburn.[45] All life on Earth, outside of ocean life, would eventually wilt under the endless barrage of UV radiation were it not for the significant degree of atmospheric filtration that's currently present.[46] Even with this protection in place, skin cancer, cataracts and immune system suppression have all been directly linked to UV radiation.[47]

X-rays – We commonly think of X-rays in terms of the process more so than the electromagnetic radiation that is the actual spectrum of light. X-rays possess the power to penetrate an external surface and produce a signature of the internal structure the naked eye can't observe. Whether revealing skeletal bone or the contents of carry-on luggage at an airport terminal check point, penetrating radiation is at work. It sounds super-mechanical and scientific, but in reality X-rays are simply another identified band in the overall naturally occurring spectrum of light. They are one of the two shortest wavelengths and are always invisible to the naked eye.[48] Knowing that X-rays have the ability to penetrate surface structure should also be a clue as to their inherent destructive properties,[49] which include increasing the potential for cancer.[50]

Gamma rays – This shortest measureable wavelength is very close to that of X-rays.[51] The prevailing thought is that gamma rays are produced by nuclear fusion and high-energy explosions deep in space,[52] but the Sun also produces gamma rays. Gamma rays are produced at the core of the Sun, and their journey to the surface involves a conversion process in which they become infrared, visible light, or UV.[53] However, some studies have shown that the Sun also produces gamma radiation that extends out into the solar system and reaches Earth.[54] Although a large portion of the gamma radiation that reaches Earth is absorbed by the atmosphere while in transit, gamma rays possess an even greater power to penetrate than X-rays and are therefore considered to be potentially the most overall harmful ray in the electromagnetic spectrum for life on Earth.[55]

So, if all of these various waves of light that are generated by the Sun are washing over the planet continually, which provides the most benefit? And which is thought to be the most harmful? It's easy to see that as the spectrum gravitates from radio waves (longest wavelength) to gamma rays (shortest wavelength) the intensity and danger levels increase each step of the way. The shorter the wavelength, the more penetration capability and destructive power is associated with it.

And, of all these various rays of light, which penetrates Earth's atmosphere with the greatest degree of efficiency? In this case, the scale seems to favor a longer wavelength over a shorter one. Very little infrared light is blocked and although visible light is sometimes diffused or obscured by cloud cover, most of it gets through. Enough UV light gets through to make sunscreen a top seller for skin protection, but some of the UV is blocked. X-rays and gamma rays make the journey through the atmosphere in diminishing amounts respectively.

So, we're in good shape. Safe. It's all good. Right? Consider this quote from The National Science Foundation Polar Programs UV Monitoring Network: "The energy contained in the infrared rays causes the molecules of the substance it hits to vibrate back and forth. However, the energy contained in ultraviolet rays is higher, so instead of just causing the molecules to shake, it actually can knock electrons away from the atoms, or cause molecules to split. This results in a change in the chemical structure of the molecule. This change is especially detrimental to living organisms, as it can cause cell damage and deformities by actually mutating its genetic code." [56]

The emissions from the Sun that bring light and heat to

the planet also bring with them destructive forces that are capable of causing a sunburn on the "*Ratz!*" end of the scale, and diseases such as cancer, cataracts, immune system suppression or even cellular DNA damage that could possibly mutate genetic code on the "*Are you freaking kidding me???*" end of the scale.

In essence, the same Sun that brings with it the potential for life also destroys life on a cellular level. And that's if the Sun happens to be having a normal, everyday, "I'm happy and I'm not going to blast you with solar flares, storms or coronal mass ejections" kind of day.

In reading the last few verses of the creation account from Genesis, chapter 1, we find that God said that everything was not only good, but that it was very good. How could it be very good, if the "Greater Light" that was created on Day 4 to rule the day (Gen. 1:16) was given the power to light things up and roast them at the same time? If that's how it was, the Serpent could have gotten on Eve's good side by introducing her to cocoa butter long before tempting her with forbidden fruit. They were supposedly naked from head to toe, after all.

Seriously, a planet under the constant bombardment of radiation that burns the skin, causes cancer, and leads to cataracts? Does that does sound like anything that anyone with clear understanding would call good?

Getting Back to Good

Cracks in the crust, frozen wastelands, bone-dry deserts, falling space rock, and a constant bombardment of life destroying radiation from the Sun; this is home. This is a part of life on planet Earth. Less than 20% of this planet is actually inhabitable, and that comes with constant peril from the planet itself and the space through which it transverses, but it's all we've ever known and we've adjusted just fine.

Areas we haven't discussed, for the sake of not bogging down in total despair over the planet's shortcomings, include: volcanic eruptions, calamitous weather flare-ups such as tornado generating storm cells or hurricanes, raging fires sparked by a lightning strike that go on to torch thousands of acres of forests, massive sinkholes that cause the ground to open up and swallow everything nearby, or even the insane worldwide philosophy that peace can be brought through war. And, just so you'll know, there were a reported 2,053 nuclear explosions at various sites around the globe between 1945 and 1998.[57]

As things currently stand, it seems reasonable to conclude that "Paradise" does leave a little something to be desired. At the close of creation, however, God said that what He had created was not only good, but that it was *very good*, which begs the question: Is what we experience today anything like the finished product that left the Creator so pleased with the results? Is there any imaginable way that it could be?

The statement, "it was good," is repeated seven times in the first chapter of Genesis. Step by step, day by day, the Creator marked the progress as beneficial. When all was done, He graded it as "very good" and then rested. This isn't an indication that somehow, after all the activity, the Creator God was tired or drained of energy and needed to recuperate. The word used in Genesis 2:2 is the Hebrew word, *"shabath"*[58] (shä•vath'), meaning to cease or to desist. It's the same terminology that might be used in a court of law when an attorney has presented his entire case to such a degree of finality that he is satisfied with the completed work – the attorney rests. Nothing has been added to the works of creation by the Creator anywhere in the universe after Day 6. He concluded his work and rested.

Everything that he was going to create was created. Everything that he was going to make was, at that point, made. He concluded his work at the close of Day 6 and we're left with a pair of alternatives: either the world he created included all of the previously mentioned flaws and perils that we experience today and the Creator was okay with the short-comings, or it absolutely did not exhibit any of the previously mentioned flaws and perils, meaning that it was indeed as he had declared – *very good.*

If the world he created included all the flaws and perils that we see today, then how can we possibly reconcile the Creator's assessment that it was not only good, but very good? In answering this question, we're drawn to one of three possible explanations:

> First Option – A divine being known as God does not actually exist. The concept of God and the details of the creation account have been completely and elaborately fabricated by man in an effort to explain his own origin. In this instance, not only is the creator fabricated, but Adam, Eve, and all of their immediate offspring are also fictitious. Everything that was supposedly created in that ancient time has been creatively woven into the setting of a perfect environment that no living being ever actually experienced.

The question would be, who's responsible for imagineering the intricate saga and whose curiosity were they attempting to satisfy? Furthermore, how long did ancient man live without any concept of a creator before someone somewhere determined that a divine creator was an absolute necessity?

Is it even feasible that a large population of human beings existed, or possibly numerous populations in separate civilizations around the globe, with no knowledge of each other and no concept of their own origin until someone of respected character in each civilization began to weave the underpinnings of a backstory that pointed to a singular conclusion — that is, man was created by God? Wouldn't such imagined sagas have taken on drastically different concepts or ideas in each society with regard to the source of man's origin?

In the first scenario proposed, there's no logical reason to portray the world that we now experience as having been measurably different at some specific point in the past. If the history of man were to be constructed by man himself, the world we currently know would suffice as the world that has forever been known, and there would be no need to construct a previously perfect environment that didn't include the perils and flaws that are present around the world today. Since no one in the ancient history of man would have ever actually experienced anything other than the world that we experience today, how could they, with any sense of accuracy, imagine something different?

Second Option – There was a being or group of beings, who was or were far superior to ancient man, and thereby took advantage of ancient man's ignorance by contriving a historical account of how he or they (that being or group of beings) was or were responsible for bringing into existence everything that ancient man could see and experience. Ancient man bought into the story and passed it along to his descendants. After a number of generations, the superior being or group of beings became recognized and worshipped as the god or gods who brought everything into existence.

This same concept, complete with a similar story that man was created by a god or multiple beings recognized as gods, was also introduced to all of the existing tribes of ancient man in their own language at or about the same time in man's ancient past. It was then passed down through their generations faithfully to the point that each civilization points back to a time of their distant ancestry and thereby tells the story of how they were created by a god or group of gods.

Proliferating this option leads not to the question of whether this being (or group of beings) existed at some point in man's ancient past, but rather the question of who this being (or group of beings) was. It also leaves us with follow-up questions to consider, such as: Why did the being (or group of beings) come here in the first place? And where did he (or they) go when they left? We might even ask the question: Should we anticipate a continued relationship on some level? Or look toward a future return?

In this second scenario, there's no issue with portraying the world that we now experience as the world that always was in time past. There's no reason that a being (or group of beings) who sought to deceive ancient man and thereby be accepted as a god (or gods) would have any need to portray the planet as having been vastly different at a previous point in time. Would such a being (or group of beings) even have a concept of how the observable planet would have been different prior to his (or their) arrival? Would there be any logical reason for a being (or group of beings) to portray the planet as anything other than what we see and experience today?

Third Option – The Genesis account exhibits validity, but everything in the account is expressed in the terms of what the first man, Adam, and the first woman, Eve, would have experienced; thereby, the description is local. Everything was perfect and there were no flaws and perils in the limited paradise to which Adam and Eve were exposed. It was only as the population grew and their descendants began to migrate outside of the local area that they began to discover a stark contrast to the paradise in which they were born.

In this scenario there's no issue with portraying the world that we now experience as the world that always was, if we include the concept that the Creator God withheld information from Adam and Eve or deliberately misled them to believe that what they were experiencing was all that there was to experience. Thus Eden was paradise, but the rest of the world contained the flaws and perils we have today.

The biggest snag with this proposal is that the timeline of creation events as recorded in Genesis clearly states that man, Adam, was created outside of Eden and introduced to life in the garden after having experienced the world outside of it (Gen. 2:8 & 15). Surely, if the world outside of the garden was anything like the previously described world that was filled with flaws and perils, Adam would have known.

The record of Creation, as recorded in Genesis, depicts something vastly different than the world that we experience today with all of its flaws and perils. Let's take a brief look at the instances in which the Creator declares that something "is good."

Genesis 1:3-5 details the establishment of light.

> Verse 4 says that, "God saw the light *and it was good.*" The Hebrew word that is translated "good" is the word *"towb"*[59] (tōve), meaning good, pleasant or agreeable to the senses. Verse 4 goes on to tell us that God divided light from darkness (a process discussed in chapter 5) and verse 5 indicates that these actions took place on "the first day."

Genesis 1:9-10 details the initial appearance of dry land.

> Verse 9 describes the activity and verse 10 tells us that God named the dry land, Earth, and called the waters, seas. Verse 10 goes on to tell us that God says, *"it was good."* The Hebrew word that is translated "good" is the same word that was used previously.

Genesis 1:11-12 details the arrival of vegetation.

> Verse 11 highlights God's creative decree that the newly established dry land bring forth grass, herbs and fruit trees that were "yielding fruit." Verse 12 tells us that the earth immediately responded by producing grass, herbs and fruit trees that were "yielding fruit," indicating that they were fully mature and producing food from the very moment that they were created. Verse 12 also records God's affirmation that "*it was good.*" Genesis 1:13 tells us that the pair of declarations recorded in verse 10 and verse 12 transpired on "the third day."

Genesis 1:14-19 recounts the creation of things that were not on the earth.

> Verse 14 speaks of lights in the firmament for the purpose of dividing the day from the night. It's noted that these lights also serve the purpose of identifying signs and seasons and are helpful in tracking days and years. Verse 15 specifies that the primary purpose for these heavenly objects is to house light. Verse 16 states that the sources of light were separated into two categories: a greater light to rule the day (the sun) and a lesser light to rule the night (the stars). Verse 17, they are set into their assigned places. Verse 18, "*and God saw that it was good.*" According to verse 19, these events transpired on "the fourth day."

Genesis 1:20-23 describes the appearance of the first living creatures.

> Verse 20 says that creatures spring forth from the waters upon God's command. These are further identified as

moving creatures that have life and fowls that fly. The Hebrew word that is translated "creature" is the word *"sherets"*[60] (sheh'•rets), meaning teeming or swarming things. Most likely, these are insects. Verse 21 speaks of the waters bringing forth an abundant amount of sea life and closes with the declaration from God that, *"it was good."* Verse 23 states that these events transpired on "the fifth day."

Genesis 1:24-25 addresses the initial appearance of land animals.

Verse 24 specifies living creatures, cattle and creeping things spring forth from the earth (dry land) upon God's command. The Hebrew word that is translated "creature" is the word *"nephesh"*[61] (neh'•fesh), meaning things that breathe. It further implies that these are things with souls, minds, desires and emotions. Verse 25 acknowledges that the earth responded to the command of the Creator and living creatures, cattle, beasts of the field, and creeping things came into existence. At the close of verse 25 is our repetitious phrase of approval, "and God saw that *it was good."*

Genesis 1:26-31 speaks to the direct creation of the first man, Adam, and of the first woman, Eve.

As previously detailed, these verses spell out in general what is expounded upon in great detail in Genesis chapter 2. Verse 26 outlines the specific decision that God made to fashion man after his own likeness. Verse 27 tells us that God followed through with his plan and that man and woman were created in the image of God.

Verses 28-30 reveal a variety of different decrees that are given.

> Of everything that was created, man was designed and appointed to be the dominant life form. Man is told that all things in nature are to be nurtured and cared for by him. Plants are not considered living things, but rather have been given by God to all living things for the purpose of food. Everything is designed to reproduce after its kind and fill the earth with life. Verse 31 tells us that this all transpired on "the sixth day" and that everything "*was very good.*"

Having closely examined the details of the Genesis account of creation, the only logical conclusion is that the flaws and perils, previously described in this chapter, were not present in the original creation, or else the Genesis account of creation paints an inaccurate and falsified picture of the world into which Adam, Eve, and all living creatures were born.

The Crossroads of Possibility

There comes a point when things that are diametrically opposed to one another force a difficult decision. This is such a point. The world in which we live can be seen, explored, experienced, appreciated, and questioned, but it cannot be reconciled with the world described in the initial chapters of Genesis. While there may be a transition from that world to this, the journey has to fall into the realm of logical, systematic, progression that is in harmony with geological science. Supernatural intervention can only suffice when mixed appropriately with faith.

In times like these, the question is often raised, "Is there anything too hard for God?" The implied answer, the only answer, is *no*. For at the moment something becomes too hard, too difficult, too complicated for the Almighty, he ceases being the Almighty. For those unescorted by faith, the question is wholly inappropriate when it comes to bridging this gap.

The purpose of this writing from the onset was never to raise the question of whether something was too hard for God, or if God had the power to destroy the world by flood. Rather, if there is truth to the story that he chose to do so, under what realm of understandable possibility could it have been done? In essence, if the world that we know today was at some point in the past destroyed and reconfigured by a worldwide deluge, how was it possible?

One of my favorite scenes from the six-year TV epic "LOST" takes place in season five.[62] A quiet conversation ensues in a small Catholic Church sanctuary between a character named Jack Shephard and another known as Benjamin Linus. Ben calls Jack's attention to a painting, "The Incredulity of Saint Thomas," by Caravaggio. Ben then tells Jack the story of how Jesus wanted to return to Judea and the disciples feared that if he did, he would be killed. Thomas, the disciple featured in the painting, speaks up in favor of following Jesus, "that we might die with him." The story is recorded in John, chapter 11, and serves as the backdrop for the resurrection of Lazarus.

Ben continues his story, pointing out to Jack, that Thomas is not remembered for this moment of bravery, but for a personal crossroads that he faced much later, after the death of Christ. Even though he had personally witnessed the resurrection of

Lazarus, Thomas refused to accept the testimony of his fellow disciples and acknowledge the resurrection of Christ. The words of the one who became famous for his admission of doubt can be found in John 20:25,

> *"Except I shall see in his hands the print of the nails,*
> *and put my finger into the print of the nails,*
> *and thrust my hand into his side,*
> ***I will not believe."***

Ben then explains to Jack that Thomas is often derided for expressing his deep humanity. In Ben's explanation, Thomas very much wanted to believe, but so deep was his emotion that he just couldn't wrap his mind around it. He needed to touch the wounds of the living Christ before accepting that Christ had indeed risen from the dead.

Seemingly unaware of the story's conclusion, Jack asks if Thomas was ever convinced. In somber tones, Ben assures Jack that Thomas got his wish and then adds a word of comfort for a friend who is struggling to believe, "We're all convinced sooner or later."

Remembered as the ultimate example of doubt, St. Thomas takes a lot of abuse. In reality, he is likely the one disciple with whom we all could most intimately relate. Emotionally brave, he was willing to take a stand for the cause, even if it cost him his life. He spoke up, as the other disciples tried to reason their way into the shadows. Thomas was the one who drove a stake of commitment into the ground, proclaiming, "If we die, we die. Let's go with him to Judea." He was willing to follow Christ to the point of ultimate loss and were it not for his amazing commitment, the disciples might not have witnessed the resurrection of Lazarus at all.

It is at this crossroads where I now stand as a writer and you now join me as a reader. Are we at peace with the trustworthiness of the ancient recorded testimony? Or do we, like St. Thomas, need to place a finger into a reassuring nail print? The battle rages. Our inner being wants so desperately to have faith in something greater, while the forces of reasoning caution us against being thought a fool for our beliefs.

Passion runs deep. Sentiment is continually tested and ever fragile. A confirmation of faith brings a rush of exhilaration which is often met on equal terms by waves of relief. Beliefs that are dashed sometimes give way to spirals of despair. This is common ground. Privately, we have all, at some point in life, stood in the sandals of Thomas.

Is it any wonder that Christ called for his followers to just hold to the smallest measureable amount of faith, that of a grain of mustard seed? That may be all that it takes, but at this stage, for Thomas, that was asking too much. Thomas' faith had been crushed and, as a result, Thomas was broken.

So am I, the writer, or you, the reader, to be reprimanded for the need of nail prints? Not at all. Thomas asked for proof and proof was provided. We shall move forward with eyes wide open, exploring that which we cannot prove while looking for mustard seeds of proof that we cannot deny. The decision as to whether a worldwide flood would have been logically and scientifically possible must rest with the private, personal verdict of each individual along the way.

A Visit to the Clue Store

Through the brilliant pen of Sir Arthur Conan Doyle, a generation was introduced to the wisdom and problem-solving acumen of the unflappable Sherlock Holmes. Held captive by his methodical deduction prowess, followers hung on every turn of phrase and anxiously turned page after page whilst Holmes found every nondescript puzzle piece and laid it neatly into the montage of his soon-to-be-forged solution.

Time after time, Holmes built upon one steadfast principle that never failed to deliver answers, "Once you eliminate the impossible, whatever remains, no matter how improbable, must be the truth."

At the heart of our journey, one quiet obstacle has patiently awaited our arrival: What about the water? If the earth is to be flooded, it must be flooded with water and that key ingredient has been grinning silently from the end of the main hallway as we have spent time opening every available unlocked door throughout our approach. To this point, it remains firmly planted as the poster child for the impossible.

Where Did It Come From? And Where Did It Go?

The question is often raised regarding the volume of water that would be needed to inundate the earth to the extent described in the Old Testament text. Where did all this water come from? And where did it go once the flood ended?

The question is a legitimate one, worthy of a closer look. To

what extent was the earth flooded? And how much water
would be needed to do so?

Genesis 7:19-20

> *(19) "And the waters prevailed exceedingly*
> *upon the earth; and all the high hills,*
> *that were under the whole heaven, were covered.*
>
> *(20) "Fifteen cubits upward did the waters prevail;*
> *and the mountains were covered."*

Our text describes with sufficient detail the degree to
which the level of water increased. Verse 19 eliminates any
possibility that this was a localized flood event, as it identifies
the expanse of the flood as covering "all the high hills that
were under the whole heaven." Any attempt to classify this as
a localized event calls into question the validity of the text. The
word that is translated as "the whole heaven" in the Hebrew
text is *"shamayim"*[1] (shä•mah'•yim), meaning the visible sky
or abode of the stars. It's the same word used in the creation
account to describe the establishment of open, unrestricted
area above the surface of the earth where birds were to fly
(Genesis 1:8) and in the command for the waters "under the
heaven" to be gathered together into one place (Genesis 1:9).

In both cases, as in the Genesis 7:19 reference, the term is
singular in nature and identifies the heaven as a singular
expansive component, not an isolated portion of the visible
sky. Thus the phrase, "all the high hills that were under the
whole heaven," in verse 19 is intended to be a reference that is
global in perspective, not local.

Verse 20 tells us that the waters prevailed upwards 15 cubits and the mountains, presumably all of the mountains in accordance with our understanding of verse 19, were covered. As it stands, this passage could be interpreted in one of two ways: 1) the mountains weren't very tall at the time and a mere 15-cubit swell in sea level was all that was needed to cover them; or 2) the waters continued to rise until the mountains were submerged under at least 15 cubits of water.

Sticking with the same translation for the measurement of the cubit that we proposed earlier in this book (1 cubit = 20.4 inches), we can convert the 15 cubits to 25 feet 6 inches. It would be difficult to imagine that there was no mountain on Earth taller than 25½ feet or that 25 feet of water would be sufficient to lift a vessel the size of the ark and its occupants from its moorings while managing to drown every living creature on Earth at the same time.

Whereas the intended meaning of verse 20 could be debated, the only meaning that really makes sense is option 2 – the prevailing water covered the top of the highest mountains by at least 15 cubits or 25 feet and 6 inches.

If that's the case, it becomes fairly easy to determine the amount of water that would be needed to flood the entire globe to such a degree. The formula for finding the volume of a sphere is: 4 divided by 3, multiplied by the value of pi (3.14), multiplied by the value of the radius cubed.

How do you find The Volume of a Sphere?

$V = 4/3\pi r^3$

Volume Equals Four Divided By Three Times Pi Times the Radius Cubed

Figure 18

(See Figure 18). That may sound daunting, but the dots aren't too difficult to connect and it provides a facts-based answer to the question.

The radius of the earth has been estimated in a number of different ways over time, but today's modern technology provides a fairly accurate measurement. Science has determined that the earth is not an exact sphere, as once thought. Because of Earth's rotation, there's a bit of a bulge at the equator, making the earth a little pudgy around the midsection. The distance around the earth at the equator is about 24,902 miles (40,075 km). This is known as the Equatorial Circumference. When measuring the distance in a north-to-south fashion that passes through the poles, the earth is only 24,860 miles (40,008 km). This is Earth's Meridianal Circumference (by way of the meridian lines). It's a difference of only about 40 miles, but it's enough to change the proper description of Earth's shape from sphere (perfectly round) to oblate spheroid.[2]

Given this fact, it is necessary to take a number of distance measurements from different angles of circumference to establish an average and fairly accurate measurement of Earth's mean or average radius. Plenty of research has been done in this area and the generally accepted consensus for Earth's average radius is 3,959 miles or 6,371 km.[3]

Since the rest of the world measures in kilometers, let's use that form of measurement as we apply the formula to the commonly accepted mean radius of the earth. Based on this, Earth's current overall volume is just under 1 billion,

$4/3 = 1.333$

$1.333 \times \pi = 4.18666666667$

$6,371^3 = 258,596,602,811 \text{ km}^3$

$4.18666666667 \times 6,371^3 = V1$

$V1 = 1,082,657,777,112 \text{ km}^3$

Chart #11

83 million cubic kilometers. (See Chart #11.)

Now we need to determine the highest point on the planet above sea level. Most would immediately identify this as the 29,035-foot peak of Mount Everest, but that's not actually the case. Although Mount Everest is the highest elevation on Earth, it's a pretty good distance from the equator. The highest point on the earth from the center of the earth actually belongs to the peak of a volcanic mountain named Chimborazo in Ecuador, standing at 20,561 feet above sea level. Its location near the equator means that it actually reaches much farther into space than Everest.[4] If water levels exceeded Chimborazo's peak, Everest would also be totally submerged.

For the ultra-curious, the tallest mountain on Earth from base to peak is actually Mauna Kea in Hawaii at 33,480 feet. It doesn't qualify as the highest elevation or greatest distance from the center of the earth because more than half of the volcano is actually below sea level.

The accurate measurement for establishing the highest point above sea level would be to use the Chimborazo volcano in Ecuador. But, since we're adding raw numbers to a previously established average radius measurement, let's use the larger elevation number of Everest. At 5,280 feet per mile, Everest adds 5.499 miles or 8.85 km to our previous radius. Let's round it up to 9 km to make calculations easier and to ensure that we're well above the highest peak of Everest. This puts us approximately 500 feet above Everest, significantly adding to the depth of the overall global water level.

Adding this additional volume to our existing measurements establishes the cubic volume of a secondary sphere that exceeds the height of the highest known land mass on Earth today by nearly 20 times the measurement given in the Genesis passage. In going absurdly above and beyond the height of current mountain peaks, the question as to the height of the highest places on Earth at the time of the flood can be pushed aside as irrelevant. (See Figure 19.)

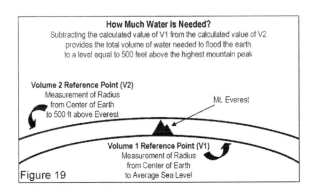

How Much Water Is Needed?
Subtracting the calculated value of V1 from the calculated value of V2 provides the total volume of water needed to flood the earth to a level equal to 500 feet above the highest mountain peak

Volume 2 Reference Point (V2)
Measurement of Radius
from Center of Earth
to 500 ft above Everest

Mt. Everest

Volume 1 Reference Point (V1)
Measurement of Radius
from Center of Earth
to Average Sea Level

Figure 19

Applying the formula for determining volume to our new measurements of 6,380 km, we come to a value that is a little more than 1 billion, 87 million cubic kilometers. (See Chart #12.) When we subtract the previously established volume

V2 > V1 by 9km
4/3 = 1.333
1.333 x π = 4.18666666667
6,380³ = 259,694,072,000 km³
4.18666666667 x 6,380³ = V2
V2 = 1,087,252,514,774 km³

Chart #12

from the newly established volume, we can get an idea of exactly how much water would be needed to flood the entire globe as we know it today, to the extent of the Biblical proportions given in Genesis 7:19-20.

In short, it would require almost 4.6 billion cubic kilometers of water to get the job done. (See Chart #13.) As expected, that's a huge number and pretty difficult to envision. At this point, a more basic visual illustration might make it a little easier to comprehend.

| V2 - V1 = Volume Difference |
| V Diff = Amt of Water Needed |
| V2 - V1 = 4,594,737,662 km³ |
| Total Need = 4.6 Billion km³ |

Chart #13

It has been estimated that the combined quantity of water on this planet is equal to 1,386,000,000 cubic kilometers.[5] Suppose we could — in some magical way — fit all that water into a single gallon-sized milk container. We'd need to fill at least 3.315 additional containers, or find more than three times as much water than we can currently measure on the surface of the earth, if we wanted to achieve the goal of flooding the earth to 500 feet *above* the peak of Mount Everest.

There's a notion that if the polar caps were to melt, the entire planet would be flooded. Whereas the water levels would significantly rise, those standing near the summit of Everest would not be in any immediate danger. The same resource that provided the numbers for the current volume of water on the surface of the planet goes on to break it down as 96% ocean water, 2% ice caps, about 1% freshwater lakes and streams, and the remainder exists as water vapor in Earth's atmosphere.[6] It sounds like they've covered all angles and even if they had left the polar regions out of the conversation, 2% would scarcely match the amount needed.

There is also the thought that raising the ocean floor would make for shallower oceans and easily flood the planet. That certainly makes sense. After all, the Mariana Trench is 1,580 miles long and averages about 43 miles in width. That's more than five times the length of the Grand Canyon. It's also been measured at 36,201 feet deep. That's nearly seven miles. At its deepest point, it measures over one-and-one-third miles deeper than Everest is tall.[7] If we somehow managed to fill

275

that thing in, the rising tide levels might become cause for concern.

There's also scientific data. Just plain, out-in-the-open research documentation that is available for all to see and consider. According to a March 2002 report, while trying to reproduce in the lab the environment and conditions that were projected to exist deep in the earth, Japanese scientists discovered an amazing amount of water. It wasn't exactly what they were looking for, but their experiments indicated that more water is probably present deep within Earth's crust than is currently present on the surface, *"as much as 5 times more."*[8]

Okay, now we're getting somewhere. Is there enough water present on the planet to flood all of the existing land masses? Our volume calculations indicated that we needed at least three-and-one-third times more water than we can currently measure on the surface of the earth, and science indicates that there is at least that amount with plenty to spare.

If there's any validity at all to the Old Testament text, then the fact that this vast reserve of water was discovered beneath the crust of the earth should really come as no surprise. Verses throughout the early chapters of Genesis allude to the presence of large amounts of water beneath Earth's crust (Genesis 1:2; 1:6; 1:7; 1:9; 1:10; 7:11). It's also poetically referenced by King David in the Old Testament book of Psalms: *"The earth is the Lord's, and the fullness thereof; the world, and they that dwell therein. For, He hath founded it upon the seas, and established it upon the floods."* (Psalm 24:1-2) *"To him that stretched out the earth above the waters...."* (Psalm 136:6).

Getting THERE from HERE

Finding enough water is an important factor, but it really only indicates that the resources exist. The mechanism by which the flood occurred continues to cast a long shadow across the pathway of understanding. Theories and ideas abound. Some are quite well thought out. Others are just mind-numbingly absurd. All are easily researchable.

Any theory presented is just that, a best guess or contrived supposition. Our story says that only the eight people aboard the ark survived the flood and not one of them is around to question about the details. Even if they were, there's no indication that they would be able to give a great deal of insight as to the overall chain of events. It's entirely possible that not a single person aboard the ark had any comprehension of what was going on outside. According to Genesis 7:7-10, they were safely tucked away behind the sealed door a full seven days prior to the start of the flood.

The ancient record gives some particulars, but little in the way of step-by-step progression. And of the information that is clearly spelled out, much of it has been so poorly represented by those aspiring to tell the Biblical version that the end result is a fuzzy mess at best. This is no simple tale, and the elements involved cannot be characterized in a short and sweet, neatly wrapped, weather report segment suitable for the nightly news.

The chain reaction of events that brought about global flooding unfolded methodically over a period of several days. Each occurrence led to the next result. Each happening signaled the onset of the next soon-to-arrive calamity. Once the judgment began, each sequential incident fell within the established laws of nature. Make no mistake; the great flood of Noah was an extinction-level event that exceeded any modern-day catastrophic devastation to which we can relate. The planet that had sustained life for 1,657 years came apart at the seams, and what we see today is the resulting aftermath of that wreckage.

Perhaps the greatest source of our collective blindness to what was, is our current satisfaction in the knowledge of what is, and the sense that it has always been as we currently experience it. Even though we have a multitude of scientific data indicating that our planet has not always been as it is today, we somehow envision that the differences apply to a period of time in the far distant past, prior to man's existence.

However, all of the ancient records that have served as our resource material to this point indicate that man has been in place since Day 6. Therefore, unless there were drastic atmospheric changes between Days 5 and 6 that went unrecorded by those compiling the ancient texts, Noah and his family came from *that* world.

It was a world that consisted primarily of one land mass as opposed to the seven distinct continents that we recognize today. It was a world that had smaller bodies of water, as opposed to the enormous oceans that we experience today. It was a world that enjoyed a singular source of flowing water, which sprang from Eden and divided into four rivers that carried an uninterrupted current throughout the entire globe, including vast underground caverns that we know today as subterranean caves. It was a smaller planet, with less seasonal fluctuation and less temperature variation.

According to a 2011 *National Geographic* article, "Why Giant Bugs Once Roamed the Earth," it was a planet with a 30% to 50% higher oxygen content.[9] This same article attributes that massively enriched oxygen content to "the rise of vast lowland swamp forests." Evidence reveals that *that* world had a much thicker and richer proliferation of plant life. A teaching guide, recommended for elementary and middle schools, describes ancient forests filled with ferns approaching 10 meters in height (about 32 feet 9 inches) and other giant plants (not trees) nearing 30 meters tall (about 98 feet 6 inches).[10]

Is it possible that there were any human beings around during this period of time? Unless the plant life that Genesis asserts came into being on Day 4 had died out and been replaced by scaled-down replica versions before the formation of Adam from the dust, those who accept the ancient texts as factual are left with no other alternative. This was the world in which Noah lived.

There's also ample evidence that Earth's magnetic field is undergoing a significant process of change. Most agree conclusively that, from the point wherein technology has been able to measure it, the field has shown a steady pattern of weakening.[11] Some assert that this decline is part of a natural process or cycle that will result in an eventual reversal of the magnetic field. This reversal process is a theory that has both support and opposition.[12] The projected period of time for this cyclical process has been estimated at about 250,000 years, but the same studies indicate that there has not been a reversal in over 800,000 years.[13]

This commonly accepted research data indicates that the world in which Noah lived had a stronger magnetic field.

Whatever may be included in the complete bundle of benefits that a stronger magnetic field provides, one question that it leaves open is whether a definitive layer of water was present in the upper atmosphere.

The theory of a pre-flood canopy has been openly purported and discredited since being initially proposed by Isaac Vail in 1874.[14] Having been hotly debated for well over 100 years, it's hardly a topic that stands the slightest chance of being resolved by a few short paragraphs at this point. The potential existence of a canopy has been supportively detailed by such writers as Dr. Carl E. Baugh[15] and adamantly opposed by such theorists as Walter Brown.[16] Although both men are staunch "Creationists" and wholeheartedly share the same viewpoint on origins, they present elaborate research and persuasive scientific data to support their opposing views on the existence of a pre-flood canopy. Both men are wrestling with the same Genesis passage. Both are interpreting the same historical and scientific evidence. And both come to opposing conclusions.

From this standpoint, it may be beneficial to reach beyond the 1874 time frame of Isaac Vail and once again review the ancient historical documents for reference.

> *"After this, on the second day, he placed the heaven over the whole world, and separated it from the other parts, and he determined it should stand by itself.* **He also placed a crystalline [firmament] round it,** *and put it together in a manner agreeable to the earth, and fitted it for giving moisture and rain, and for affording the advantage of dews."*
> *- Flavius Josephus*[17]

Josephus, a first-century Jewish historian, was commissioned by the Roman Empire to write and preserve the history of the Hebrews. We can't say for certain that he possessed any divine knowledge of the past, but he most likely was highly familiar with traditional knowledge that had been passed down through the generations. In some cases he references "to this day" as a point of identifying information as being either verified by first-hand experience or gleaned from reliable contemporary resources. Although that was the case with his recorded testimony regarding the existence of the ark (seen in this book's introductory pages) and concerning the Prophecy Pillars erected by Adam,[18] that is not the case with the reference shown above.

Whenever any writer or speaker makes a statement, it is always good to ask yourself the question, "Does he *think* that or does he *know* that?" No speaker, teacher, professor, or writer should be exempt from this rule. In general, both speakers and writers word things authoritatively and their statements come across as confirmed factual data, but that's not always the case. Helpful secondary questions to ask might be, "What makes him think that?" or "How does he know that?"

In this instance, Josephus is speaking from passed-down tradition, not verified knowledge. Based on tradition, Josephus thinks or believes that there was a crystalline canopy of some sort that surrounded Earth's upper atmosphere and there might have been, but he never saw it and he does not know anyone who personally saw it. Therefore, he thinks it, but he does not know it for certain.

2nd Peter 3:5-6

(5) "For this they willingly are ignorant of,
that by the word of God the heavens were of old,
and the earth standing out of the water and in the water:

(6) "Whereby the world that then was,
being overflowed with water, perished:"

Written around 66 AD,[19] these two verses in the second epistle of Peter give some insight into Peter's understanding of the ancient event. Peter was a disciple of Jesus and, according to the gospel records, seems to have often enjoyed private conversations with Christ. Perhaps the events of Noah's great flood were discussed on such occasions. There is no question that Christ presented the event as historically factual in his teachings (Matthew 24:39).

The opening phrase of verse 5 refers to a group of people who are "willingly ignorant" of the creation of the world by God. Peter had previously identified this group of people as "scoffers" in verse 3 and declares that they will be prevalent among society in "the last days" prior to the return of Christ, which is referenced in verses 10 and following. These verses were not included in the quoted text above because our interest is not in a dissertation about who Peter's "scoffers" were, nor is it drawn to Peter's insight as to the return of Christ. The focal point, for us, is Peter's perspective of the original creation.

In the latter portion of verse 5, Peter describes the newly created Earth as "standing out of the water" and "in the water." Verse 6 opens with the word "Whereby," indicating that the previous statement from verse 5 identifies the cause or reason for the events of verse 6: the ancient world was overflowed by water and perished.

Peter identifies two distinct positionings of the ancient Earth.

It came "out of the water" and yet it was "in the water" and, according to Peter, both of these water sources factor into the flooding of the earth. How can Earth be "out of the water" and "in the water" at the same time, unless there are two recognized locations of the water?

In 1950, Dutch astronomer Jan Oort proposed the idea of a cluster of icy solar bodies surrounding the known solar system. This realm was thought to be on the outer reaches of the Sun's gravitational limits. The existence of this icy region of space is now regarded by science as the potential origin of long-period comets. This proposed region has become known as the Oort Cloud.[20]

This visualization is that of an all-encompassing icy sphere that surrounds our entire solar system at its extreme outer edges. Although Earth clearly is not positioned in this "outer edges" region, it would be acceptable to say that Earth exists "in" or "inside of" the Oort Cloud.

This same visual principle could be assigned to Peter's description of the newly created Earth as "standing out of the water" but yet being positioned "in the water." However, Josephus' understanding is that this all-encompassing canopy was in some way a part of Earth's upper atmosphere and that it came into being on Day 2 of creation.

The "standing out of the water" portion of Peter's assessment was covered earlier, in chapter 5, as we examined the meaning of Genesis 1:9, *"Let the waters under the heaven be gathered together unto one place, and let the dry land appear...."* This description seems to clearly fit the concept of the inhabitable surface of the earth coming into existence through the process of "standing out of the water."

But what of Peter's "in the water" reference? He may be alluding to his understanding of Genesis 1:6, *"And God said, 'Let there be a firmament in the midst of the waters, and let it divide the waters from the waters."* In chapter 5, we hinted at the idea that this "firmament" or separation of waters from waters may have been the result of Earth's magnetic field being established.

The use of the term "firmament" is somewhat foreign to us and thus understanding what is meant when the term is used can be somewhat confusing. This doesn't mean that the term is vague, but rather that the concept isn't something to which we can easily relate.

Genesis 1:14 and 15 refer to it as the location of the Sun and stars. Genesis 1:20 identifies it as the place where the birds fly. Ezekiel 1:25 and 26 seem to indicate that the Throne of God is located "above the firmament," presumably a reference to a region that is above or beyond the stars. These are clearly three distinctly different locations, which leads me to disassociate the definition of the firmament as Earth's atmosphere and think of it in a much broader sense – the realm of magnetic fields within the cosmos.

It is commonly believed that Earth's magnetic field is the result of the liquid core of the earth circulating around a smaller, solid core.[21] That's apparently how it sustains itself, but what started the movement? What jump-started the supposed current circulation?

In 1971, Dr. Thomas Barnes, then professor of physics at the University of Texas-El Paso, published a study proclaiming that the strength of Earth's magnetic field was decreasing.[22] In 1983, Dr. Russell Humphreys, a physicist at the Sandia National Laboratories in Albuquerque, New Mexico, expanded Barnes' work to theorize how and why Earth's magnetic field was initialized.[23]

In Humphreys' view, water was the key ingredient. As Humphreys explains, "Atoms of many elements, such as hydrogen, have spinning nuclei. Such a nucleus has a small magnetic field like that of a bar magnet lined up with the spin axis."

In theory, when the water was separated from the water (Gen. 1:6) the atomic nuclei may have temporarily lined up with their spin pointing in the same direction. The accumulation of so many atomic nuclei lined up would have the power to ignite the electromagnetic flow of the field.

In chapter 5 we proposed that while the prevailing thought is that the separation of water from water was an Earth-related event, the principle may have applied throughout the universe. A year after his initial paper, Humphreys applied his ignited-by-water-nuclei theory to planets throughout the solar system and got astounding results.[24] Humphreys not only projected accurate measurements for many planetary magnetic fields, but also the presence of a verifiable magnetic signature associated with galaxies in general.[25]

In recent history, scientists have discovered and begun studying a phenomenon known as Noctilucent Clouds. First observed in 1885, two years after the massive eruption of

Krakatoa, these clouds were initially thought to be connected to the amount of volcanic debris in the atmosphere.[26] German polar researcher Alfred Wegener made a study of the clouds and concluded in 1912 that they were primarily composed of frozen water particles, not volcanic debris that had gotten trapped in Earth's upper atmosphere.[27] Recognized as the highest altitudinal clouds in Earth's atmosphere, their glow is most often observed in the summer months as the sun dips below the horizon at latitudes between 50° and 70° north and south of the equator.[28] Could their presence, primarily at these latitudes, be in any way associated with Earth's magnetic field?

Although it was once believed that water took on one of three physical properties – liquid, vapor, or solid – it is now known that there are as many as 15 different phases of solid water or ice crystals. There may be even more, but in 2009 it was discovered that ice began to take on metallic properties at Phase XV (15), thus becoming malleable.[29,30] Theoretically, at this phase ice does not shatter when struck, but responds as a metal would and can be beaten into thin layers. What an intriguing thought!

Could the increased strength of Earth's pre-flood magnetic field have supported a thin layer of super-cold, highly pressurized ice in a state such as Phase XV? If so, could it have formed some type of upper atmosphere crystalline canopy around the earth? Some early historians, such as Josephus, certainly envisioned it.

Another question that often goes unasked is perhaps the most telling of all: If there was a crystalline canopy that was transparent, would it have been seen at all by those living under its protective expanse? It's a question that is arguably worthy of being asked and most certainly deserving of a rational response.

If it existed, it is not there now. So, we are left with one of two conclusions: 1) It was imagined by early historians with no supportable evidence other than a misinterpretation of the Genesis firmament description and therefore never actually existed; or 2) it existed before the flood, and a catastrophic event that was connected to the flood led to its ultimate destruction and demise. In the second option, there should be some residual evidence to support its pre-flood existence.

Research has broadened my understanding of the potential consequences of a flood, such as Noah's. While the scope was previously wrapped around global markers of the devastation's aftermath, now it has turned outward. In essence, if Noah's flood is a reality of Earth's past history, the physical cause, consequence and post-event markers should be perceptible not only on this planet, but also throughout the solar system. Not only should the earth exhibit post-flood disfigurement, but other heavenly bodies should show the scars as well.

A Parade of Planets

If what modern science tells us about the formation of our solar system is true, we should be able to observe several consistencies among the planets. They should be composed of similar material. They should follow some basic scientific laws with regard to rotations and orbits. The behavior of their satellites (moons) should fall within a certain predictable pattern.

Keeping in mind that scientific theories of origin are just that — theories — observations outside the norm could indicate that they were not formed the way modern science proposes. These anomalies might also indicate that something occurred between the time they were formed and our present day that bears influence on what we see today.

In reality, we've discovered that each of the planets harbors its own singularity. As a collective group, the main thing they have in common is the star that they orbit. Other than that, they just aren't very similar at all. One might imagine that Mercury, the planet closest to our Sun, would have developed a precise circular orbital path over the years. It is, after all, the smallest planet in the bunch (now that Pluto has been reassigned) and it would seem reasonable to expect that, after 4.6 billion years,[31] its small mass combined with the Sun's massive gravitational tug would keep it locked into a fairly consistent trip around the block. However, just the opposite is true; Mercury's orbit is strangely abstruse. Mercury's flight path is the most elliptical of all the planets, taking it within 46 million kilometers of the Sun at one point and ranging out to 70 million kilometers at another.[32]

NASA's Mariner 10 spacecraft made a series of three fly-bys in 1974 and 1975, sending back images of the planet's surface before dying in space. The photos showed that Mercury's surface is literally covered with impact craters, including one of the largest impact craters known to exist anywhere in the solar system.[33] So, the planet that is just a little larger than Earth's moon and stays tucked away in the constant breeze of the solar winds, with little to no atmosphere and a magnetic field that is strength-wise barely equivalent to 1% of Earth's, features wall-to-wall impact craters? Either it's under a constant bombardment of space debris or this must have been one gigantic meteor shower.

If the Sun was a 12-foot by 12-foot accent wall in your living room, Mercury could be represented on the wall by the head of a thumbtack. The thumbtack has very little gravity. By comparison, the accent wall has a massive amount. Hang the thumbtack from the ceiling by a string about a foot away from the wall. Stand across the room and try to hit the tack by using a teaspoon to launch two or three poppy seeds at it. It sounds silly, but that's the visual of Mercury being hit by stray meteors as they plummet toward the Sun. If it was under constant bombardment, surely NASA's Mariner 10 probe in 1974/75 or NASA's Messenger probe in 2008 would have captured visuals of ongoing impacts as they occurred.

Venus was long thought to be Earth's twin. Only slightly smaller, it was imagined that the two planets might exhibit a lot of similarities. In reality, they couldn't be more different. The gravity on Venus is about 9% less, but the pressure generated by the thick Venusian atmosphere is 92 times greater. It would be the equivalent of trying to survive at a depth of nearly a mile deep in the ocean.[34] Earth rotates over a period of 24 hours and takes 365 days to circle the Sun; it takes Venus about 5,832 hours (243 of our days) to complete a single rotation, but only 225 days (62% of our year or the time from January 1st to August 14th) to complete its annual orbit.

Venus is also the only planet in the solar system to rotate backwards, meaning that if the Sun rose in the west on January 1st, it would eventually set in the east around the 1st of September.[35] It takes nearly a full day and a half for the Sun to move one degree in the Venusian sky. That same single degree of movement across the sky happens on Earth in only eight minutes.

Venus has very few impact craters by comparison to other planets, and most of them are in the same general area of the planet. This has led scientists to theorize that the planet has undergone a global resurfacing event in the recent past (projected at 300 to 500 million years ago).[36] Thus, the surface appears to be relatively young and observable impact craters, are limited to certain areas that were presumably unaffected by the resurfacing.

We're fairly familiar with our moon. We're used to seeing it in the sky, tracking the phases and going through "oooh, ahhh" contractions about every 27 days when it's full. There's nothing unusual here, right? Open your internet browser and pull up a photo of the lunar surface. Where are the impact craters? You'll notice that the impact craters are anything but evenly spaced. There is a large concentration of craters towards the "north pole" area and one very large crater with streaks radiating in all directions to the south. This is known as the Tycho impact basin.[37] Take a look at the back side of the moon. It couldn't be more drastically different than the side that continually faces the earth. Could the clustering be more indicative of a series of impacts that occurred as a result of a specific event, as opposed to independent, unconnected impacts that are spread out over millions of years?

From an earthbound perspective, the moon and the Sun look to be the same size in the sky even though the Sun is physically 400 times larger. This is because the Sun is also about 400 times farther away.[38] This exceptional positioning makes Earth the only planet in the Solar System that can experience a total eclipse of the Sun. The positioning is also quite peculiar because there's strong evidence to support a measurable drift of the moon into a more distant orbit. As the moon continues to drift away, our ability to experience total eclipses of the Sun will diminish.

Mars is the closest planet as we move outward, away from the Sun. Mars is about half the size of Earth and has only about 33% of the gravity. It's known as the "Red Planet" because the large amount of oxidizing iron minerals present in the soil gives it a red appearance.[39] It has two fairly small moons, one of which is projected to break up and eventually crash to the surface of the planet.[40] Pull up an image of Mars on your internet browser and you'll notice that nearly 90% of all the impact craters on Mars are positioned in the southern hemisphere. You'll also see that the southern hemisphere of the planet is home to a massive impact crater. Although Mars, like Earth, orbits the Sun in a counter-clockwise motion, it is not on the same orbital plane. The orbit of Mars is at a slight angle, by comparison to Earth's.[41]

The Asteroid Belt is another anomaly. We think of it as a single, scattered cluster of rock fragments suspended between Mars and Jupiter, but we're learning that it is so much more. A few asteroids have been identified as being particularly large by comparison to most objects in the field. It is suspected that more than half of the total mass of the belt is composed by Ceres, Vesta, Pallas, and Hygiea. Ceres, alone, is thought to be equal to nearly 25% of the Asteroid Belt's mass.[42] But we are still identifying new components of the field.

Astronomers have also identified three additional fields on the outermost portion, in Jupiter's neighborhood. These are known as the Trojans, the Greeks and the Hildas. The Trojans and Greeks are considered a part of Jupiter's orbit and are thought of as related fields with 65% of the mass (the Trojans) being out in front of the planet's orbit and the remaining 35% (the Greeks) trailing behind.[43] The Hildas also mirror Jupiter's orbital plane, but are located on the opposite side of Jupiter's orbital path.[44]

Perhaps the most interesting and telling thing about Jupiter is the perturbation of its orbit. Perturbation is a term used to describe the complex motion of a planetary body that is subject to the forces of pull from more than one additional planetary body.[45] In other words, the orbit of Jupiter is not affected by the pull of the Sun alone; Saturn also has some tug that shows up as a noticeable "perturbation."[46]

It was through the understanding of this principle that other planets were discovered. Every planet from Mercury to Saturn can be observed in the nighttime sky with the naked eye. It was thought for a while that only these six planetary bodies existed. Once we understood the principles of perturbation, we could see that Saturn's orbit was indeed affected by another body, which prompted astronomers to look for additional planets. Uranus was found by chance in 1781 by Britain's Sir John Herschel.[47] Since its orbit was also perturbed, astronomers continued to search. Mathematical formulas helped to project the whereabouts of another body and eventually the planet Neptune was found in September of 1846, by British astronomer Johann Gottfried Galle, based on the mathematical advice he was given from a French mathematician, U.J.J. LeVerrier.[48]

These same principles were put to the test again when it was observed that Neptune's orbit was also perturbed by another object and the discovery of Neptune did not sufficiently explain all of the "outlaw behavior" exhibited by Uranus. In June of 1930, *Popular Science Monthly* ran the story of the discovery of Pluto by Clyde W. Tombaugh.[49]

Pluto lost its planetary status, however, when in August of 2006, the General Assembly of the International Astronomical Union agreed to a new set of planetary definitions:

1. A planet must orbit around the sun (check).

2. A planet must have enough gravity to pull its mass into a spherical shape (check).

3. A planet must have "cleared the neighborhood" of its orbit (uh-oh, this is where Pluto falls short in the new agreed-upon definition).

Pluto was reclassified as a "dwarf planet" that exists along with a multitude of other dwarf planets on the fringes of the Kuiper Belt. It has been estimated that there may be more than 70,000 such objects and at least one of them, Eris, is larger than Pluto.[50]

In essence, Pluto doesn't have enough mass to generate the observed perturbation of the outer planets. So, the search continues.

In 1983, *New York Times* "Ideas and Trends" researcher John Noble Wilford wrote, "Something out there beyond the farthest reaches of the known solar system seems to be tugging at Uranus and Neptune. Some gravitational force keeps perturbing the two giant planets, causing irregularities in their orbits."[51]

The article goes on to reference the work of Dr. Thomas C. Van Flandern and Dr. Robert Harrington of the U.S. Naval Observatory, disclosing that they attribute the anomaly to the tug of a single undiscovered planetary body that is as much as five times more massive than Earth and has a highly elliptical orbit that extends well beyond Pluto (outside of the region we know today as the Kuiper Belt).

The article also quotes Dr. Ray T. Reynolds of the Ames Research Center in Mountain View, California: "Astronomers are so sure of the 10th planet, they think there is nothing left but to name it."

That would have been highly premature in 1983 and although writer Zechariah Sitchen gave it a name in his 1976 book, *The 12th Planet*, it still seems a bit presumptuous. Project as we will, try as we might, since the discovery of Neptune in 1846, we still haven't discovered an additional planetary body that meets the criteria and perturbs the orbits of the two outermost planets to the degree observed, but the search continues.

In July of 1972, *Popular Science Magazine* again reported a possible discovery. Joseph L. Brady, a scientist at the Lawrence Livermore Laboratory at the University of California, reported that his computer models showed the influence of such a planetary body on the orbit of Halley's Comet, thus accounting for the comet's eccentric behavior.[52] The search continued.

March 2, 1972 — NASA launched the Pioneer 10 space probe

with an express mission to explore the asteroid belt and Jupiter. It made its first contact with Jupiter in December of 1973 and sent back historic data about the planet. No signal has been received from Pioneer 10 since January 23, 2006, and on March 4, 2006, NASA officially stopped attempting to reestablish contact with the craft.[53]

April 5, 1973 — NASA launched the Pioneer 11 space probe, sending it to explore a region of the solar system that was directly opposite the flight path assigned to its predecessor. Pioneer 11 passed Jupiter on December 2, 1974, and Saturn on September 1, 1979. All contact with Pioneer 11 was lost in November 1995.[54]

NASA launched a pair of space probes named Voyager in 1977 — Voyager 2 launched first, on August 20th, followed by Voyager 1 on September 5th. Both probes were sent to the same region of space, just a few degrees to either side of where Pioneer 11 had been sent. Both are still active. One of the primary missions shared by the two probes is to conduct magnetic field investigation[55] (one way of searching for unknown or yet-to-be discovered planetary objects).

In 1983, NASA's Infrared Astronomical Satellite (IRAS) tracked an object at the edge of the solar system.[56] The Washington Post reported the discovery on page A1 that December. The article detailed two sightings of a mysterious object some 50 billion miles from Earth. While that may seem to be a great distance, a member of the IRAS research team, Dr. James Houck, was quoted as saying, "If it really is that close, it would be a part of our solar system." Houck went on to say, "I don't know how the world's planetary scientists would even begin to classify it."

The object was spotted by the IRAS research team on two separate occasions, six months apart. Speculation as to what the object could be ranged from a comet, to a Jupiter-sized planet, to an object that "started out to become a star eons ago, but never got hot enough." Such objects are typically classified as Brown Dwarfs.

The article also noted that the object exhibited no discernable change of location between the two sightings. Thus, comet was eliminated as a possible identification and planet was pushed to the fringe. Admittedly, six months of time at that great of distance is a fairly small amount of data to project movement.

Dr. Gerry Neugebauer, the director of the Palomar Observatory for Cal Tech, added these thoughts, "All I can tell you is that we don't know what it is." He went on to say that he hoped that the discovery "is a distant galaxy either so young that its stars have not begun to shine or so surrounded by dust that its starlight cannot penetrate the shroud."

The article concludes with the disclosure of plans to search for the object with the world's largest telescopes. Follow-up papers were published by Houck and others in 1985 and 1987. The papers identified the IRAS observations as a distant, ultra-luminous young galaxy and a filamentary structure known as "infrared cirrus" floating in intergalactic space.[57] Not a planet.

And... the search continues.

The End of All Flesh

Genesis 6:13

"And God said unto Noah,
The end of all flesh is come before me;"

Having read that statement, I have to pause and let the gravity of such a declaration sink in. In an earlier chapter we noted that Noah was one of only two people of whom it was said *"(he) walked with God."* (Gen. 6:9). Clearly he enjoyed a bond with the Almighty that was not common to others living in his day. It was during this type of one-on-one interaction that Noah was made aware of a soon-to-come future event – *the end of all flesh.*

When such a statement is made, a couple of things immediately come into play. Does the source of the comment have the power to follow through? And does the source of the comment have the resolve to follow through?

We often hear those around us lash out with threatening language. We hear it so often, in fact, that for the most part we simply dismiss such comments out of hand as idle and meaningless. We even have a coined phrase to categorize such ominous announcements as someone who is "blowing off steam." However, if the person making such a comment has the power and the resolve to follow through with their threatening pronouncement, we tend to give more credence to the possibility that actions will follow the expressive statements.

In this instance, the one who is speaking to Noah is the same one of whom it was written, *"In the beginning...."* This is the Creator. This is the all-powerful being who spoke and brought light into existence. This is the one who called out for the waters to gather together into one place, and they obeyed. This is the being who fashioned a great light to rule the day and scattered lesser lights across the expanse of space to rule the night. This is the one who called forth grass, plants and fruit-bearing trees out of the dry land. This is the one who, at his will, caused birds and fish to spring to life from the waters. This is the one whose command brought forth cattle, creeping things and beasts of the field from the undisturbed soil of the earth.

This is the one who formed Adam from dust and breathed into his nostrils the breath of life. This is the one who commissioned Adam and Eve to bring other living human beings into the world and then endowed them with the power to create new life together. This is the one who answered when Abel's blood cried up from the ground.

This is the being whose power caused the Watchers to tremble in fear as they contemplated the consequences that would surely follow their yet to be consummated treasonous revolt. This is the one to whom the archangels turned for instructions when the Watchers were to finally be judged.

This is the one who called Enoch away to solitude so that he might reveal to him the secrets of the universe. This is the one who now walks with Noah and suspends all other activity so that he might personally announce to him the incredibly sobering verdict.

Noah is fully aware that the one with whom he is talking not only has the power to do it, but that he, without question, has the resolve as well. That must have been a heart-stopping moment of spine-chilling awareness.

Think for a moment of the most mind-numbing announcement you've ever heard. Maybe it was a phone call about a child or family member who was involved in a horrific accident and is being rushed to a medical facility. Maybe it was the confirmation of a medical diagnosis that you had tried to dismiss as days passed slowly while you lived in fear of the news. There are many things and situations that would stop us in our tracks and cause us to emotionally crumble to our knees. Not one of these instances could be compared with the news that Noah has been told.

"The end of all flesh is come before me."

Personal Disclaimer:

What you are about to read over the course of the next few pages is my mental image of how the flood may have unfolded. This is not the mental image that I would have attempted to relate a mere six months ago. Research has broadened my perspective and opened my eyes to things that previously I would not have considered, nor thought possible. This is my visual image and I openly admit that I cannot in any way prove it beyond the premise of theory.

This is not my attempt at gripping fiction. This is my attempt to relate what may very well be a part of the past history of our planet. Some of the things I have uncovered have kept me up at night and some things have caused vivid nightmares;

because research indicates that if this is a part of our past, it most assuredly will be a part of our future (Matthew 24:37).

My theory as to how things may have transpired has been influenced by a number of factors, some of which I will make an effort to explain along the way. Everything that I attempt to articulate over these next few pages is drawn from things commonly accepted as factual, or based upon theoretical supposition that is supported by things commonly accepted as factual.

Let me state again that this is only a theory. As such, it may not be what actually happened, and in the future my thoughts on the matter may change. But for now, what you are about to read is my best attempt to assemble all the pieces that I have uncovered into a logical timeline of events.

I realize that while some of the details that I have included in my theory may resonate with some, they may be viewed as perposterous by others. But, I assure you, not a single thing that I have included do I consider to be purely fictional.

We Have Nothing to Fear Except...

Fear is a primal emotion that only steps to the forefront when we are confronted with possibilities. Regret may feed on the past. Indecision may thrive in the present. But fear... fear relies only upon the soon-to-emerge aspects of what is yet future. Most often it's tied to things unknown. In some instances fear is driven by something that is known, but not yet experienced. In either case, fear is a very real and present companion on some level.

When his disciples persisted in their desire to know things that were yet future, Jesus opened a window and gave them a collective visual of the events that one day would be. Earlier we referenced his allusion to the "Days of Noah," and positioned it simply as a testimonial record that Christ, himself, did not view the story of a man named Noah, nor the events that were said to have transpired in his day, as metaphorical. Christ spoke of Noah (spelled Noe in Matthew and Luke) as a historical figure and decidedly positioned the events of Noah's day as historical fact.

The reference is found in two separate gospel accounts. Matthew records it in chapter 24 and Luke in chapter 17. The pressing question asked by the disciples is, *"What shall be the sign of thy coming and of the end of the world?"* (Matt. 24:3). In Luke 17:20, it's the religious leaders of the day who are asking when the kingdom of God will come. In both instances, it's in the responses of Jesus that the name of Noah is referenced.

The focal point in the conversation is drawn to the comparison of the "Days of Noah" (history) and the prophesied arrival of "God's kingdom" (future). Most often the phrase is associated with the social activities of Noah's day and the overall lack of awareness that the flood of Noah's day was imminent. The reference is to the carrying on of life as if tomorrow, next week, and next month, were a certainty. *"They did eat, they drank, they married wives, they were given in marriage...."* (Luke 17:27, Matt. 24:38).

However, a more thorough reading of both passages, and the continuation passage in Luke 21, gives a much different perspective. The telltale signs are not the events that happen around the consumption of food, beverage or even marital practices, but rather what is going on in the heavens.

Matthew 24:29-30

> *(29) "Immediately after the tribulation of those days*
> *shall the sun be darkened, and the moon shall not give her light,*
> *and the stars shall fall from heaven,*
> *and the powers of the heavens shall be shaken:*
>
> *(30) "And then shall appear the sign of the Son of man in heaven:*
> *and then shall all the tribes of the earth mourn,*
> *and they shall see the Son of man coming*
> *in the clouds of heaven with power and great glory."*

Luke 17:24

> *"For as the lightning, that lighteneth*
> *out of the one part under heaven,*
> *shineth unto the other part under heaven;*
> *so shall also the Son of man be in his day."*

Luke 21:25-27

> *(25) "And there shall be signs in the sun, and in the moon,*
> *and in the stars; and upon the earth distress of nations,*
> *with perplexity; the sea and the waves roaring;*
>
> *(26) "Men's hearts failing them for fear,*
> *and for looking after those things which are coming on the earth:*
> *for the powers of heaven shall be shaken.*
>
> *(27) "And then shall they see the Son of man*
> *coming in a cloud with power and great glory."*

In each of the three settings, Christ directs the attention of those listening toward the heavens. In each case, it is *after* things become clearly observable in the heavens that "the Son of man" (Christ) is revealed. Both Matthew 24 and Luke 21 speak of the powers of heavens being "shaken."

The word translated "powers" is the Greek word *"dynamis"* (dü'-nä-mēs).[1] It is used to describe something that has great inherent strength by virtue of its nature. It is strong. It has great stamina. It is steadfast and imposing because its very construct is *dynamic*.

The word translated as "shaken" is the Greek word *"saleuō"* (sä-lyü'-ō).[2] It's often used to reference something that's affected by a prevailing wind, storm or the constant force of water currents. It implies that something has been stressed to the point of tottering and is giving way under the intense, unrelenting strain. What could possibly cause the powers of the heavens to *"saleuō"*?

Luke 17 says that it will be as a flash of lightning that fills the sky – even if you aren't looking for the flash, your attention is stirred by the illumination. This event will not go unnoticed. There won't be some who happen to catch it because they were looking in the right place at the right time and others who are oblivious to it altogether. The event being described in this instance is spellbinding on every level. Everyone will see it. Everyone will be aware.

Luke 24 says that men's hearts will fail them because of the overwhelming fear that is associated with "those things which are coming on the earth." This will not suddenly appear and then be gone and forgotten. This event will linger and play out over time. This event will cause mental anguish and emotional dread.

Fear. It relies on our perception of things that are a part of the soon-to-arrive future. Sometimes it is fear of the unknown. But it would seem that the most paralyzing fear is the fear of that which is known, but not yet experienced. This is the fear of which Christ speaks when he refers to "things which are coming." This is something that is widely known by all to be "on the way." This is what precluded the arrival of the flood in the days of Noah. Noah and his family saw it prior to boarding the ark and being sealed inside.

Many of the documented flood legends that have been pulled from cultures around the world include a complete blackening of the sky just prior to the flood. In Matthew 24:19 we read that the Sun would be darkened, the moon would not give light, and it would appear that the stars themselves were falling from the heavens. This is complete and utter blackness. The only light, it would seem, originates from the falling stars.

This same portrait is painted in Mark 13:24, Luke 21:25, and even in Old Testament passages such as Isaiah 13:10, Ezekiel 32:7, and Joel 2:31. What in the world is going on?

There are also numerous references among the various flood legends to a massive earthquake that was associated with the start of the flood. The Book of Jasher speaks of the same: *"And on that day, the Lord caused the whole earth to shake, and the sun darkened, and the foundations of the world raged, and the whole earth was moved violently, and the lightning flashed, and the thunder roared,"* (Jasher 6:11a). Verse 13 time stamps the happenings as taking place seven days before the flood, which was the same day Noah and his family entered the ark (Genesis 7:1-10).

The prophet Isaiah speaks of a future time of final judgment when the earth *"shall reel to and fro like a drunkard"* (Isaiah 24:20). Revelation 16:18 also warns of a great earthquake in the days of final judgment: *"....and there was a great earthquake, such as was not since men were upon the earth, so mighty an earthquake, and so great."* Again, the parallel is between the events of Noah's day and a day yet future; a day spoken of by Christ when asked about the signs of his coming and the end of the world.

Dr. W. Bruce Masse states in his research that nearly half of the 175 flood legends that he studied associated a "supernatural entity" with the arrival of the flood. In 38 cases, Masse says that there are detailed descriptions of a giant object in the sky. Among the different cultures, the object is envisioned as a snake, a water serpent, a bird, a catfish, a horned snake, an elongated fish-like creature with a long snout, a crocodile, a dragon, or a giant lizard. In each, the mysterious object that appeared in the sky was directly associated with a blanket of darkness, a great earthquake and the raging flood.[3]

Masse credits these depictions as attempts to describe a fiery object that blazed across the pre-flood sky – in his words, a comet. But what comet has ever blocked out the light of the Sun? Someone might suggest that a comet impact would accomplish this element of the story, but who then would be around to record such a happening if the blackness only followed the impact?

The only known event that blocks out the radiating light of the Sun is a solar eclipse. This occurs when the moon blocks out the light of the Sun for a short period of time. The event is also limited to a small geographic location, as opposed to a large land mass, country or even hemisphere. For something to block the light of the Sun in an eclipse-like fashion, it would have to be either larger in size than our moon or closer in distance than our moon.

The moon is able to do this because the combination of its size and distance from the earth makes it appear to be the same size as the Sun from our earthbound perspective. If an object that was smaller than our moon were to block the Sun's light in such a manner, it would have to be proportionally closer to the earth. If the object were greater in overall size than our moon, it could be considerably farther away and still block out the light of the Sun by passing between the earth and the Sun.

Forgive me for temporarily under-appreciating the majesty of such an event as the earth (or any portion of the earth) being temporarily sheltered from the direct light of the Sun, but solar eclipses are mundane by comparison to something that blocks out the Sun, the moon, and makes it appear as though the very stars are falling from the heavens. I do not believe that what is being so vividly depicted in so many ancient flood legends is merely a comet.

Comets do not arrest the attention of the masses. Certainly not everyone worldwide is aware of their approach, and many of those who are aware, are blatantly apathetic. Also, in our present day and age of enlightenment, the approach of a comet would not cause "men's hearts to fail for fear," as Christ so boldly prophesied.

The impact of a comet would certainly cause the ground in the nearby region to violently tremble, but would even a large comet be enough to cause the entire earth to *reel to and fro like a drunkard*" (Isaiah 24:20) or possess the power to move the earth *"out of her place"* (Isaiah 13:13)? I do not believe that what broached the sky in Noah's day was merely a comet. Nor does the pending arrival of a comet fit the somber tone of events as they are described by Christ.

Let me pause at this point to briefly address the previously quoted testimony of Christ. Some who are reading this may profess themselves as believers in Christ, and I realize that just as many, if not more, may not profess such a belief. If you are among those who do, be aware that Christ clearly, and without apology, declared himself to be the Son of God multiple times during his life. Prior to his crucifixion, he blatantly declared himself the Son of God, answering the High Priest by simply saying, *"I AM"* (Mark 14:61-62). Either Christ is who he claimed to be, and he was not vague about this in any way, or he was perhaps the most deceitful of all human flesh. You are free to choose either perspective; but know this, at no point do the words he spoke regarding the days of Noah or the days prior to his return appear to be allegorical in any manner.

Honey... You've Gotta See This!

When it comes to understanding and interpretation, the Book of Revelation is perhaps the most hotly debated portion of all scripture. Expositors have put their slant and spin on selected portions and individual verses for generations, all attempting to match the written word with the unfolding of current events. How much of it is literal, versus how much of it is symbolic, will no doubt continue to be argued for as long as there is time to disagree. However, for our purposes, we would do well to consider a mesmerizing sky portrait that is painted in chapter 12 by the book's writer.

Revelation 12:1

> *"And there appeared a great wonder in heaven;*
> *a woman clothed with the sun, and the moon under her feet,*
> *and upon her head a crown of twelve stars:"*

Notice that the writer identifies what he is about to disclose as "a great wonder" that appears "in heaven." It's the first of seven wonders that John sees and the purpose here is not to seek out a detailed interpretation (hence we have not included verse 2), but rather to call attention to the location of where this "wonder" is revealed. John specifies that it is in the heavens. This calls to remembrance the declaration of Christ to his followers when they asked about the end of the world. Christ said, *"And there shall be signs in the sun, and in the moon, and in the stars...."* (Luke 21:25). This being the case, perhaps John's description of such things should not be wholly dismissed as symbolic.

This "wonder in heaven" has been broadly adopted by the Catholic Church as a heavenly image of the Virgin Mary. A famous stained glass window in the St. Francis of Assisi Catholic Parish is only one of many artistic depictions that feature Mary, standing upon a crescent moon, basking in the light of sunshine, with 12 stars encircling her head.[4]

There is, of course, an astronomical "wonder in heaven" known for centuries as the constellation Virgo. Primarily visible in the springtime sky, there are times that Virgo is positioned in an almost upright manner against the night sky and the moon is positioned below the constellation, thus giving the visual of a woman in the heavens with the moon under her feet.

Directly over the head of the Virgo constellation would be the Leo constellation, which is comprised primarily of nine stars, but at times can be accompanied by the positioning of Mercury, Venus, Mars, Jupiter or Saturn within the constellation. A proper positioning of any three planets would make the Leo constellation appear as a collection of twelve stars that are positioned over the head of the Virgo constellation. Such a composite configuration would be rare and could indeed be considered a heavenly wonder.

Revelation 12:3

> *"And there appeared another wonder in heaven;*
> *and behold a great red dragon, having seven heads*
> *and ten horns, and seven crowns upon his heads."*

The second wonder that appeared in the heavens for John to see is vividly described as a Great Red Dragon. We have the assignment of color and the association with an animal counterpart, much as we saw in many versions of the various flood legends. We also have the descriptive term: *great*. This word can be used to portray a number of characteristics. It can describe the status of a thing or an individual as being of substantial importance or rank. It can define the quality of something as being top-notch or standout. It can also denote size or weight. In this case, the Greek word *"megas"* (me'-gäs) is used in an adjective form to imply mass.[5] As we will see, the object John describes as a dragon is massive in size. As a bit of a side note, this word is also used at times to identify something as being old, or of great age.

There are a variety of Biblical interpretations when it comes to what the seven heads, ten horns and seven crowns, mentioned in verse 3, may represent. Again, our interest is not in seeking out an interpretation of the passage. Our focus is on the location of the wonder that John sees and the descriptive size of the object. It is in the heavens and it is *"megas"* or *great*!

Revelation 12:4

> *"And his tail drew the third part of the stars of heaven, and did cast them to the earth: and the dragon stood before the woman which was ready to be delivered, for to devour her child as soon as it was born."*

As any properly drawn dragon would, this object has a tail and apparently the tail is monstrous in size, expanding to encompass a full one-third of the stars that are visible in the night sky. This estimation is absolutely massive. The expanse of the sky is typically divided by degrees. A full circumference of the earth would be equivalent to 360 degrees, and a span from visible horizon to visible horizon would be 180 degrees. If the tail of this object occupies one-third of the sky, it would be equal to a 60-degree spread or arc. By comparison, the Sun and moon (which are seen from Earth as being the same size in the sky) are equivalent to one-half of one degree.[6]

If this size assessment is anywhere close to accurate, then just the protruding tail of what John sees would take up the same portion of the sky as 120 side-by-side full moons. Can we now envision why Christ compared this future sign in the heavens with lightning flashing from the east to the west or warned that men's hearts would fail them for fear? Surely there's no way imaginable that what John describes could possibly go unnoticed by anyone on the planet.

John gives us a position of the Great Red Dragon as being "before the woman," which could be taken in one of two ways:

1. The Great Red Dragon is positioned in a manner so as to appear to be in front of the woman as if she is facing it in the sky. The Virgo constellation is almost always drawn facing to the left (north). The Draco (dragon) constellation would be directly in her line of sight.

2. The Great Red Dragon is positioned in such a manner that, as the Virgo constellation continues in its natural path across the sky, it would cross into the path of the Great Red Dragon. As the earth makes its annual pass through the constellations, Virgo is positioned with Leo higher in the sky (appearing to be over the woman's head). Cancer is above Leo in the progression. Thus, it would appear that the woman crowned with 12 stars is moving toward the Cancer constellation. Is this the location of the sky where John's Great Red Dragon appears?

When we call to reference constellations, make note that we are referencing ancient astronomy as opposed to modern-day astrology. The International Astronomical Union currently recognizes 88 official constellations of star groupings, many of which date back to ancient Babylon and Egypt.[7] So, yes, John would have been quite familiar with the recognized positioning of stars in the heavens and the designated depictions associated with them.

John also tells us that the Great Red Dragon appears to cast stars from the heaven to the earth. My guess is that John is seeing a massive meteor shower that unfolds as a part of this heavenly display. The Draco constellation appears to produce a meteor shower that can be seen each year in the month of October. The shower is actually composed of leftover trail debris from the comet 21P/Giacobini-Zinner, and in most cases this meteor shower is anything but dramatic.[8] We commonly refer to these leftover particles as "shooting" or "falling" stars. Could this be what Christ is describing when he tells his disciples, "the stars shall fall from heaven" (Matt. 24:29)?

SIDE NOTE: The appearance of the Virgo constellation in the springtime sky and the annual early October meteor shower, associated with the Draco constellation and known as the Draconids, are separated by five months (May, June, July, August and September). Revelation 6:12-17 describes the opening of the Sixth Seal, which brings with it a great earthquake, total eclipse of the Sun and stars falling from the heavens (massive meteor shower). As described, this is an extremely dramatic event.

Revelation chapter 8 describes a series of events that include hail and fire, mingled with blood falling from the sky to the earth (a dramatic meteor shower). An object described as being the size of a mountain falls out of the sky, but mainly impacts the oceans. This is followed by the arrival of the infamous sky object called "Wormwood." Its impact pollutes much of Earth's water supply and also darkens one-third of the sky (nuclear radiation fallout from an impact event). The events of Revelation 6 and the events of Revelation 8 appear to be separated by *five months.*

But the descriptions of John in Revelation and the proclamations of Christ during his ministry are still thought to be future events by most people and, yes, the passages are interpreted by some as being purely symbolic. Perhaps they are realistic visual images of what is to come when "the powers of heaven" are indeed being shaken (Matt. 24:29, Luke 21:26). Perhaps they are extreme overstatements for the purpose of emphasis. Everyone is left to their own understanding, interpretation and belief.

In either case, this might be a good time to stop and ask the question, "Have there been any such events recorded in our historical past?"

Both the Tulli Papyrus, written by the Egyptians, and the Mawangdui Silk Almanac, recorded by the Chinese, record a majestic object that appeared in the ancient sky over their lands. Both separate the appearance of the object by noting that it was unlike anything the official watchers of the sky from either civilization had ever observed or documented.

Each civilization dated events with regard to the onset of a ruler's reign. As such, the datelines given by the two cultures present a little bit of a variation. The Egyptians date the event as it pertains to the reign of Tuthmosis III. The Chinese document it as transpiring during the reign of Tang, the first Shang king.[9] We are left with that information as an anchor when it comes to discerning the approximate time period of the event. But the graphic details recorded by the two cultures seem to remove all doubt that they are indeed speaking of the same spectacular event.

The Chinese dates for the event point to a time period just after 1500 BC. The Egyptian papyrus gives a more precise date that has been equated to 1486 BC. The descriptions are as follows:

> *Egyptian* – The object in the sky is described as "a marvel never before known since the foundation of this land." Also, "Its body was one rod in length and one rod in width.... and extended to the limits of the four supports of heaven."[10]

> Graham Phillips, in his book, T*he End of Eden: The Comet That Changed Civilization*, gives us a better understanding and comparison of the Egyptian measurement of a rod, equating it to 100 Egyptian cubits. He goes on to state that the Egyptians measured the full moon at only five cubits wide. By comparison, the object that is described in the Tulli Papyrus is 20 times the size of the full moon.[11]

> *Chinese* – The object is also described as massive in size, but the Chinese astronomers were particular to note the number of tails that were visible. In most cases these visiting objects in the sky are described as having two, three or even up to five tails. The objects were also given names that associated them with the mythical creature they were thought to represent. The truly impressive ones were associated with and named after gods.[12]

> This particular object was noted as having 10 tails and was named "Lao-Tien-Yeh" – The Great God.[13] The Chinese, much like the Egyptians, describe the object as a disk of fire. They thought it illuminated the sky because it appeared to be burning, which is why

the Chinese also used the description of fire-breathing dragon[14] (similar to the graphic portrait painted by John in Revelation 12).

Phillips devotes an entire chapter of his book to this particular object, detailing how the appearance of this object in 1486 BC impacted numerous cultures including the Hittites, Assyrians, Mitanni, and Babylonians. All of these cultures adopted a similar depiction of a sky disk with wings and associated it in their culture with the arrival of a new god. The Egyptians also adopted a winged disk symbol that is associated with the 1486 BC appearance of this massive object in the sky. The Chinese simply portrayed it as a large circle with 10 distinct lines protruding from the edge of the circle on one side.[15]

Whatever this object was, there's no question that it arrested the attention of the world from Egypt to China and across the entire Middle East. Cultures far and wide, great and small, reacted to its presence in the sky. Many viewed the object as the appearance of a superior god and changed their religious practices accordingly.[16]

It is interesting to note that during this same historical time period the Old Testament book of Joshua details the battles of the Israelites in the land of Canaan. The recorded events transpire following the Egyptian Exodus and the 40 years of wilderness wanderings. It is during these conquests that the famed walls of Jericho crumble before the invading Israelite army. Some have suggested that an earthquake may have been involved in the leveling of Jericho's famed walls.

Joshua chapter 10 also tells the story of five kings who plotted together against a nation called Gibeon. It reveals that the Gibeonites had made a peace agreement with the Israelites. When the collective forces of the five kings finally went to war against Gibeon, Joshua and the Israelites came to their aid. As the armies of the five kings sought to flee from the Israelite army, an unrelenting shower of stones fell from the sky (Joshua 10:10-11). The passage describes it as a great slaughter, noting that more soldiers of the five armies died from the hailstones in this short period of time than were killed by the Israelites.

It's in this same passage that we find the legendary tale of the Sun and moon standing still at Joshua's command. This takes place after the shower of stones has practically laid waste to the collective armies of five kingdoms. The Sun and moon stand still so that the battle can be completed and all of the enemy can be slain.

What could possibly cause stones to rain from the sky and the rotation of the earth to slow to a complete halt? Scientifically this seems impossible to explain. It's just not something that is logically conceivable or easy to envision. However, the story is recorded in the 88th chapter of the Book of Jasher, as well as the 10th chapter of Joshua. It can also be found among legendary stories from cultures around the world.

Initially, I thought that commentary outside of Biblical sources pointing to a miraculous event would be difficult to find. I was wrong. There are numerous accounts of writers and researchers who have taken a critical and scientific approach to solving the riddle of just how such a day could be plausible. These are just a few of the resources that I was able to find:

- *A Geocentricity Primer (Introduction to Biblical Cosmology)* by Gerardus D. Bouw, Ph.D. (2004)

- *Worlds In Collision* by Immanuel Velikovsky (1950)

- *When The Earth Turned Over* by H.B. Rand (1968)

- *Joshua's Long Day and the Dial of Ahaz, A Scientific Vindication and A Midnight Cry*, 3rd Edition, by C.A.L. Trotten (1891)

My singular question was whether or not the base summary of the story could be found in other historical literature. Not only is it found, it's also specific to the declaration of an extended period of daylight or extended period of darkness, depending on the geographical origin. This would be anticipated if the story were to have any merit beyond the romantic lure of legendary tales. If one side of the globe experienced perpetual daylight, the opposing side should be immersed in extended darkness.

If we are to dismiss romantic folklore, then we're brought face to face with the need for explanation. How is it possible for such an event to occur?

First, let's deal with a shower of stones from the heavens. The Egyptian Tulli Papyrus not only records the appearance of a majestic, if not imposing object in the sky, it also details the departure or demise of the object. According the papyrus, after several days of zenith, there appeared large numbers of smaller fiery objects in the sky. These objects began to burn brighter and brighter until they outshone the brightness of the sun. The final description is that of "fish and birds" raining down from the sky.[17] The description could easily be interpreted as a colorful depiction of a large meteor storm, such as the one recorded in Joshua 10.

But what of Joshua's long day? What astronomical event could have held the Sun and the moon in place for an extended period of time on the horizon? Could the overall influence of a large luminous body, which was documented and assessed by the Egyptians to appear as 20 times the size of the full moon, include the power to initiate a slowing of Earth's rotation to such a degree that both the Sun and the moon remained stationary in the sky? Could a prolonged, increased tug, or perturbation, brought into play by an object with sufficient mass, affect the normal degree of axis tilt so as to project a mystical motionless effect with regard to the Sun and moon?

There are but two astronomical proposals that would extensively affect the movement of the Sun and moon:

1. The rotation of the earth slowed to an eventual stop or near stop, thereby giving the appearance that the Sun and moon no longer transited across their given sky treks, but instead, *stood still.*

2. The axial tilt of the earth shifted to the point of drawing the northernmost pole to a more equatorial position, thereby giving the region of Joshua's famed extended battle the perspective that might be considered a normal transition of the Sun and moon closer to the Arctic or Antarctic Circle.

Both Rand and Velikovsky propose the idea of temporary polar shift, crediting the influential force to the intervention of an abnormally close passing of Venus or Mars. A deeper understanding of the laws of planetary motions in this present day and time would appear to render both of the conjectures as fallacies.

Although there are times when the orbital paths of Venus and Mars bring them into closer proximity with the orbit of Earth, it is widely believed that neither planet has ever closed the gap sufficiently to even appear one-quarter the size of a full moon, let alone cause a dramatic temporary polar repositioning. If any orbiting solar body ever held such an influence over the earth, it most certainly was not Venus or Mars.

There have been a number of impressive comet sightings recorded in our modern day. Some were celebrated for their vivid sky displays (comets Kohoutek in 1973, Hyakutake in 1996, and McNaught in 2007); some fizzled out well short of their anticipated radiance (comet Ison 2013). These were all clearly comets and it is commonly projected that the object of 1486 BC was also a comet — albeit, clearly more astounding than the long list of modern-day comets by far.

There's also the record of Swiss astronomer Jean-Philippe de Cheseaux, who documented the appearance of an object in 1744 and described it as reaching more than eight times the size of the full moon.[18] It is also noted that it was bright enough to be seen during the day by the naked eye and displayed six, and at times seven, distinct tails that could be seen streaming upwards on the horizon just before daybreak.

Chinese observers noted that this object also produced distinct atmospheric sounds when it was at its peak.[19] It has been suggested that this was perhaps one of the closest cometary approaches on record and that audible sound was generated as a result of the object's interaction with Earth's magnetosphere.[20] Interesting!

It would be reasonable to project that, even today, in our intelligent and highly educated society, if a brightly shining object suddenly appeared in the sky that was twice the size of a typical full moon; we would be awestruck to say the least. And, if the object was four or five times the size of the moon and accompanied by a prevailing tail that swept across a full one-third of the visible heavens, it's extremely probable that such a happening would thoroughly captivate worldwide attention.

Setting the Table

So why call to reference a pair of prophetic accounts that some may consider to be purely symbolic? And why spend time researching a pair of historical accounts that some might dismiss as having been greatly exaggerated by under-educated civilizations?

Because the backdrop of documented history, mixed with that of recorded prophecy, paints the vivid picture of an object of substantial size that is a permanent part of our solar system and has a direct and powerful influence on the planet we call home.

Noah's flood did not happen because a petulant, oversensitive deity threw a temper tantrum, waved a magic wand, and caused all hell to break loose. If there was a flood, it unfolded as a result of the progression of natural laws that, once in motion, were irreversible.

The flood of Noah's day was a globally reconstructive event on every level. It decisively destroyed the world that then was, and left us with the planet that now is. The two are not comparable.

We detailed a few chapters back a world that was designed by the Creator primarily as a singular landmass. The landmass was fed by a globally connected flow of water that emanated from Eden and spread throughout the planet by way of four primary rivers. We found that portions of this water flowed beneath the surface of the planet in reservoirs referred to as fountains of the deep.

We've explored the research and proposals from prominent geologists who, working independent of each other's research, projected the existence of such a singular landmass in our planet's past, during a time when the earth was as much as 50% smaller than it is today. These geologists went to great lengths to substantiate their proposed theory of Earth's ancient construct.

We looked at magnetic fields and the role they play in the overall workings of planetary bodies. We reviewed the research of scientists who predicted, then went on to discover, the existence and prominence of magnetic fields throughout the universe. We wrestled with the concept of a pre-flood canopy that may have surrounded the planet, questioning how it could have existed, if it did, and what form it might have taken.

We examined scientific evidence of higher oxygen content in our planet's past and considered the effects of an increased atmospheric pressure. We reviewed the verification of enormous plant life and extreme amounts of vegetative growth found in fossils and coal. We evaluated documentation that provided evidence of a number of insect species that are preserved in the fossil record as being hundreds of times greater in size than their present-day counterparts.

The world that then was is not the world that now is. That is a heavily documented, undeniable fact. That world and this world are vastly different. The only question is: How did we get from there to here?

There are only two possible answers:

1. Minute, systematic changes gradually took place over extremely long periods of time, with periods of global extinction and resurrection mixed in.

2. There was a global flood that completely reconstructed the planet, bringing us from there to here over a far shorter period of time and leaving evidence in its wake.

It is my contention that if Noah's Flood did indeed occur, it would have happened as a result of a prominent and devastating influence from an object similar to the one recorded in ancient Egyptian and Chinese history. It is my belief that this object, which played a pivotal role in bringing about the end of all flesh, would also play a prominent role in the prophesied events that are yet future. As it was in the days of Noah, so shall it be....

The evidence points convincingly toward the involvement of an orbiting object; an object that could prove to be the yet-to-be-discovered source that perturbs the orbits of Uranus and Neptune and bends the orbital paths of some comets into irregular cycles of appearance.

When it comes to the potential of an unknown or unrecognized planetary body that could be a force of great destruction if ever its path brought it into the inner solar system, there is no shortage of theories and doomsday prognostications. In most cases the conspiratorial rogue planet is referred to as "Planet X" (the original designation given by NASA for any yet-to-be-discovered planet). In some cases the name popularized by the works of Zecharia Sitchen, Nibiru, is used.

Likewise, there are a wide variety of solar system diagrams depicting the interaction of this undiscovered orbiting body with the inner reaches of our solar system. Of all the printed material and diagrams from Sitchen to NASA that I have researched (and I have spent hours in diligent research), I've only come across one person's work that stands up to scrutiny and matches the prophetic portrait of John's "wonder in heaven."

His research is extensive and his diagrams are elaborate. While I am not completely on board with every detail, his projections fill the gaps in the puzzle almost seamlessly. He is an amateur astronomer from Louisiana named Gill Broussard, and his work can easily be found by searching the term "Planet-7x." I do not have permission to print his charts or diagrams, but having had a number of lengthy phone conversations with him during my research, I feel that I can mention him as a prominent source of plausible data and give credit where it is most certainly due.

When I initially began to consider the possibility of an outside force being involved as the impetus for Noah's flood, my research led me early and often to comets. As you've read earlier, I became quite comfortable with the conclusion that a comet would not fully possess the properties to have the level of impact needed to trigger a global devastation such as the flood.

Hours of research regarding the discovery of the planets beyond Saturn, and the continued search to find the cause of the perturbations of the orbits of Uranus and Neptune, led me to broaden my research and open my mind to other possibilities. At this stage, I think it is entirely possible that there remains a yet-to-be-discovered or yet-to-be-disclosed planetary body that interacts with the inner portions of our solar system. The object would exhibit an elongated orbital path that takes it beyond what we know as the Kuiper Belt and brings it back toward the Sun over a course of several hundred years.

Some have gone so far as to speculate about the length of time that could be assigned to the orbital cycle of such an object. Sitchen famously defined it as a 3,600-year orbit. Broussard seems to favor a more frequent and slightly irregular course of about 360 years. The difference lies in the well documented translation issues with the number zero in the ancient languages from which the information is drawn.

I am not convinced of a certain number of years with regard to the time frame of the object's orbit. I am, however, convinced of three things that must be a part of the final projections:

1. It must be on the same general orbital plane as the earth, not a highly tilted plane.

2. It must follow the same counterclockwise orbit as the earth, not orbit in an opposing directional path.

3. Its orbit must intersect with the obital path of Earth at entry and exit intervals that are separated by 150 to 151 days (5 months). This is the time that it takes the Earth to transverse the distance between the entry and exit points.

If it exists, if it was the catalyst of Noah's Great Flood, then these three parameters are vital for its projected influence to be realized. A fourth parameter is based solely on NASA's mission to find the object that perturbs the orbits of the outer planets. The orbit of this object takes it through the section of deep space studied by the Voyager 1 and Voyager 2 space probes.

One unknown factor that cannot be projected is the composition of such an orbital body. When it comes to speculating unknowns about an unknown, the limb gets pretty thin. However, the potential composition seems to hold the key to a wide number of variables. For instance, Saturn is recognized as one of the largest planets in our solar system, but it's also the least dense. The density of Saturn (0.687 grams per cubic centimeter) is less than that of water (1 gram per cm^3), meaning that Saturn should actually float if you could find a puddle big enough to test the theory.[21]

However, Saturn maintains enough continuous tug to sustain a collection of ice crystals that take on the form of magnificent rings around the planet. It also holds 62 known moons in orbital tow.

The one thing that can be projected is the minimum requirements to produce the observed effects. This is similar to the Law of Displacement, also known as Archimedes' Principle. Archimedes was a third-century BC mathematician and physicist who was charged by King Hiero II to measure the amount of gold in his crown. The king had given a certain amount of the royal gold to a blacksmith and entrusted him with the design and forging.

Apparently the king was distrusting of the blacksmith and wanted Archimedes to verify that all of the gold that had been given had been used to forge the crown and that the blacksmith had not substituted another less precious metal to balance out the weight differential. With the crown being an irregularly shaped object, Archimedes was perplexed as to how he might measure its overall gold content without melting it down. While taking a bath, he observed that the level of water in the tub rose as he got in. He then realized that the crown would do the same, and that by dividing the mass of the crown by the volume of water that it displaced once submerged, he could resolve the king's dilemma.

As the story goes, Archimedes then got so excited that he jumped out of the bath and ran through the streets naked, screaming "Eureka!" (Greek for "I have found it."). After he settled down and presumably found a robe, the test was performed and it was determined that the crown contained silver, as well as gold.[22]

The base principle is that the overall composition of the

object would greatly determine its potential effect as it neared other planetary bodies in the solar system. For minimum projections, I go back to amateur astronomer Gill Broussard, who projects the object to be at least seven times the overall mass of the earth, thus his given designation of "Planet-7x."

There is also the size/distance equation. This is most easily seen in our relationship with the moon during a total solar eclipse. Because of the size/distance ratio, the moon is capable of blocking out the entire mass of the sun when it is in optimum position. This results in near darkness, leaving only the Sun's corona visible, during what would otherwise be a normal, bright, sunny day.

If the moon orbited closer to the earth, it would appear to be larger and thus block out the corona as well. If it were farther away, it would only block out a portion of the Sun even though perfectly aligned during the pass. With this principle in consideration, we can see how the object recorded by the Egyptians and Chinese in 1486 BC as 20 times the size of the full moon and the object observed by Swiss astronomer Jean-Philippe de Cheseaux in 1744 as eight times the size of the full moon could be the same object, but at vastly different distances. (This statement is for illustration purposes only. I am not stating that the object seen in 1486 BC and the object seen in 1744 was the same object, only that it could be.)

Since we're considering the impact of a physical pull or tug on other objects in the solar system, the Inverse Square Law is also in play. Basically, the intensity of the tug on an object is inversely proportional to the square of the distance from the source of the tug. Simply put, every time the distance is cut in half, the force of the tug is quadrupled.[23]

The rules of the Inverse Square Law apply when you are dealing with gravity, light, magnetism and the people to whom you are attracted. In our case, we are primarily drawn to the forces of magnetism between two objects as they approach each other (this could also be thought of in terms of gravitational pull, as the lines between magnetism and gravity are continuing to blur in scientific circles). The closer the objects are to each other, the greater the force and influence of the tug or pull.

Ending The Beginning

It is my contention that a large orbiting object exists within our solar system and that it possesses sufficient size and the necessary properties to disrupt life on this planet on a globally destructive scale. I believe this object was known to ancient civilizations such as Sumer, Assryia, Babylon, Egypt and China. I believe it was observed and documented by the royal sky observers of these cultures and that they tried, to the best of their abilities, to explain its nature.

If we were to take the 1486 BC record of the Egyptians and Chinese and begin counting forward in rough 360-year cycles from that date, we come across some interesting points in time such as the 1053-1054 AD time frame where the Chinese documented and tracked the appearance of a strange object in the sky and the 1744 time frame for de Cheseaux's amazing sky object.

Most astronomers identify the appearance of the documented Chinese "Guest Star" of 1053-1054 as an exploding star or supernova that formed the Crab Nebula.[24] But some point to the fact that the Chinese documented movement of the "Guest

Star" and dismiss the supernova theory in favor of a large object in motion that possesses a greatly extended orbit.[25] In the case of the "Guest Star" the dates align with a 360-year cycle within 20 years, not a huge time window variation over 2,500+ years of time.

De Cheseaux's massive comet comes within nine years of hitting a 360-year cycle squarely on the nose. Again, this is not a huge variation for a span of over 3,200 years. See Appendix 4 for a timeline chart, mapping a 360-year cycle.

If we started at 1486 BC and counted backward in time, using the same rough 360-year cycle of years, we come surprisingly close to an appropriate time window for Noah's Flood — 2926 BC. Some date the time of the Flood to between 2950 and 3000 BC.[26] Again, over an approximate 1,500-year period of loosely calculated dates, the time gap doesn't seem to be substantial.

Another prominent event is documented during the reign of King Uzziah in Judah. A prophet named Amos uses this event to time-stamp the period in which he prophesied, or preached, to the nation of Israel.

Amos 1:1

> "The words of Amos, who was among the herdmen of Tekoa, which he saw concerning Israel in the days of Uzziah king of Judah, and in the days of Jeroboam the son of Joash king of Israel, two years before the earthquake."

The time period is framed by the reigns of King Uzziah in Judah and King Jereboam, the son of Joash, in Israel. Jereboam reigned briefly with his father, Joash, but became the sole regent of Israel in 781 BC. Uzziah's reign in Judah began about 768 BC. Jereboam died in 753 BC, while Uzziah was still king. Therefore, the date of the referenced earthquake has to fall between 768 BC (when Uzziah began to reign in Judah) and 753 BC (when Jereboam died).

Apparently, the earthquake was substantial and became a point of reference for the entire region of the Middle East. The prophet Zechariah references it as a point of illustration in his description of an earthquake that he says will occur when the Messiah returns to the earth at the end of days.

Zechariah 14:4-5

> *(4) "And his feet [Christ] shall stand in that day*
> *upon the mount of Olives, which is before Jerusalem*
> *on the east, and the mount of Olives shall cleave*
> *in the midst thereof toward the east and toward the west,*
> *and there shall be a very great valley; and half of the mountain*
> *shall remove toward the north, and half of it toward the south.*
>
> *(5) "And ye shall flee to the valley of the mountains;*
> *for the valley of the mountains shall reach unto Azal:*
> *yea, ye shall flee, like as ye fled from before the earthquake*
> *in the days of Uzziah king of Judah: and the LORD my God*
> *shall come, and all the saints with thee."*

Since the Mount of Olives is currently intact, we can conclude that Zechariah describes a day that has not yet arrived. If his prophetic words are accurate, there remains a day in the future, when the Mount of Olives in Jerusalem will split from east to west and separate from north to south. The separation will be so wide that it will create "a very great valley," according to verse 4. He then says that this will be similar to the earthquake that happened in the days of Uzziah. Again, the message is quite clear that the earthquake in the days of Uzziah was substantial.

Based on archeological excavations in the area, geologists estimate the quake to be of at least 8.2 in magnitude and suggest that the regions affected by the tremor included Israel, Jordan, Lebanon and Syria.[27] The proposed time period is 750 BC, plus or minus 25 years. The time frame, as defined by the rule of the two kings mentioned by Amos, would be 768 BC to 753 BC.

Amos also gives us another point of reference. Keeping in mind that he states in his introduction that his ministry began two years prior to the earthquake, we can also consider his prophetic reference of a coming judgment on Israel in chapter 8 of his book.

Amos 8:8-9

> (8) "Shall not the land tremble for this, and every one mourn
> that dwelleth therein? and it shall rise up wholly as a flood;
> and it shall be cast out and drowned, as by the flood of Egypt.

> (9) "And it shall come to pass in that day, saith the Lord GOD,
> that I will cause the sun to go down at noon,
> and I will darken the earth in the clear day:"

The idea of trembling land in verse 8 could certainly be the foreshadowing of an earthquake, but what of the reference to the darkening of the earth in verse 9? A total eclipse is documented by the Assyrians around this time and scholars have pinpointed the date as June 15, 763 BC.[28] The broadly verified date also falls so nicely into the time window of Amos that some secular references even identify it as linked to the Amos passage.

If we started our calendar in 1486 BC and subtracted a pair of 360-year orbital cycles (720 years) we arrive at 766 BC. Once again, we are missing a direct hit by only a matter of a few years.

Moving into the 1st century AD, we find that the crucifixion of Christ in 32 AD falls into the time window, if we allow for a little variation in orbital cycles over a 1,500-year period. During the time when Christ hung on the cross, there is a documented interval of midday darkness that lasted approximately three hours and a great earthquake (Matthew 27:45-51, Mark 15:33, & Luke 23:44-45). References to this span of darkness can also be found in the 1st-century writings of Origen, Thallus and Phlegon.[29]

Some have associated the darkness with a solar eclipse, but Julius Africanus expounded upon the writings of Phlegon in the 3rd century, noting that the crucifixion event took place around Passover, meaning that it would be at the time of a full moon, thereby negating the possibility of the period of darkness being the result of a solar eclipse.[30] Also, a solar eclipse would span a matter of minutes as opposed to a time frame encompassing three hours.

The time period from 1486 BC to 1744 AD equates to a span of 3,230 years. Adding a year for the year zero brings the total count to 3,231. This number may not be entirely accurate due to the way the passage of time was marked in ancient times, but it is a reasonable and commonly accepted representation of years.

Divide the proposed number of years (3,231) by the projected orbit interval (360 years) and you arrive at a total of 8.975 orbital cycles over that period of time. Since we are beginning the count of years with the verified sighting of a remarkable object in the sky and ending with another extraordinary event, we want to round the 8.975 average to the nearest whole number — 9. This is indicative of one appearance on each end of the time span and seven in between. If we divide the total number of years (3,231) by 9, we come to an average of 359 years between appearances. That number nails the proposed 360-year orbital cycle almost exactly.

The projected orbit of the object in question takes it through the Asteroid and Kuiper Belts; both are regions where it meets with resistance on some level. It is also highly probable that, since it influences the orbits of other planetary bodies, the object is affected to some degree by them in return. Thus, an irregular orbital journey that fluctuates to a certain degree in length would be a logical expectation.

If we set a proposed date of 3,000 BC for Noah's flood, then add up the years between that date and 1744 AD, we come to a total of 4,745 years. If we divide that number by the proposed 360-year orbital cycle, we come to 13.18. If we were to divide the total number of years (4,745) by 13 orbital cycles, we come to an average of 365 years per cycle. Again, we see that we are not far removed from the projected cycle of 360 years. Over a span of 4,745 years, the fluctuation is less than 1.4%.

I believe that there is a very real possibility that the existence of this planetary body may have been confirmed at some point in the last few decades, but it has not yet been disclosed to the general public due to concerns regarding the influence that this object could have on our planet.

If it was suddenly made known that there is a large orbiting object in our solar system, which carries with it the potential to trigger substantial environmental chaos as its orbit brings it closer to the inner solar system, it would have a subversive effect on world culture, undermine world commerce and demoralize social stability.

Such information would only be made known to the general public when there was no other alternative. It would also be disseminated very cautiously and methodically over an extended period of time. In 1998, Paramount Pictures released a movie entitled "Deep Impact," starring Robert Duvall, Téa Leoni, and Morgan Freeman. In the first 20 minutes of the film, they got it right. They got it so eerily right!

I believe that there is an object and that this object has not only left a lasting impression on this planet, but also on other orbiting bodies within our solar system. The composition of this object generates a massive magnetic field that perturbs the orbit of other planetary bodies. In the past, it has also caused smaller orbiting objects such as moons to shift in their orbits, collide with other orbiting objects, or even tear violently apart under the relentless strain that it can cause.

The orbit of this object exceeds the boundary of the Kuiper Belt and, as it orbits, it draws with it smaller objects from the Kuiper Belt and Oort Cloud, carrying them along in its orbital path until they are caught up in the tug of other large planetary bodies such as Neptune, Uranus, Saturn or Jupiter. It may be responsible in part for the extremely angled and elliptical orbit of Pluto, which crosses the orbit of Neptune and at times draws close to the orbit of Uranus.

In a previous chapter (page 192), we learned that activity confined to a planet, such as earthquakes and volcanic eruptions may cause a shift of the planet's figure axis, but only the external force of gravity (in this case, magnetic field interaction) can affect a planet's actual degree of axial tilt. As such, the potency of this object's magnetic influence on other planetary bodies could be the explanation of their degree of tilt.[31]

We are familiar with the 23.4393° tilt of the earth. It's why the earth has a distinct northern and southern hemisphere and why we experience drastic seasonal changes during the year. Neptune is tilted at 28.3°, Saturn at 26.7°, and Mars at 25.2°, meaning that they also experience the effect of seasonal weather. On the other hand, Jupiter sits almost upright, displaying only a slight 3.1° tilt, and Mercury has no measurable axis tilt at all.

Uranus and Venus display the opposite extreme. Uranus is tilted at 97.8° degrees, meaning that it appears to roll on its side as it orbits the Sun, and Venus is completely upside down, tilted at 177.3°, which is why the Sun rises in the west and sets in the east from the Venusian perspective.

Many propose that the extreme tilt of Uranus was caused by a large impact at some point in the planet's past, but there are no definitive signs of such an impact, and the question could be asked, "With what did it collide?" Could the magnetism of this rogue orbiting object have locked into the magnetic field of Uranus, pulling it to an extreme axial tilt and a new, permanent position of rotation?

We think of magnetic fields as being a flow of energy that is essentially disconnected from the physical planet. However, the flow of the magnetic field originates from the core of the planet, meaning that its flow is merely representative of the planet's north/south axial orientation.[32]

Could this object have also flipped Venus upside down as it passed, causing a massive amount of volcanic activity and leading to the near-complete resurfacing of the planet that astronomers observe? Could such a violent event have also resulted in the blanket-thick gaseous atmospheric conditions?

Could the debris trail of this object be responsible for the development of rings around the three outer planets? Could it be responsible for dragging a multitude of objects out of the Oort Cloud and Kuiper Belt, resulting in each of those huge planets having multiple moons? (Jupiter has 67, Saturn, 62, Uranus, 27, Neptune, 14.)

Could the debris fields known as the Trojans, the Greeks and the Hildas, which are locked into the orbital path of Jupiter, be former moons that were torn apart as they were caught in a tug-o'-war or subjected to a massive electromagnetic discharge between this object and Jupiter during a pass?

Could the primary asteroid belt be the remains of another small planetary body that was torn apart either by a collision or the extreme force of being caught between the intense pull of this object and Jupiter? Could debris left behind from such a dismantling then spread throughout the vast gap between

Mars and Jupiter over thousands of years as Jupiter and Mars continued their orbital path?

Could a blast of debris from a small planet being torn apart by this object and Jupiter be what struck the southern portion of Mars, causing the majority of impact craters and nudging it into a slightly angular orbit? Could this be the origin of the huge scar on the southern surface of Mars? Could it be the trigger for the immense volcanic activity in the Tharsis region of the planet?

It is assumed that at some point in the past, Mars had a rich supply of water. This assumption seemed to be supported by the presence of a massive canyon on the planet's surface that dwarfs the Grand Canyon. It was presumed that the 2,500-mile-long Valles Marineris Canyon System formed over a period of a few short weeks or months due to massive flooding and water erosion.[33] The theory is challenged by some who believe that the canyon may be the result of massive volcanic activity in the Tharsis region, which caused colossal fractures to develop across a section of the planet's surface and later sink.[34]

A third possibility for the source of the canyon is that of an intensely powerful electro-magnetic strike, perhaps millions of times more powerful than a bolt of lightning.

More than 40 years ago electrical engineer Ralph Juergens of Flagstaff, Arizona, identified the canyon on Mars as a gigantic electrical arc scar. He went on to publish an extensive study, comparing the Valles Marineris Canyon System on Mars with the Grand Canyon. He said, "...to me this entire region resembles nothing so much as an area sapped by a powerful electric arc advancing unsteadily across the surface, occasionally splitting in two, and now and then-weakening, so that its traces narrow and even degrade into lines of disconnected craters...." Juergens went on to say, "I can only wonder: Is it possible that Mars was bled of several million cubic kilometers of soil and rock in a single encounter with another planetary body?"[35] Might such an encounter also explain why Mars has so little atmosphere?

Could the debris trail of this object be responsible for the large number of impact craters that we see positioned in specific locations on the inner planets and our moon? We noted earlier that while Mercury is riddled with craters, Venus has visible craters in only one location. The back side of our moon is heavily cratered, while the side facing Earth is primarily shielded. And 97% of the impact craters on Mars are in the extreme southern hemisphere.

Could a tug-o'-war between this object and the Sun be the source of Mercury's strange elliptical orbit? A distant pass every 1,500 years or so would be plenty sufficient to stretch the orbital path of Mercury without ripping it completely from its orbit around the Sun.

Let me stop to make it clear that I do not think all of the questions raised in the previous paragraphs could be answered by a single pass through the solar system of any solitary object, regardless the size or intensity of magnetic (or gravitational) pull. It seems that it would clearly take multiple passes and thousands of years of orbital time for repeated interactions and evidentiary results to transpire.

The real question is not the specific effects this orbiting body could have had on other objects throughout the solar system, so much as the question of how it might have affected the earth and been directly involved in triggering Noah's Flood. Thus far, plenty of questions have been raised about what may have caused the myriad of anomalies that are clearly observable throughout the solar system. It's finally time to project what happened when this mysterious orbiting body made its closest ever pass by of Earth and ripped asunder the planet we call home.

Enoch's First Dream Vision — Book of Enoch 83:3, 4a

> *(3) "I had just lain down in my grandfather Mahalalel's house, when I saw the heavens collapse and fall to the earth.*

> *(4a) "This caused the earth to be swallowed up in a great abyss...."*

I believe that there is a deep space object with an enormous amount of mass and a devastating magnetic field. This object is on a highly elliptical orbit that takes it to the outer reaches of the Oort Cloud at its apogee and brings it into the interior part of our solar system at its perigee. It makes its orbital

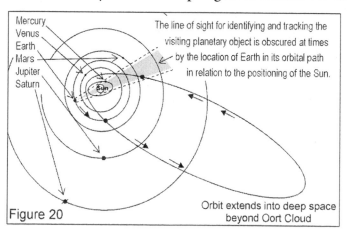

Mercury
Venus
Earth
Mars
Jupiter
Saturn
Sun

The line of sight for identifying and tracking the visiting planetary object is obscured at times by the location of Earth in its orbital path in relation to the positioning of the Sun.

Figure 20

Orbit extends into deep space beyond Oort Cloud

sweep around the Sun on the same orbital plane as the earth and follows the same counterclockwise direction. It becomes faintly visible as it passes inside of Saturn's orbit and nears that of Jupiter. Depending on the positioning of the earth in conjunction with the Sun, it may or may not be visible during the latter stages of its approach. (See Figure 20.) Diagrams are not accurate to scale or planetary positioning. They are for illustration purposes only.

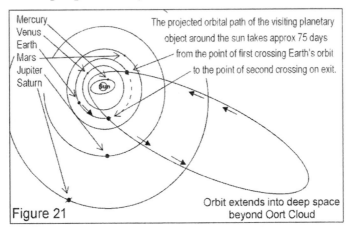

Mercury
Venus
Earth
Mars
Jupiter
Saturn

Sun

The projected orbital path of the visiting planetary object around the sun takes approx 75 days from the point of first crossing Earth's orbit to the point of second crossing on exit.

Orbit extends into deep space beyond Oort Cloud

Figure 21

From the time the object crosses Earth's orbital plane on its entrance, until it is about to cross Earth's orbital plane on its exit, is a period of approximately 75 days. (See Figure 21.) There are times during this 75-day period when the alignment between it, the earth and the Sun hide it from view. In some cases its orbit brings it close enough for it to be clearly seen even though it is on the daytime side of Earth's orbit.

As it exited Earth's orbital plane in Noah's day, it was on a path that brought it close to a collision point with the earth. It crossed the orbital path of the earth mere hours before the earth arrived at that same point in space. (See Figure 22.)

It had never come that close before and has not come that close since.

During its exit, it passed between the earth and the Sun. This resulted in an eclipse of total darkness that lasted for several

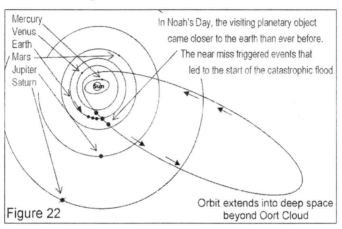

Mercury
Venus
Earth
Mars
Jupiter
Saturn

In Noah's Day, the visiting planetary object came closer to the earth than ever before. The near miss triggered events that led to the start of the catastrophic flood.

Orbit extends into deep space beyond Oort Cloud

Figure 22

hours. The object was visible in the sky as it approached the Sun and would have been visible after the eclipse. During this eclipse the Sun and most of the visible stars were completely blacked out. Earth had entered a period of extreme darkness, a blanket of black so thick that it could be felt.

The majority of the following events happened simultaneously. A few events unfolded as connected elements in a series of chain reactions that played out over the course of 48-60 hours. Although most of them were initialized as the object moved into position between the earth and the Sun, some were triggered as the object passed and began to pull away from the earth. The next few paragraphs will detail each element individually and attempt to blend them together into a logical progression.

Upon its approach to the inner portions of the solar system, the object in the sky first appeared as a faint glimmering addition to a familiar nighttime constellation. As the days passed, the brightness slowly intensified into a resonating glow that stood out from the familiar stars and planets. This was something new. This was something that the inhabitants of Earth had never before seen.

The Watchers that had spawned the Nephilim had been judged centuries earlier and confined to a place the Greeks would later call Tartarus (2nd Peter 2:4). Those who were not judged as rebellious emissaries had long since lost their influence with man. It is possible that many of the Watchers left, and those few who remained interacted with Noah only. Aside from Noah and his family, all flesh had corrupted its way upon the earth and, as a result, wanted no part of anything that involved a Creator God (Genesis 6:12). Thus, mankind was left to its own collective imagination as to the origin of this new object in the sky.

Over a period of about nine months, the object continued to grow in size and in intensity. A natural argument ensued: Was the object getting bigger and brighter? Or was it in fact getting closer to the earth? As its path brought it inside the orbit of Jupiter and eventually Mars, no doubt talk of its presence and purpose became a primary curiosity and quite possibly a cause for worry and concern.

As it closed the gap between Mars and Earth, it became easier to get a clear visual of the object against the night sky. By this time, a debris trail would have given off its own majestic glow, such as we see as modern-day comets approach the Sun. It may have even been possible to make out a number of smaller, yet distinguishable objects, that it held in tow. The ancient Sumerians would write in detail about such an object centuries later.

As it continued to close the gap, its position in the night sky gradually got lower and lower on the horizon. Earth's orbit was now taking it into a position where the Sun was between it and the new object in the sky. Eventually, it was completely blocked from view. It would seem that it had disappeared. How odd this must have been! Would those who had attentively paid attention to the object have understood the nature of the repositioning that was actually taking place in the heavens? At this point, would they have been recording its progress and positioning in the same manner we would today?

On the back side of the Sun, the object's orbit brought it closer and closer to the orbital path of the earth and the impact it had on the earth was building. Not that it hadn't been in effect throughout the approach, but this is where the principle of the Inverse Square Law would have begun to play a prominent role. As the distance between the two objects was cut in half, the resulting intensity of the interaction was magnified four times. This principle was playing out as the object moved inside the orbit of Jupiter and eventually Mars, but it may not have exhibited a noticeable effect on the earth at such a distance.

Once it was on the back side of the Sun, however, the changes were swift and dramatic. As the gap closed, the two bodies became locked into an interstellar tug of war. As it emerged from the glare of the Sun, the object suddenly became visible in the daytime sky. Now, it is significantly greater in size than when it had disappeared.

At this point it begins to feel as if the object is about to fall out of the sky and crash to the earth, but it is still several million miles away. Over the next month, the object grows gradually larger in the sky each day. It rises with the morning Sun and sets each evening. Only a few days ago it appeared to be about the same size as the Sun, now it looms larger and continues to grow.

The reaction between it and the earth is barely discerned by the inhabitants of the planet, but the two magnetic fields have now locked themselves into a synchronicity of sorts. As the days pass, the object continues to draw closer and the first electrical discharges between the two bodies begin to jettison across the gap in space.

The object now dwarfs the Sun in the sky, appearing 25 to 30 times larger. Massive streaks of lightning repeatedly rip across an otherwise clear blue sky. What in the world is going on? Surely, the inhabitants of the earth must have wondered. By now there would have been much speculation, probably even widespread concern and worry. What should we do? How should we prepare? What are we preparing for? would have all be relevant questions that became a fixture in prevailing thought. By this time Noah and his family have taken shelter in the ark.

The larger body is slightly influenced in its orbital path by the constant attraction of the smaller, but still formidable, planet Earth. The insurgent power of its transit through the solar system is plenty strong enough to keep it moving along the course that currently carries it away from the pivotal hub of the Sun and back out into the outer reaches of space.

The pull of the larger object on the planet Earth has an even greater influence. The tug is dynamic and unrelenting. Earth, though inherently resistant, is no match and bends to the will of the incessant draw. Slowly the north-south magnetic poles of the earth begin to align, pointing in the direction of the powerful electromagnetic attraction. Earth, which prior to this sat nearly upright on its polar axis at a one-half-degree tilt, begins to roll to its side.

In the same way that a wooden shed begins to slowly weaken as one side is pushed to the point of nails giving way, eventually, the earth reaches a tipping point and the rushing momentum of the collapse races to ruin. The one time jewel of God's creation is now on its side and in full tow. As a result, the Sun appears to take a strange trek across the mid-morning sky. Having initially risen in the east, it slowly redirects from the familiar pattern of passing overhead

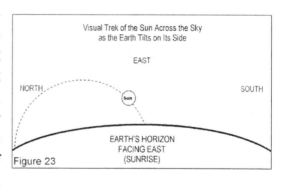

and proceeds on a curved journey across the horizon from east to north. (See Figure 23.) The prophecy of Amos 8, verse 9, *"I will cause the sun to go down at noon, and I will darken the earth in the clear day,"* had played out in Noah's day. For us, it's the words of Christ that reverberate, *"as it was... so shall it be."*

Earth is bathed in the glow of midday twilight. As the two objects continue to draw closer, the electromagnetic storm grows to unprecedented proportions. The atmosphere above the earth tingles, as bolts of electricity roar relentlessly across the surface of Earth's protective crystalline canopy of ice.

Imperceptible to those experiencing the steady progression of events on the surface, the magnetic field of the earth becomes elongated, stretching deeper into space toward the invading object of destruction. A few weeks after this encounter with Earth, the object will pass by Mars on its way back into the outer portions of the solar system. This same type of close encounter will strip Mars, a smaller planet with a less powerful magnetic field, of the vast majority of its magnetic field and much of its atmosphere, virtually killing the red planet and leaving a massive 2,500-mile-long crater behind as a calling card.

The much stronger magnetic field of the earth is holding up, but weakening against the increased strain. The crystalline canopy, composed of malleable ice, groans under the tension and starts to elongate as well, stretching more than 50% of it to the northern regions and leaving a smaller portion clinging to the magnetic anchor of the southern pole.

The sky overhead now looks to be greatly distorted. The smooth, pleasant appearance of a convex dome has been traded for a strange manifestation in the north of something that is more conical in shape. The strangely elongated heavens now appear to be rushing to the north and surges of lightning wrap themselves tighter and tighter around the ever-developing cone in the northern sky. The entire northern horizon is taking on the appearance of an inverted tornado funnel. The sky is engulfed by the massive atmospheric display. It's as if the earth is being swallowed.

The visual of the invading object becomes somewhat skewed. As the northern sky transforms into a vast tunnel that tapers off with distance, the object seems to gradually decrease in size. Slowly, the object vanishes into a pinpoint. Only the flashes of lightning remain. The prevailing energy of the invading object has rolled the earth completely onto its side as it passes between the earth and the Sun.

Twilight gives way to complete darkness as the Sun is blocked from view. Portions of the night sky emerge low on the distant southern horizon. The majority of the sky is an empty blackness. The only light comes from flashes of lightning swirling around the inverted cone to the north.

I cannot speculate that the inhabitants of the earth would have been aware of the earth tipping to one side. The earth currently races through space at speeds in excess of 67,000 miles per hour,[36] and we do not feel the effect of being in motion. The current rotation of the earth has a distinct wobble, yet we do not notice. The common rotation of the earth, which causes the Sun to rise in the east and set in the west, takes place at 1,040 miles per hour,[37] and we are equally insensitive to the motion.

A piercing ray of light flickers in the northwest and the first glimmer of the Sun's glow begins to emerge. The appearance of an early morning sunrise draws attention to the northwestern sky. It's not morning, however; it's late afternoon. A period of just over six hours has passed since the sky ran to the north and the Sun gave way to darkness. This is the first phase of the object moving beyond the direct alignment between the earth and the Sun.

As it crosses the boundary of Earth's orbit, darkness is traded for twilight and the object once again appears to slowly grow in size. The hours that have passed means the earth is in its late afternoon or early evening time frame. As a result, everything is now unfolding in the northwestern sky.

The same chain of events begin to work in reverse. The object is now separating itself from our reeling planet. Its orbital journey leads back into the outer reaches of the solar system and it dutifully stays the course. In the process of passing, Earth has been dragged into a slightly deeper position of orbit before finally breaking free of the traction which ferried it through space for nearly half a day. We will confirm this alteration of orbit later, using evidence provided in the ancient writings of Enoch.

The inverted cone-shaped appearance of the northern sky begins to broaden as Earth rebounds from the tremendous strain of the prolonged tug-o'-war. Recoiling from being dragged on its side, the earth begins to realign into an upright axial tilt. However, its orbital path takes it directly into the swath of an extended trail of space debris that has been following the invading body throughout its transit. The crystalline ice canopy, still stretched and strained from the encounter, is under full assault.

Meteor after meteor pummels the canopy, many of them larger in size than a 3,500-square-foot, two-story house. The onslaught is violent and continual. The canopy holds up under the barrage for a period of time, but eventually begins to crack. From the surface of the earth, this is the first time any evidence of the long-rumored crystalline canopy has been observed. The pounding of the meteors sends shockwave after shockwave through the atmosphere. The sound of the cracking ice is louder than the most ear-rattling crash of thunder.

Finally, it gives way. Fracture lines race across the surface in the same way a pane of tempered glass shatters into micro-bits before crumbling. Splitting asunder, it rolls up like a scroll (Revelation 6:14). A large portion of the ice follows the flow of the magnetic field to a still-recovering northern pole. A smaller portion tracks the flow to the south. The heat released from the collapsing ice soars to astronomical proportions. We know this principle today as the Latent Heat of Condensation.[38] Much of the collapsing ice begins to melt as it races to the poles, but such a vast amount travelling the same pathway in unison preserves a cold channel where large amounts of it begins to plummet to Earth's surface. As it crashes to the poles, it quickly accumulates, first as chunks of ice and later as heavy snow.

This collapse buries both poles under ice and snow in a matter of hours, trapping vegetation, animals and possibly even some human life under a rapidly accumulating blanket. The incredible weight of the crumbling canopy that accumulates at each of the polar regions creates an imbalance in Earth's distribution of mass. The inertia of Earth's rotational spin is disrupted by the catastrophic energy of the falling canopy, causing the planet to wobble violently. The resulting violent tremors can be felt throughout the world, as the very foundation of the planet begins to split.

Fissures race through the crust of the earth out of control. Cracks race blindly through the path of least resistance until encountering another crack. The massive underground chambers of water, which previously provided passage for the flow of subterranean water throughout the globe, begin to seep without remedy. The weight of the crust can no longer be supported by the fractured foundations.

Portions of Earth's surface begin to disintegrate, as massive sinkholes riddle the planet. The chain reaction of caving crust forces torrents of water to the surface. The release of water in turn opens up caverns in the crust, which crumble under the increasing weight of the ever-changing surface. The fountains of the deep are irreparably broken up. Subterranean water bleeds to the surface of the planet from countless wounds.

Meanwhile, the mixture of freezing cold air at the newly forming poles and the offsetting heat generated in the process triggers a widespread outbreak of violent storms. Super-heated air compressing against fronts that are blowing across the frozen polar regions generate tornados and hurricanes supremely more intense than anything experienced in our modern world. Torrential rainfall continues non-stop across the planet.

The process repeats as the heat from the storms continues to clash with the blasts of arctic air pouring forth from the poles. This pattern continues in an uninterrupted cycle as the thermostatic imbalance gradually begins to find equilibrium. The process takes 40 days.

The water levels steadily rise as the growing surface pressure continues to force reserves from the fountains of the deep. This too must find balance, but this process will continue unabated for months.

The inhabitants of Earth, both humans and animals, that have not fallen prey to the violent storms, earthquakes or the perils of gargantuan sinkholes, frantically seek higher ground. Water levels continue to rise, but pace has slowed. Perhaps the words of Enoch's dream vision haunt their memory...

Enoch 83:3-5

(3) *"I had just lain down in my grandfather Mahalalel's house, when I saw the heavens collapse and fall to the earth.*

(4) *"This caused the earth to be swallowed up in a great abyss. Mountains were suspended upon mountains, hills sank down on hills, and high trees were ripped up from the ground and hurled into the abyss.*

(5) *"I suddenly cried out from my sleep, 'The earth is destroyed!'"*

When the Dust Settles, It's Underwater

Genesis 7:18

*"And the waters prevailed,
and were increased greatly upon the earth;
and the ark went upon the face of the waters."*

The waters prevailed. What an interesting declaration. It's a word that is extremely limited in its suitable usage. Prevailed must wait in the wings until the last out is made, or the final seconds have ticked off the clock. It's fated to sit idly by until the resounding hand slap of the mat signals that the opponent has been pinned. Only then, only after finality has positioned itself properly, can the descriptive term be used — *prevailed!*

For 1,000 years a battle had raged. It started with a small band of Watchers committing themselves to a subversive mission that was never their calling. At some point during the days of Jared, they propped up their courage with the false hope that together they could prevail, and pledged their allegiance one to another by sacred oath. Enoch told us bluntly that they had hoped to establish an eternal presence in the earth where they would rule as gods and mankind would become their dutiful slaves (Enoch 10).

For 1,000 years, violence had reigned. For a millennium, all of creation had been under assault. For generations, man had chosen deceit and treachery in an effort to rise. Having an open door to serve and worship the creator, man had worshipped the creation instead and had been committed to serving themselves. This was a world where the strong survived and the weak were plowed under. *This world* was now underwater, because the waters prevailed.

I find it interesting that the word translated as "prevailed" and used to declare finality is basically the same word used to describe the "mighty men which were of old," in Genesis 6:4. There the word is *"gibbowr"* (ghib·bōre').[1] Here we find the root word, *"gabar"* (gä·var').[2] The difference is that the first is a descriptive term, an adjective, the second is an active verb. The first speaks to appearance and assessment: He has the power to prevail; therefore, he appears to be mighty. The second speaks of result: The last out has been made; the final seconds have ticked off the clock; the opponent has been pinned. It signals irrevocability. A conclusion has been reached.

Counting the Days

There is a misconception when it comes to the number of days it actually took to flood the earth. In most cases a time period of 40 days and 40 nights is stamped across the event, but a careful read of the text would indicate that the period of 40 days applies to something else altogether. The entire earth was not flooded after 40 days, but there is an important reason for the specific mention.

Genesis 7:17

> *"And the flood was forty days upon the earth;*
> *and the waters increased, and bare up the ark,*
> *and it was lift up above the earth."*

This verse is actually the third reference to a 40-day period found in Genesis, chapter 7. The initial mention is in verse 4. There, Noah is told that there will be a 40-day period of rain and that it will begin after he and his family have been in the ark for seven days. The second reference is in verses 11 and

12. These verses tell us the specific day that the rain began and that it continued uninterrupted for exactly 40 days and 40 nights.

Verse 17 clarifies for us that it took the entire 40-day period of rain before the ark was lifted from the earth and set afloat by the increasing water level. In our opening chapter, we estimated the height of the ark at 51 feet. If the rising water line increased steadily by one foot each day, then the dry ground upon which the ark was built would have become home to a sea 40 feet in depth over the 40-day period. Surely, 40 feet of water would have been sufficient to buoy the ark.

Research provides a wide range of depths required to float the average cargo ship. The measurable statistic is known as the ship's draft, and the actual draft of any particular ship is affected by the total weight of the ship's cargo. The average draft ranges between 27 feet, on the low end, and 52½ feet, at the top of the scale. The majority of vessels fall somewhere between 39⅓ and 46 feet.[3] When it comes to cruise ships, the numbers trend toward the lower end of the scale.

Having a few numbers to consider, it would be reasonable to anticipate that a little less than 40 feet of water would have been needed to achieve flotation. It also seems realistic to envision the ark sitting firmly in place after several days of rain, regardless of the intensity. Certainly more than six to eight feet of standing water would have been needed to move the ark. The 40-day milestone stands out because at that stage the ark began to float and the journey to a new world was underway.

We referenced 40 days in the previous chapter as the possible period of time that it took for the newly established arctic air and the heat generated by the collapsing ice canopy to reach a point of equilibrium. The effects of sweltering hot air colliding with the cycling bands of frigid fronts being generated by the ice cap formations at both poles would have ignited ferocious storm systems and produced torrents of continual rain. The process would have repeated itself over and over, before eventually leveling off and subsiding.

Still, a specified 40-day period of time stands out as an odd numerical value. Although 40 is a round number, it's not equivalent to a lunar cycle or the count of a calendar month. It's not divisible by weeks, nor is it a nice, even percentage of a calendar year. There are numerous other references in scripture to events that transpired over a period of 40 days, and we would be remiss not to at least provide a quick listing of those events and ponder the question: Why 40 days?

- Moses spent 40 days and 40 nights on Mount Sinai (Exodus 24:18).

- Spies searched out the "Promised Land" for 40 days (Numbers 13:25).

- The Israelites spent 40 years in the wilderness, literally one year for each of the 40 days spent sizing up the "Promised Land," as designated (Numbers 14:34).

- Goliath taunted the army of Israel for 40 days before David showed up and slew him (1st Samuel 17:16).

- Jonah's message to Nineveh was, *"Yet 40 days, and Nineveh shall be overthrown."* (Jonah 3:4).

- Jesus was tempted by Satan in the wilderness for a period of 40 days (Matthew 4:2, Mark 1:13, Luke 4:2).

- Jesus spent 40 days on Earth after his resurrection (Acts 1:3).

So stands the list of the more prominent mentions, and while there are a few intriguing elements in the list, there's one, yet to be mentioned, 40-day event that may prove to be the most interesting of all. Prior to Moses' Mount Sinai conference, prior to David's plunking of Goliath between the eyes with a river rock via his deadly sling, prior to Jonah's swim with the fishes and subsequent announcement to the Assyrian city of Nineveh, there was a man named Joseph.

The last few chapters of the Old Testament book of Genesis chronicle his life with intriguing detail. Joseph was one of 12 sons fathered by a man named Jacob. Favored by his father, but resented by his brothers, Joseph's story takes a strange turn when he is still quite young.

While a child, Joseph has a very elaborate dream. Excited by the vivid nature of the dream, he shares the dream with his family. One could envision any young child doing this. The symbolism of the dream blatantly infers that Joseph will one day become a ruler and that his family, including his father and mother, will bow in obedience to him.

The dream revelation annoys the older brothers beyond their breaking point and they conspire to rid the family of "this dreamer." Their plans result in Joseph being cast into a pit that the brothers had dug far out in the fields. After discussion, the brothers agree to spare Joseph's life, opting to sell him to passing merchants as a slave. In the end, Joseph finally lands in Egypt. The complete story is recorded in the 37th chapter of Genesis.

The next 13 chapters of Genesis detail Joseph's life in Egypt, including his rise in power to second in command, answering only to the Pharaoh himself (Gen. 41:41-43). It's on the heels of Joseph's rise to power that a widespread famine forces his brothers to journey to Egypt in search of food. The Egyptian authority who oversees all food distribution is Joseph, but his brothers identify him only as Egyptian hierarchy. Joseph recognizes them, however, and plots to have them held over until they come to realize who he is. Once the connection is made, Joseph requests that the entire family, including his father, move to Egypt (Gen. 45:9-10).

Joseph's proposal is met with the full support of the Pharaoh, and the entire household of Jacob relocates to Egypt. Seventeen years later, Joseph's father, Jacob, dies (Gen. 47:28). This is where things get interesting. Just before his passing, Jacob calls together all of his sons and gives them the complete rundown on the family history. He also specifies a place where his grandfather, Abraham, and his father, Isaac, are buried with their wives. He makes the brothers swear an oath to bury him in the same sacred place.

Genesis 50:1-3

> *(1) "And Joseph fell upon his father's face,*
> *and wept upon him, and kissed him.*
>
> *(2) "And Joseph commanded his servants*
> *the physicians to embalm his father:*
> *and the physicians embalmed Israel* [Jacob].[4]

> *(3) "And forty days were fulfilled for him; for so are fulfilled the days of those which are embalmed: and the Egyptians mourned for him threescore and ten days."*

The Egyptian embalming process is more widely known as mummification. This is the first mention of it in the Old Testament text, and I find it quite curious that it is specified as a practice that plays out over a period of 40 days. One might initially think that it just took about 40 days or so for the corpse to cure, but the wording of verse 3 indicates otherwise.

There is a Hebrew word that's commonly used to indicate that something has come and gone, including the passing of an indiscriminate amount of time. It is the word *"'abar"* (ä·var') and it's used 559 times in the Old Testament text.[5] It simply means to go beyond, to pass by, or to migrate from one point to the next. That word could be used in this passage, but it is not.

The word used in verse 3 is the Hebrew word, *"male'"* (mä·lä') and it signifies that a specific requirement has been met. It is used 249 times in the Old Testament text and often translated as fill, full or fulfill.[6] It carries with it the idea that something has been accomplished or satisfied. There is a marker or a goal that is not reached until the container is completely full, or the explicit conditions have been met.

The days were "fulfilled," because the guidelines of the ritual had been strictly followed. After the 40 days have been fulfilled, the actual journey of the mummified person to the new world begins. During the 40 days, the deceased is in a state of transitional lingering; dead to the old world, but not yet enroute to the new. This is a purposeful observation of a specified period of time, and quite possibly it mirrors the 40 days that mark the passage of time between the start of Noah's cataclysm and the point at which the ark was *"lift up above the earth,"* (Gen. 7:17).

In both cases there is a purposeful preparation for a passage that's designed to permanently separate from life in the present world and establish life in a new one. In each case, the transition involves passing over a body of legendary water. For the ark, it was the waters of the flood. For the Egyptians, it became a crossing of the Nile Delta, to reach the Field of Reeds.[7]

I've chosen the progressive term, "became," because much of the popularized information that we have available to us regarding this Egyptian ritual is found in a composited text known today as *The Egyptian Book of the Dead*. The text dates to the latter period of ancient Egypt, 1550 BC to 50 BC, and the name more literally translates as *Book of Coming Forth by Day*.[8]

If we are to determine how the text relates to the 40-day embalming process that's described for Jacob, we have to identify the time period in which Joseph ruled in Egypt and, more importantly, the time period in which Jacob died. Do either of these Old Testament patriarchs have a verifiable presence in Egyptian history?

Perhaps Dr. Ken Johnson can help answer the question. In his book, *Ancient Post-Flood History*, he makes a striking comparison between the Hebrew recorded history of Joseph and the Egyptian recorded history of a viceroy who served under Pharaoh Djoser, known to the Egyptians as Imhotep.[9] The stated time periods for Joseph and Imhotep coincide. Both are said to have assisted as second in command during a seven-year period of great famine. And both Joseph and Imhotep are said to have lived exactly 110 years.

Johnson also records an event that happened late in the life of Imhotep. New court officials plotted to test Imhotep's wisdom in his old age by challenging him to create an oasis in the desert. According to Johnson, "He engineered a feeder canal from the Nile to his man-made lake. Today, in the region of El-Fayoum, southwest of Cairo, there still remains a man-made fresh water lake called Birqet Qarun. It is fed by a canal stretching from the Nile to the Basin. The canal is known as Bahr Yousef, or the Sea of Joseph!"[10]

The agreed-upon time period for the life of Imhotep is a full 1,000 years earlier than the first appearance of a compiled *Book of the Dead* in Egypt.[11] Although the burial ritual was once reserved for royalty, it took on a broader scope in later Egyptian dynasties, and the handbook for navigating life after death became a must-have resource.

Widespread demand led to a progressive marketing of the manual, including the availability of personalized volumes.[12] This growing popularity resulted in a more and more elaborate text. Therefore, we cannot make a connection with every reference contained within the Egyptian death manual for adventures in the afterlife.

It would be reasonable to deduce that during the time of Joseph the ritual would have been much more traditional and a lot less elaborate. Still, there are obvious connections, including the fact that the Egyptians sealed the person into an enclosure (vessel) that was explicitly created for the journey.

The Egyptian burial coffin is known to us as a sarcophagus.

The Egyptians called it *"neb-ankh,"* which is translated as "the lord of life," or "the possessor of life."[13] How interesting that the proper name for the item used to house a dead body was thought of as being a carrier of life, rather than a container for the dead. Could this stem from the Egyptian's perception of the personal journey that was to be undertaken by the person so encased?

The burial boxes were often carved or painted with representations from the lifetime of the person who was enclosed. Personal artifacts and possessions were also included in the entombment, so that they might assist the person in their journey or be used by the person when they reached the end of their journey and embraced life in another realm.[14] With some of the Pharaohs these preparations were made years in advance and were subject to the approval of the Pharaoh.

Another parallel can be drawn to the ark. It was expressly built for Noah's journey from the old world to the new. Some supplies were taken for the journey itself; other things were preserved for use once Noah and his family concluded their passage and embarked on life in the new world.

Other metaphorical connections might include the belief that the heart was to be weighed at the onset of the journey and that the mouth needed to be opened so that the *"Ba"* could be released.

The weighing of the heart determined whether the person was worthy to proceed. The evaluation of purity was determined by placing the person's heart, a symbol of the soul, on one side of a set of balancing scales. A feather from the headdress of the representative deity of the Egyptian concept of truth and morality, Ma'at, was placed on the other. If the scales balanced, the person was judged worthy and the journey to life in the new world continued.[15]

In Genesis 6, we initially read that the entire world was corrupt and that judgment was pronounced upon all flesh. However, in the 8th verse of the chapter we're told that Noah *"found grace in the eyes of the LORD."* Verse 9 tells us why: because he *"was a just man and perfect in his generations."*

The Egyptians also believed that each person had a spirit and that a doorway or window needed to be left open so that, though entombed, the spirit could leave and return to the physical body. They referred to it as the *"Ba,"* and burial practices called for the person's mouth to be left open as the transitional pathway. The *"Ba"* was often portrayed in Egyptian artwork as a human-headed bird that was free to roam the skies by day and return each night.[16] Could this practice be equated with Noah's daily release of a dove and the dove's nightly return?

A number of other comparisons could easily be made. In fact, there is so much here, that one could easily bog down in the details. Perhaps, to a small degree, we already have.

One might also claim that preposterous presumptions are being made, and such an accusation might stand firm, were it not for the mitigating connection of Joseph. His story is a foundation stone in the history of the Hebrews, and his lineage is carefully traced in Genesis 11:10-26 from Abraham (his great grandfather) back to Noah's son, Shem.

The post-flood details given in the Book of Jasher about Noah and the descendants of his three sons are riveting. We don't have the time, nor the space, to review the complete text in this volume, but it serves us well to note that a direct line from Noah to Abraham (known from birth as Abram) is drawn in chapters 9, 10 and 11. Abraham, the father of Isaac, the father of Jacob, the father of Joseph, learned about the flood and the world that it destroyed from the very one who survived it — *Noah!*

Abraham is born nearly 300 years after the flood.[17] By that time, the family tree of Noah's sons has expanded by nine generations. Noah is nearing the end of his life, and much of the world's population has already forsaken the Creator God and chosen to worship handcrafted idols. In fact, Abraham's father is a beloved high priest of worship in the court of the king.

The three referenced chapters from the Book of Jasher reveal a series of events that result in Abraham being separated from his father's house as an infant. After being cared for in secret by his mother for 10 years, he is sent to live with Noah. For the next 39 years, Noah and his son Shem teach Abraham about the pre-flood world, the Creator God, and how civilization was established after the flood.

Having been personally taught by Noah and Shem about the Creator God, a 49-year-old Abraham confronts not only his father, but also the reigning king, regarding their idol worship. Both refuse to heed his counsel. Three years later, a 52-year-old Abraham finally convinces his father to abandon the king and leave the ancient city of Ur.

Forsaking the city of his birth, with only his closest family members and a few servants by his side, Abraham seeks to establish refuge in a new land. His express desire is to separate his family from the prevailing idolatry and raise his descendants in the knowledge and wisdom of the Creator. A major portion of Abraham's mission is to teach and preserve all the things that he had learned directly from Noah.

Abraham went on to become a great leader, but reached the latter years of his life without fathering a rightful heir to the family birthright. Late in life, Abraham finally fathered a son through his wife, Sarah, who was also well into her golden years. They named the child Isaac.

Isaac fathered a famous set of twins, Jacob and Esau. Shortly before passing away, Isaac bequeathed the family birthright and inheritance upon Jacob. Being the firstborn twin Esau thought of himself as the rightful heir and was bitterly angry that he was passed over. The lingering resentment led to constant conflict between the two brothers and numerous battles being fought between their descendants, some of which continue to this day.

Through two wives and two handmaidens, Jacob fathered a total of 12 sons (Gen. 35:22-26). The descendants of the 12 sons eventually gave rise to the 12 tribes of the Hebrew nation. Although he grew from adolescence to manhood in Egypt, Joseph was initially parented as one of the 12 sons and, therefore, he cannot be casually dismissed.

When we point to Joseph as the son of Jacob, who was the son of Isaac, who was the son of Abraham, we're making a very strong connection between the life experiences of Noah and the family history that Joseph learned as a child and brought with him to Egypt.

Memories of Noah's personal experiences, his insight regarding first-hand interaction with the Creator and the Watchers, and quite possibly many pre-flood artifacts would have naturally been passed down and preserved through Abraham's lineage. As such, it's not only possible, but also probable, that some pre-flood relics may have been transferred with the birthright and included among the keepsakes of Jacob.

It's so easy to see the connections and symbolism that only a minimal amount of open-mindedness is needed. The 40 days mark a transcendent point of separation; so transcendent that 600 years later[18] it is memorialized through an elaborate burial ritual when Joseph's father, Jacob, dies in Egypt.

After 40 days of rain, the ark was lifted up from the earth and Noah's journey began; a journey that would forever change the planet itself and the life that calls it home.

We've Only Just Begun

The ark is afloat and the journey is underway, but we are far, far away from a conclusion. There are still a number of imposing question marks to explore:

- How long were they on the ark?

- How did they feed themselves?

- What about fresh drinking water?

- How did they take care of the animals?

- What about sea life? Was it in peril?

There are so many things left to explore. If the proposed

cataclysm actually took place, then the world that Noah and his family found on the other side of the flood would have been remarkably different. Reestablishing civilization and culture would have been a daunting task. How did an eight-person campsite develop into ancient world empires?

Spending some time to research the lives of Shem, Ham, Japheth and their descendants is of critical value to the story. What footprints, if any, did they leave in the sands of time? Are these simply the tales of lore and legend, or do they ring true with verified history?

The Linguistic Society of America reports that at least a portion of *The Bible* has been translated into 2,508 different languages. The group goes on to state that there are currently 6,909 definitively different languages recognized in today's society.[19] Depending on the source, it's generally agreed that there are four distinct racial families from which the world's diverse ethnicities originate (African, American Indian, Asian, and Caucasian) and perhaps as many as five (Polynesian).[20] If all modern civilizations supposedly sprang from the family tree of one of Noah's three sons, how did the different races and languages emerge?

What old-world artifacts did Noah bring into the new world? Surely, anyone who was given time to prepare for a one-way trip would take things of practical use, as well as things of sentimental value. Could Noah be thought of any differently? Are there things that we have in our modern-day world that can be directly traced back to Noah's epic journey?

Genesis 6:4 says *"There were giants in the earth in those days and also after that."* Did the giants reemerge after the flood? Did the deceitful Watchers somehow escape their judgment and revisit their schemes? Did other shrewdly manipulative beings establish a presence in the post-flood world and actively seek to influence mankind? If remarkable beings, referred to as giants, are a part of the post-flood testimony, then it's imperative for any worthy research to trace their origin.

What about the legendary tale of the Tower of Babel? Are there any historical references to its construction or demise outside of the Old Testament book of Genesis? Is this yet another case where a supreme deity felt threatened by the progress of mankind and threw a temper tantrum to put man in his place? Perhaps the entire story is just an ancient allegory that has lost its interpretive meaning over time.

In the chain of events that were proposed as the catalyst for the legendary flood, we mentioned a repositioning of the earth into a different orbit. We also hinted at an alteration of the orbit of the moon. The change in the axial tilt of the earth was also left as a dangling thread in the sweater, just waiting to be pulled. That's just not right. If we are to find a satisfactory conclusion, these loose ends must be tied up. Could information in the ancient writings of Enoch help unravel this mystery?

It's been a long journey. It's been an amazing journey. It's been a challenge to my personal beliefs, understanding and perspective. But we're not anywhere close to a reaching an acceptable resolution of issues. Each question has led to another question. Each researched pathway has revealed additional, less-obvious trails that scream for exploration.

The Beginning may have come to an end, but Noah's journey has just begun. And, in a very real sense, so has ours. Another desk drawer is waiting to be filled with notes and research.

Another shelf calls for additional research volumes and text.

As we look back and seek to uncover the past, perhaps we can look forward and better understand the things that are yet future. Having a penchant for thought-provoking quotes, I close with the words of Christ,

"As it was... so shall it be."

Face to Face with the Question of God

"Doubt is not a pleasant condition,
but certainty is absurd."
- Voltaire

In truth, God either does or he does not exist. He does not exist simply because someone believes that he does. Nor does he cease to exist because someone believes that he does not. If he does exist, it might serve me well to ask who he is and what he wants of me. If I choose to turn a blind eye, a deaf ear, and a cold shoulder in his direction and declare of my own conscious will that he does not exist, can he be blamed in any way for honoring my decision and granting me an understanding and dedication to a life that is free from his existence?

I do not believe that most people are angry with God, so much as they are offended by those who claim to be his ambassadors. Most are angered by the self-assumed mission of the emissaries to persistently invade and conquer areas that have clearly been marked with signs stating that God, or more specifically his self-appointed representatives, are not welcome to trespass.

If there exists a person who is truly beyond redemption, it can only be that person who has determined within their own private convictions that they don't want to be redeemed. That conviction is between the individual and God, and it would be honorable for people of all faiths to respect their choice. Most assuredly God, if he does indeed exist, has already complied with their wishes.

There was a time when Noah and Methuselah stood before the people and proclaimed the message that the Creator tasked them to convey. Once the message was rejected, they were directed to withdraw and prepare for the day in which God would reveal himself.

Centuries later, Christ specifically told his own disciples to dust off their sandals and be on their way if they were not openly received. He called them to be the salt of the Earth, a seasoning of sorts. While he did not set restrictions on the scope of their outreach, I don't see where he commissioned them to argue a single unreceptive individual into submission.

Throughout history, mankind has consistently wrestled with feeble attempts to define God or, even more disgracefully, to speak self-servingly on his behalf. It's all a matter of record that cannot be denied, nor excused. We get in our own way more often than not and ultimately trumpet our own message of conformity as if it came from the Almighty.

It seems abundantly clear that, if God exists, then by his very nature he is a big boy who is not in any way overmatched. It would also seem that his overall plan, if indeed he does have one, is not subject to reactionary changes based on the collective state of society. He is who he is, without regard to mankind's approval or assessment. Ultimately, he will do what he will do without the need for humanity's mutual consent to do so, or a collaborative opinion as to how it should be done.

Either God exists, or he does not exist at all. If he does exist, it might serve me well to ask who he is and what he wants of me. If I sincerely seek to know him in truth, the onus is now on him, and the challenge would seem to be no challenge at all, if indeed he is God.

Appendix 1

The Unedited Lineage of Seth from Chapter 2

This was the original portion of text found in chapter 2 prior to editing:

It's evident that Cain is not the only branch in the family tree. But did Adam and Eve give birth to anyone else who left a documented legacy?

Genesis 4:25

> "And Adam knew his wife again; and she bare a son, and called his name Seth: For God, said she, hath appointed me another seed instead of Abel, whom Cain slew."

The Book of Jubilees notes that Adam and Eve mourned the loss of Abel for nearly 30 years (Jubilees 4:7). It identifies this time period as years 99 through 127 (the third Jubilee, weeks 1 through 4). Eventually the mourning comes to an end and life returns to some form of normal. Then, in the year 130, Seth is born (Jubilees 4:7) and Eve rejoices exceedingly.

A daughter is born to Adam and Eve a few years later. She is named Azûrâ (Jubilees 4:8). At some point during the fifth week of the fifth Jubilee (years 225 through 231), Seth takes Azûrâ to be his wife (Jubilees 4:11). In the fourth year of the sixth week (year 235) Seth and Azûrâ give birth to a son and name him Enos (Jubilees 4:11). Seth is 105 years of age when Enos is born. This same timeline is documented in Genesis 5:6.

Thus begins the narration of Genesis 5, which details more than 1,000 years of family lineage traceable through Seth all the way back to Adam. Being Seth's family records, it's likely that most of it was personally witnessed and recorded by Seth himself. The inclusions of the time of death for both Adam and Seth make it clear that another prominent family member takes on the responsibility of preserving the record. It's also noteworthy that in this lineage the specific birth year is listed, as opposed to a loosely defined "week" of years.

As the lineage unfolds, we see the birth of several dynamic individuals:

- Enos – In whose time people began to seek knowledge from God (Jub. 4:12).

- Cainan – Previously referenced as the highest ranking monarch and father of Adah and Zillah (Jasher 2:10-16).

- Enoch – Noted as a person who *"walked with God"* (Gen. 5:21-24), wrote about many mystical revelations and apparently never died.

- Methuselah – Famous as the one who lived longer than any other person in world history (969 years, according to Gen. 5:25-27).

- And eventually, Noah – the builder of the ark.

The lineage is also spelled out in great detail by the Book of Jubilees. We'll use both the Book of Jubilees and the Biblical text as we work our way through the documented dawn of human history. Genesis provides an accurate time stamp of both the births and the deaths of each person listed. The Book of Jubilees adds insight as to each person's wife and even gives her heritage. All listed dates are A.M. (Anno Mundi) or the "Year of the World" (from the creation of Adam).

Sometime between years 309 and 315 (the third week of the seventh Jubilee), we find that Enos, the son of Seth, takes a woman named Noam to be his wife (Jubilees 4:13). Noam is identified as the sister of Enos, presumably his blood sister as opposed to half-sister.

Genesis 4:26 states that during the time period into which Enos was born, men began to call on the name of the Lord. No specific year is given as to when this began to occur, but it is noteworthy and the Book of Jasher adds that Seth names his son Enos for this very reason (Jasher 2:2). The word translated "call" in the Genesis passage is used in a variety of ways, including the concept of crying aloud for help.

Although God once walked in the Garden with Adam during the cool of the day (Gen. 3:8), now there are a multitude of people living on the earth and apparently personal communication with God had become a thing of the past.

In the third year of the fifth week of the seventh Jubilee (year 325), Enos and Noam have a son named Kenan (Jub. 4:13). He is called Cainan in the Biblical text. Enos is 90 years of age when Kenan/Cainan is born. This same timeline is documented in Genesis 5:9.

You may remember the name Cainan from the family of Cain. In fact, you may see several names over the next few paragraphs that match names recorded in Cain's lineage.

Don't let it become confusing. The names mentioned in Seth's genealogy are completely different people from those mentioned in the genealogy of Cain.

At the close of the eighth Jubilee, presumably at some point during the seventh week (years 386 through 392), Kenan/Cainan takes his sister, Mûalêlêth, to be his wife (Jub. 4:14). As we saw in the case of Seth and of Enos, Mûalêlêth is also Kenan/Cainan's blood sister.

In the third year of the first week of the ninth Jubilee (year 395), Kenan/Cainan and Mûalêlêth have a son named Mahalaleel (Jub. 4:14). This same time frame is documented in Genesis 5:12. Kenan/Cainan is 70 years of age when Mahalaleel is born.

> SIDE NOTE: This is the same Cainan who later fathers Adah and Zillah, the two wives of Lamech in the previously reviewed lineage of Cain. He is also noted in the Book of Jasher as the ruling monarch (Ch. 2:11-14). Thus, the rest of the names that are listed in this lineage are a part of a royal line of descendants.

During the second week of the tenth Jubilee (years 449 through 455), Mahalaleel takes Dinah as his wife. She is identified as the daughter of Barakiel, who is the brother of Kenan/Cainan (Jub. 4:15). It's noteworthy that from this generation forward the tradition of taking a sister as a wife is replaced with the practice of taking the daughter of your father's brother – your first cousin.

In the sixth year of the third week of the tenth Jubilee (year 461) Mahalaleel and Dinah give birth to a son and name him

Jared (Jub. 4:15). Mahalaleel is 65 years of age when Jared is born (Gen. 5:15). It would seem that the Book of Jubilees lists the age of Mahalaleel at 66, but keep in mind that it only lists years, not months. There's really not a discrepancy here between the Book of Jubilees and the Genesis text. The synchronization of dates does tend to fall apart after this, however.

Jared takes a woman named Baraka as his wife at some point during Jubilee (years 519 through 525). Baraka is the daughter of Rasujal, who is the brother of Jared's father, Mahalaleel, making her Jared's first cousin (Jub. 4:16).

Jared is 162 years of age when the couple gives birth to a son whom they name Enoch (Gen. 5:18). This is year number 623. Enoch is a mysterious central figure of early world history and his writings, once thought by some to be forever lost, have become particularly relevant within the last 75 years.

> SIDE NOTE: Enoch is recognized in the Book of Jasher as the ruling monarch who reigns over a number of kings, princes and judges at their request. This information can be found in Jasher 3:9 and following.

Beginning with the birth of Enoch, the timeline in the Book of Jubilees begins to break down. Keep in mind that Jubilees and the Old Testament text have matched up precisely year for year to this point. As discrepancies in the timeline arise, we'll rely on the Biblical text because it is more highly esteemed for its accuracy.

Enoch takes a woman named Edna as his wife. She is the daughter of Enoch's uncle, a man named Danel, making her

Enoch's first cousin (Jubilees 4:20). Genesis 5:21 tells us that Enoch is 65 years old when he and Edna give birth to a son, Methuselah. This is year 688.

Methuselah enjoys a longer recorded life span than any other person who ever lived. He dies at 969 years of age. The great flood begins in the same year that Methuselah died. That would be year 1657 for those who are itching to jump ahead. Writers know who you are!

The name given for Methuselah's wife is also Edna. She is identified as the daughter of Azrial, who is listed as the brother of Enoch (Jubilees 4:27). I'd mention that she's Methuselah's first cousin, but you've probably caught on to that by now and it's starting to sound repetitive.

Genesis 5:25 states that Methuselah was 187 years of age when he and Edna gave birth to a son whom they named Lamech. We are now at year 875. Adam, who lived to be 930 years of age, still has 55 years of life ahead of him. It seems doubtful that he personally knew all of his grandchildren and their children, etc. But logistically, it's possible.

Lamech takes a woman named Betenos as his wife. She is identified in the Book of Jubilees as the daughter of Methusaleh's brother Barakiil (Jub. 4:28). When he is age 182, Betenos gives birth to a son whom they name Noah (Genesis 5:28-29). This is year 1057 and Adam has been dead for 127 years.

Late in his life, Noah, the son of Lamech and Betenos, becomes the builder of the ark. The flood begins 600 years, one month and 17 days after Noah is born.

SIDE NOTE: Genesis 7:11 plainly states that the flood begins in the 600th year of Noah's life, in the second month and on the 17th day. This is Year of the World 1657. Jasher 4:13 indicates that Noah was born on the first day of the new year. The Book of Jubilees gives a precise calendar date for the fall of man in the Garden of Eden – the 17th day of the second month of Year of the World 8 (Jubilees 3:17). Could it be possible that the flood began exactly 1,650 years from the fall of man to the day?

Appendix 2

A Closer Look at
The 70 Generations Prophecy

Enoch 10:11-13

> *(11)* *"And the Lord said unto Michael:*
> *'Go, bind Semjaza and his associates who have united them-*
> *selves with women so as to have defiled themselves with them in*
> *all their uncleanness.*

> *(12)* *"'And when their sons have slain one another,*
> *and they have seen the destruction of their beloved ones,*
> *bind them fast for seventy generations in the valleys of the earth,*
> *till the day of their judgment and of their consummation,*
> *till the judgment that is forever and ever is consummated.*

> *(13)* *"'In those days they shall be led off to the abyss of fire:*
> *and to the torment and the prison in which*
> *they shall be confined forever.'"*

This is an interesting reference to a period of confinement that is specified as a personal punishment for the Watchers who abandoned their original commission. We cover their actions in great detail in chapter 3: There's New Kids on the Block.

The term used to outline their period of confinement is a stipulation of generations, as opposed to a number of years. Some have attempted to convert this number to a period of years by citing a reference in the Psalms that describes the lifespan of man as being seventy or eighty years in length.

Psalm 90:10

> *"The days of our years are threescore years and ten;*
> *and if by reason of strength they be fourscore years,*
> *yet is their strength labour and sorrow;*
> *for it is soon cut off, and we fly away."*

The focus of those who attempt to make this connection appears to be an effort to determine a release date for the imprisoned Watchers. In reading and rereading the Enoch passage, I cannot find any hint to a future release. The passage simply specifies that 70 generations will pass before the consummation of their judgment, or until their fate is completely sealed.

Remembering that this entire ancient battle was an attempt by the fallen to cut off mankind from the rightful position as anointed steward of all things created, it would seem that this reference also is tied to the protection of the royal bloodline that would eventually result in the birth of the messiah (Christ). It is this bloodline that is meticulously traced through Seth to Noah and then preserved through Noah's son, Shem. The bloodline is then tracked for another ten generations in Genesis 11:10-32.

As we have detailed in chapter 8, the bloodline traces through Abraham to Isaac, then to Jacob and through one of his 12 sons, Judah (whom we did not name in chapter 8).

This is the royal bloodline and it can be found in its entirety in Luke, chapter 3. The names listed by Luke may appear somewhat different as they are the Aramaic or Greek rendering of the original Hebrew name. Beginning with the birth of Jesus and counting backward through the bloodline, Enoch is generation number 70.

The prophecy of Enoch 10 is not pointing to a future release of the incarcerated Watchers, but rather a distinct timeline of generations that would be born leading up to the birth of Christ. Just as Noah was prophesied to be the one who would preserve creation through the judgment of the flood, so Jesus was prophesied to be the culmination of the royal bloodline and the one appointed to redeem all of mankind, preserving them through the ultimate judgment of sin. From Enoch to the messiah would be 70 generations. Once Christ was born, the prophecy was fulfilled and the Watchers' fate was forever sealed.

The following is the genealogy of Christ as compiled by Luke and presented in the third chapter of his gospel account. The genealogy begins with Christ and goes all the way back to Adam, who is listed as being directly descendent from God. This is Luke's testimony that the Adam written about in the early chapters of Genesis was the beginning point of all human history.

1. And Jesus himself began to be about thirty years of age,

2. being (as was supposed) the son of Joseph,

3. which was the son of Heli,

4. which was the son of Matthat,

5. which was the son of Levi,

6. which was the son of Melchi,

7. which was the son of Janna,

8. which was the son of Joseph,

9. which was the son of Mattathias,

10. which was the son of Amos,

11. which was the son of Naum,

12. which was the son of Esli,

13. which was the son of Nagge,

14. which was the son of Maath,

15. which was the son of Mattathias,

16. which was the son of Semei,

17. which was the son of Joseph,

18. which was the son of Juda,

19. which was the son of Joanna,

20. which was the son of Rhesa,

21. which was the son of Zorobabel,

22. which was the son of Salathiel,

23. which was the son of Neri,

24. which was the son of Melchi,

25. which was the son of Addi,

26. which was the son of Cosam,

27. which was the son of Elmodam,

28. which was the son of Er,

29. which was the son of Jose,

30. which was the son of Eliezer,

31. which was the son of Jorim,

32. which was the son of Matthat,

33. which was the son of Levi,

34. which was the son of Simeon,

35. which was the son of Judah,

36. which was the son of Joseph,

37. which was the son of Jonan,

38. which was the son of Eliakim,

39. which was the son of Melea,

40. which was the son of Menan,

41. which was the son of Mattatha,

42. which was the son of Nathan,

43. which was the son of David,

44. which was the son of Jesse,

45. which was the son of Obed,

46. which was the son of Booz,

47. which was the son of Salmon,

48. which was the son of Naasson,

49. which was the son of Aminadab,

50. which was the son of Aram,

51. which was the son of Esrom,

52. which was the son of Phares,

53. which was the son of Juda,

54. which was the son of Jacob,

55. which was the son of Isaac,

56. which was the son of Abraham,

57. which was the son of Thara,

58. which was the son of Nachor,

59. which was the son of Saruch,

60. which was the son of Ragau,

61. which was the son of Phalec,

62. which was the son of Heber,

63. which was the son of Sala,

64. which was the son of Cainan,

65. which was the son of Arphaxad,

66. which was the son of Sem,

67. which was the son of Noe,

68. which was the son of Lamech,

69. which was the son of Mathusala,

70. which was the son of Enoch,

71. which was the son of Jared,

72. which was the son of Maleleel,

73. which was the son of Cainan,

74. which was the son of Enos,

75. which was the son of Seth,

76. which was the son of Adam,

77. which was the son of God.

Appendix 3

Timeline for Births & Deaths for Noah's Sons and the Descendants of Seth from Arphaxad to Joseph

The following is footnotes and references for each person listed in the timeline chart of births and deaths found on page 395. Please keep in mind that dates are estimated from the information given and the information that is given does not specify a certain year. Dates are referenced by the listed age of the father at the time that the son was born.

Although we have a document indicating that a person fathered a child at 24 years of age, we do not have enough information to determine the exact year in which the child was born, only a window. Even if you are given the month and year, March 1961, for example, you still are working with a 12 month window of possibility that cannot be narrowed any further based solely on the knowledge that the child was born when the father was 24. The date of birth for the child could fall anywhere between March of 1985 and February of 1986.

Likewise, in the timeline chart of births and deaths, time is marked more generally than specifically. The purpose of the chart is to provide a point of reference showing how the lifespan of one person most likely overlapped that of another, not to provide an accurate calendar count of years.

1. **Methuselah:** a son of Enoch. Enoch is listed as being 65 years of age when Methuselah is born (Gen. 5:21), hence we place the birth of Methuselah as happening in Year of the World 688. Genesis 5:27 states that Methuselah lived 969 years, placing his death in year 1657. The year of his death coincides with the beginning of the flood. We detail this connection in a section of the book called, "My Three Sons (and Their Wives)" found in Chapter 4.

2. **Lamech:** a son of Methuselah. We list the year of his birth as Year of the World 875. This is taken from the reference to Methuselah being 187 years of age when Lamech is born (Gen. 5:25). Lamech dies at 777 years of age (Gen. 5:31). This is Year of the World 1652, five years before the flood.

3. **Noah:** a son of Lamech. We list the year of his birth as Year of the World 1057. This is taken from the reference to Lamech being 182 years of age when Noah is born (Gen. 5:28-29). Noah dies at 950 years of age (Gen. 9:29) this is 350 years after the flood. We have marked his death at Year of the world 2007. According to the Book of Jasher, Noah's wife was the daughter of Enoch and thus the sister of his mentor, Methuselah (Jas. 5:14-16). Noah lived long after the flood enough to see 10 generations born. He also lived well into the lifetime of Abraham and long enough to experience the Tower of Babel event.

4. **Japheth:** a son of Noah. We cannot be specific about the age of Japheth. We can only deduce that he is the firstborn son of Noah (Gen. 9:24, 10:21)

and that he was born after Noah was 500 years of age (Gen. 5:32). The book of Jasher states that his mother was Naamah (Jas. 5:17) and goes on to say that Noah named him Japheth because he was to be the father of a great population of people. We have no specific record of his passing. We have associated Japheth's time of death with the Tower of Babel event because there is an indication that many of his sons were involved in the building of the tower and there is no record of Japheth that extends beyond that time frame. It is also possible that he died prior to the tower event.

5. **Shem:** a son of Noah. We list the year of his birth as Year of the World 1559. This positions him as the second son born to Noah and correlates to the earliest possible age for the birth of his firstborn son, two years after the flood. The details of Shem being either 97 or 98 years of age at the beginning of the Flood are spelled out in Chapter 4. Naamah is listed as his mother in Jasher 5:17. Noah names him Shem, thus tying his birth to the preservation of the sacred bloodline. According to Genesis 11:10-11, Shem dies at age 600. This would be Year of the World 2159. Thus, Shem lived past the lifetime of Abraham and was still alive at the time of the birth of Abraham's son, Isaac, as well as Isaac's twins, Jacob and Esau.

6. **Ham:** a son of Noah. Although Jasher specifically references the births of Japheth and Shem, there is no such reference to the birth of Ham. We proposed in Chapter 4 that Ham may have been much younger than his brothers and that he may have had a different mother. Likewise, there is no specific reference to his death. We have associated his death with the tower event because his grandson Nimrod was the ruling monarch at the time and it

would seem fitting for Ham to be closely associated with the events of his rule.

7. **Arphaxad:** a son of Shem. The year of his birth is marked as being 2 years after the flood (Gen. 11:10). We have put it on the calendar as being 2 years after the flood began, although it could also be interpreted as 2 years after Noah and his family left the ark. This is most likely Year of the World 1659 or 1660. Arphaxad lived a total of 438 years (Gen. 11:12-13), long enough to see the rise of Abraham and the birth of Isaac.

8. **Salah:** a son of Arphaxad. Genesis 11:12 tells us that he is born when his father is 35 years of age. This is most likely Year of the World 1694 or 1695. We are told that he fathers a son named Eber at 30 years of age and that he lives another 403 years after the birth of Eber (Gen. 11:14-15).

9. **Eber:** a son of Salah. Genesis 11:14 indicates that he is born when his father is 30 years of age. This is most likely Year of the World 1724 or 1725. We are told that he fathers a son named Peleg at age 34 and that he lived another 430 years after the birth of Peleg (Gen. 11:16-17). We have marked his lifespan at 434 years. His generation appears to be the last to enjoy a lifespan that naturally exceeds 400 years. It appears that both Eber and Salah outlive the lifetime of Abraham and were still living at the time of the birth of Isaac and later his twins, Jacob and Esau.

10. **Peleg:** a son of Eber. Genesis 11:16 indicates that he is born when his father is 34 years of age. This is most likely Year of the World 1758 or 1759. We are told that he fathers a son named Reu at age 30 and that he lived another 209 years after the birth

of Reu (Gen. 11:18-19). This makes him 239 years of age at his passing and brings us to the year of the Tower of Babel event. Jasher 10:1 indicates that Peleg dies during this time, but does not specifically say that he died in the tower event. The final verse of Jasher 9 says that, "...many of the sons of men died in that tower, a people without number."

11. **Reu:** a son of Peleg. Genesis 11:18 indicates that he is born when his father is 30 years of age. This is most likely Year of the World 1788 or 1789. We are told that he fathers a son named Serug at age 32 and that he lived another 207 years after the birth of Serug (Gen. 11:20-21). His life spans 239 years.

12. **Serug:** a son of Reu. Genesis 11:20 indicates that he is born when his father is 32 years of age. This is most likely Year of the World 1820 or 1821. We are told that he fathers a son named Nahor at age 30 and that he lived another 200 years after the birth of Nahor (Gen. 11:22-23). His life spans 230 years. He outlives his son, Nahor, and may have lived long enough to see or hear of the birth of Isaac.

13. **Nahor:** a son of Reu. Genesis 11:22 indicates that he is born when his father is 30 years of age. This is most likely Year of the World 1850 or 1851. We are told that he fathers a son named Terah at age 29 and that he lived only 119 years after the birth of Terah (Gen. 11:24-25). His life spans 148 years. Jasher 11:12 tells us that he died in the 49th year of Abraham's life which may coincide with the Tower of Babel event. By comparison, his father lived 230 years and his son lived 205 years. Perhaps the life of Nahor was cut short by the collapse of the tower.

14. **Terah:** a son of Nahor. Genesis 11:24 indicates that he is born when his father is 29 years of age. This

is most likely Year of the World 1879 or 1880. We are told that he is 70 years of age when his sons, Abram, Nahor and Haran are born (Gen. 11:26). We are told that he lives a total of 205 years (Gen. 11:32). A number of question marks have been raised regarding the timing of the births of Terah's sons and specifically his age at the time Abram (Abraham) is born. The wording seems to be similar to that found in Genesis 5 regarding the birth of Noah's three sons, but it is not. The wording of Genesis 5 indicates that Noah reached 500 years of age and the birth of his sons followed. Genesis 11 indicates that Terah lived 70 years and that the birth of his three sons transpired within that period of time. In both cases, we supplement the references in Genesis with information from other texts. In the case of Terah, we look to Jasher 7:22, which states that Terah was 38 years of age when he fathered his sons, Haran and Nahor. Jasher 7:50-51 indicates that Terah was 70 years of age when he fathered Abram (Abraham). Jasher 9:4 indicates that Abraham's brother Haran was 42 years of age when he fathers a daughter named Sarai. It goes on to state that Abraham was 10 years of age at that time. Putting all of these references together, it is apparent that Terah fathered the three sons by the time he reached age 70 and that Abraham was born to him at that point in time.

15. **Abraham:** a son of Terah. As detailed above, he is born to his father Terah when Terah is 70 years of age. This is most likely Year of the World 1949 or 1950. Abraham fathers Isaac at age 100 (Gen. 21:5) and lived a total of 175 years (Gen. 25:7).

16. **Isaac:** a son of Abraham. Genesis 21:5 indicates that he is born when his father is 100 years of age. This is most likely Year of the World 2049 or 2050.

We are told that he fathers twins at age 60 (Gen. 25:24-26). The firstborn is named Esau. The second is named Jacob. Isaac lives a total of 180 years and is buried by his twin sons (Gen. 35:28-29).

17. **Jacob:** a son of Isaac and twin brother of Esau. Genesis 25:24-26 indicates that the twins are born when Isaac is 60 years of age. Jacob is the younger of the two and is said to be holding the ankle of his brother at birth. The name Jacob means "ankle grabber." With the help of his mother, he tricks his aging father into passing the family birthright to him instead of his older brother, Esau (Gen. 27). Jacob dies in Egypt at age 147. The details of his passing are featured in Chapter 9.

18. **Esau:** a son of Isaac and twin brother of Jacob. Genesis 25:24-26 indicates that the twins are born when Isaac is 60 years of age. Esau is the firstborn of the two twins and is said to be covered with reddish hair at birth. Shortly before the death of Isaac, Esau comes in from a lengthy hunting trip and claims to be near death due to hunger. Jacob uses this moment of weakness in the life of Esau to entice Esau into selling the rights to the family birthright to him for a bowl of pottage (Gen. 25:27-34). Esau is killed during a battle that breaks out when the sons of Jacob return to the sacred burial cave to lay their father to rest (Jasher 56:61-64).

19. **Joseph:** one of the 12 sons of Jacob. We have to piece together information from a variety of references to reach a reasonable approximation of the time of Joseph's birth. Genesis 41:40-46 tells the story of Joseph's appointment to second in command in Egypt at age 30. His appointment is followed by seven years of prosperity and then followed by seven years of famine, as Joseph had foretold.

Genesis 45 tells the story of the family of Joseph relocating to Egypt. The indication is that this took place after two years of famine. This would make Joseph 39 years of age at the time. When Joseph's father, Jacob, arrives in Egypt, he tells the Pharaoh that he is 130 years old (Gen. 47:9). Jacob is said to have lived in Egypt for 17 years and died at age 147 (Gen. 47:28). This further verifies his age upon his arrival in Egypt. If we can place Jacob's age at 130 at a time when Joseph was 39, then we can deduce that Jacob was 91 years of age when Joseph was born and mark the birth of Joseph around Year of the World 2200 or 2201. Jasher 31:21 states plainly that Jacob was 91 years of age at the time Joseph was born. This further corroborates the timeline. Genesis 50:26 states that Joseph was 110 years old at the time of his death. Joshua 24:32 reveals that the bones of Joseph were taken from Egypt during the Exodus and later buried in Shechem. The burial site of Imhotep has been found in Saqqara, Egypt. The sarcophagus that was initially associated with the find was empty. As of 2014, the search for Imhotep's mummy is ongoing.

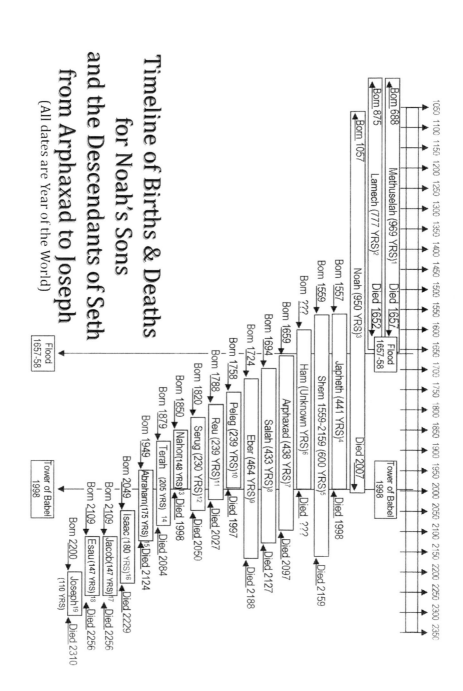

Timeline of Births & Deaths
for Noah's Sons
and the Descendants of Seth
from Arphaxad to Joseph

(All dates are Year of the World)

395

Appendix 4

Timeline of 360 year Cycles for Planetary Object

The following is listing of footnotes as they relate to explanations of dates listed in the chart of 360 year cycles on page 401. Please note: when we compiled this chart, we did not expect events to align in exact 360 year increments. Conversions from dates "Year of the World" to dates in accordance with our modern calendar are estimates. Conversion dates are difficult due to a variety of factors, not the least of which is a multitude of attempted conversions from a 360 day calendar year to a 365 day calendar year.

A study of how we came to our modern-day calendar is quite interesting and most often leads to the conclusion that we have very little idea what year in which we are actually living. The Jews mark year 2014 as Year of the World 5775. Bishop James Ussher authored the most extensive calendar count registry ever researched, *The Annals of the World*. He placed the date for the creation of the world at 4004 BC. Several others, including Sir Isaac Newton, have placed the date of creation between 3940 BC and 3942 BC. We have opted to use the estimated date of creation offered by Sir Isaac Newton, 3940 BC. We chose to use Newton's calculations solely as a starting point of reference for the timeline.

1. **Flooding of the Gihon River:** this date is marked from the date of the flood. The Book of Jasher

provides a window of time for this happening, but not an exact date. We simply plugged in a date that was 360 years prior to the flood as a point of reference.

2. **The Worldwide Flood of Noah:** this date is calculated in terms of Year of the World calendar count and is marked as having occurred 600 years after the birth of Noah.

3. **The Fall of the Tower of Babel:** this date is calculated with assistance from the Book of Jasher. Although the building of the tower spanned a great number of years, the collapse of the tower is said to have happened in the 48th year of the life of Abraham (Jasher 10:1). We previously dated the birth of Abraham in Year of the World 1949. Abraham would have most likely turned 48 in year 1997. Jasher 11:12 speaks of events that happened after the fall of the tower and indicates that Abraham was 49. We have marked the fall of the tower in Year of the World 1998 because it could not have happened any later in the timeline.

4. **Object Observed in Egypt and China 1486 BC:** this date is taken from the research cited in chapter 8. Documented by the Egyptians and the Chinese, this event is most commonly dated as having occurred in 1486 BC.

5. **No Known Event:** this is marked as a 360 year cycle from the previous date. At this time I have not uncovered any known event that seems suitable to associate with this point in the timeline

6. **The Great Earthquake in the Days of Uzziah:** this taken from the Old Testament books of Amos and Zechariah. Scholars have projected the date of this earthquake and the great eclipse that accompanied

it as having happened June 15, 763 BC. Details are given in Chapter 8.

7. **No Known Event:** this is marked as a 360 year cycle from the 763 BC event. At this time I have not uncovered any known event that seems suitable to associate with this point in the timeline.

8. **Crucifixion of Christ 32 AD:** this event included an eclipse that spanned approximately three hours and a great earthquake. Scholars commonly agree with a date of 32 AD for the crucifixion of Christ. Dr. Ken Johnson pinpoints it to the day in his book, *Ancient Prophecies Revealed: 500 Prophecies Listed In Order Of When They Were Fulfilled.*

9. **No Known Event:** this is marked as a 360 year cycle from the date of the crucifixion. At this time I have not uncovered any known event that seems suitable to associate with this point in the timeline.

10. **No Known Event:** this is marked as a 360 year cycle from the previous date. At this time I have not uncovered any known event that seems suitable to associate with this point in the timeline.

11. **The Chinese "Guest Star" in 1054 AD:** this is taken from Chinese astrological records. They tracked and documented the movement of the "Guest Star" for a period of 26 months.

12. **No Known Event:** this is marked as a 360 year cycle from the previous date. At this time I have not uncovered any known event that seems suitable to associate with this point in the timeline.

13. **de Cheseaux's Sky Object 1744 AD:** the date of this event is documented by Swiss Astronomer Jean-Philippe de Cheseaux. This would be the fifth

cycle from the date of the crucifixion. Taking the count of years between the two events (1,712) and dividing by the number of cycles (5) produces an average cycle length of 342.4 years, well within projections.

14. **No Known Event:** this date is yet future. We have simply marked 360 years from the date of Jean-Philippe de Cheseaux's sky object. We are not making projections for a future appearance.

Timeline Chart of 360 Year Cycles of Unknown Planetary Object

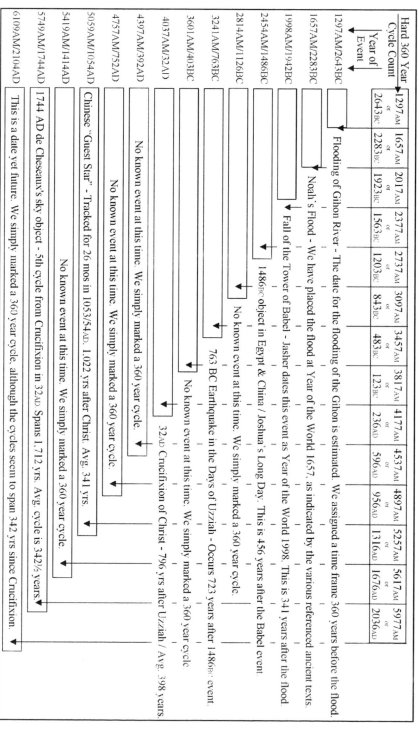

Hard 360 Year Cycle Count	Year of Event	Event
1297AM/2643BC	1657AM / 2643BC or 2283BC	Flooding of Gihon River - The date for the flooding of the Gihon is estimated. We assigned a time frame 360 years before the flood.
1657AM/2283BC	2017AM / 1923BC	Noah's Flood - We have placed the flood at Year of the World 1657, as indicated by the various referenced ancient texts.
1998AM/1942BC	2377AM / 1563BC	Fall of the Tower of Babel - Jasher dates this event as Year of the World 1998. This is 341 years after the flood.
2454AM/1486BC	2737AM / 1203BC	1486BC object in Egypt & China / Joshua's Long Day. This is 456 years after the Babel event.
2814AM/1126BC	3097AM / 843BC	No known event at this time. We simply marked a 360 year cycle.
3241AM/763BC	3457AM / 483BC	763 BC Earthquake in the Days of Uzziah - Occurs 723 years after 1486bc event.
3601AM/403BC	3817AM / 123BC	No known event at this time. We simply marked a 360 year cycle
4037AM/32AD	4177AM / 236AD	32AD Crucifixion of Christ - 796 yrs after Uzziah / Avg. 398 years.
4397AM/392AD	4537AM / 596AD	No known event at this time. We simply marked a 360 year cycle.
4757AM/752AD	4897AM / 956AD	No known event at this time. We simply marked a 360 year cycle.
5059AM/1054AD	5257AM / 1316AD	Chinese "Guest Star" - Tracked for 26 mos in 1053/54AD. 1,022 yrs after Christ. Avg. 341 yrs.
5419AM/1414AD	5617AM / 1676AD	No known event at this time. We simply marked a 360 year cycle.
5749AM/1744AD	5977AM / 2036AD	1744 AD de Cheseaux's sky object - 5th cycle from Crucifixion in 32AD. Spans 1,712 yrs. Avg. cycle is 342½ years.
6109AM/2104AD		This is a date yet future. We simply marked a 360 year cycle, although the cycles seem to span 342 yrs since Crucifixion.

401

Bibliography

These four texts, frequently quoted throughout the book, are available in a number of editions and various translations. The fifth in the list is an online resource for scripture reference and original language. The following is a list of published versions of each manuscript that was used as the primary reference resource for this book. If an alternative reference source was used, it was cited on a case by case basis in chapter footnotes for this book.

The Scofield Reference Bible: Authorized Version. New York: For Oxford UP, American Branch, 1909. Print.

The Book of Enoch. London: R.H. Charles, D. Litt., D.D. Society for Promoting Christian Knowledge, 1917. Print.

The Book of Jasher: Faithfully Translated (1840) from the Original Hebrew into English. Salt Lake City: J.H. Parry, 1887. Print.

The Book of Jubilees. From the Apocrypha and Pseudepigrapha of the Old Testament by R.H. Charles, D. Litt., D.D. Oxford: Clarendon Press, 1913. Scanned and Edited by Joshua Williams, Northwest Nazarene College. No Date. Web. <http://www.pseudepigrapha.com/jubilees/index.htm>.

Strong's Concordance with Hebrew and Greek Lexicon. EliYah, No Date. Web. <http://www.eliyah/lexicon.html>.

Footnotes by Chapter

Chapter 1 - You Want Me To Do What?

1. Simpson, D. P. *Cassell's Latin Dictionary: Latin-English*, English-Latin. London: Cassell, 1977. Print.

2. W. Gunther Plaut, Bernard J. Bamberger, William W. Hallo (eds.) (1981). *The Torah*. New York: Union of American Hebrew Congregations. Footnote to Gen. 6:15: "...figuring a cubit to be about 18 inches."

3. Marshall Clagett (1999), *Ancient Egyptian Science, A Source Book. Volume Three: Ancient Egyptian Mathematics*, Philadelphia: American Philosophical Society.

4. YRC Freight, Shipping Resources, Semi-Trailer Dimensions, <http://www.yrc.com/shippers/semi-trailer-dimensions.html>

5. Dimensions sourced from retailer product specifications for 3.4 cubic feet capacity top loading washer.

6. *Ibid.* YRC Freight, Shipping Resources.

7. Jewish Encyclopedia dot-com, *The Unedited Full Text of the 1906 Jewish Encyclopedia*, Nippur, <http://www.jewishencyclopedia.com/articles/11551-nippur>

8. *Acta praehistorica et archaeologica Volumes 7–8*. Berliner Gesellschaft für Anthropologie, Ethnologie und Urgeschichte; Ibero-Amerikanisches Institut (Berlin, Germany); Staatliche Museen Preussischer Kulturbesitz. Berlin: Bruno Hessling Verlag, 1976. p. 49.

9. Lyle, Anthony, *Ancient History: A Revised Chronology, Volume 1*, Author House, 2012, pg. 108.

10. *Acta praehistorica et archaeologica Volumes 7–8*. Berliner Gesellschaft für Anthropologie, Ethnologie und Urgeschichte; Ibero-Amerikanisches Institut (Berlin, Germany); Staatliche Museen Preussischer Kulturbesitz. Berlin: Bruno Hessling Verlag, 1976. p. 49.

11. Telephone Pole source information taken from "My Florida Public Service Commission" website, section 14, <http://www.floridapsc.com/consumers/utilitypole/en/AllUtilityPoleInfo.aspx>

12. Interstate Highway Standards, Wikipedia, July 2007, *Vertical Clearance*.

13. Reference to fictional pop-culture icon Sheldon Cooper from CBS Television's "The Big Bang Theory" sit-com.

14. Tim Knight, *The Woodworker's Journal*, "How Much Lumber is in a Log?" August 3, 2011. <http://www.woodworkersjournal.com/woodworking_blog/index.php/how-much-lumber-is-in-a-log/> <http://www.heartwoods.com/html/calculator.html>

15. Dimensions sourced from retailer product specifications for 25.5 cubic foot side-by-side refrigerator.

16. Growth data and projections taken from the California Forest Foundation, <http://www.calforestfoundation.org/pdf/RESTORING-REDWOOD-FORESTS.pdf>

17. "Hughes HK-1 (H-4) 'Spruce Goose,'" The Aviation Zone.com, <http://www.theaviationzone.com/factsheets/hk1.asp>

18. "Spruce Goose." Evergreen Aviation Museum.org, <http://evergreenmuseum.org/the-museum/aircraft-exhibits/the-spruce-goose/>

19. Claxton, Capt. R. N., *History and Description of the Steamship Great Britain*, J. Smith Homans, New York. 1845.

20. <http://www.ssgreatbritain.org/>

21. <http://www.ssjeremiahobrien.org/>

22. Hurricanes: Science and Society, "Hurricane Impacts Due to Storm Surge, Wave, and Coastal Flooding," <http://www.hurricanescience.org/society/impacts/stormsurge/>

23. Jess Baker, "Japan 2011 Earthquake and Tsunami Disaster: Revealing Before and After Photos 3 Years Later," *The Weather Channel*, March 11, 2014. <http://www.weather.com/news/japan-earthquake-tsunami-3-years-later-photos-20140310>

24. "The Deadliest Tsunami in History?" *National Geographic News*. National Geographic Society, 28 Oct. 2010. Web. Retrieved Dec. 3, 2013. <http://news.nationalgeographic.com/news/2004/12/1227_041226_tsunami.html>.

25. Jackson, J.B., *A Dictionary of Scripture Proper Names*, Loizeaux Brothers, June 1909, pg. 26.

26. National Geographic Channel, Episodes, "The Truth Behind The Ark," <http://channel.nationalgeographic.com/channel/episodes/the-ark/>

27. "Tests Show Drogue Stones Effectiveness on Noah's Ark." *YouTube*. Anchor Stones, 14 Dec. 2010. Web. Retrieved Feb. 8, 2014. <https://www.youtube.com/watch?v=108wGjwyS7o>.

28. Lovett, Tim. "Noah's Ark Through History." *WorldwideFlood.com*, June 2007. Web. Retrieved Dec. 5, 2013. <http://worldwideflood.org/general/ark_history.htm>.

29. "Safety Investigation of Noah's Ark in a Seaway," *Answers in Genesis Ministries*, 2003. Retrieved Dec. 5, 2013. <http://worldwideflood.org/ark/safety_aig/safety_aig.htm>

Chapter 2 - There Goes The Neighborhood

1. History World, *History of Civilization*, <http://www.historyworld.net/wrldhis/plaintexthistories.asp?historyid=ab25#ixzz2jlFonnL8>

2. History World, *Mesopotamia and Egypt: 3100 BC*, <http://www.historyworld.net/wrldhis/plaintexthistories.asp?historyid=ab25#ixzz2jlFonnL8>

3. Flavius Josephus, *Antiquities of the Jews*, Book 1, Chapter 2, Paragraph 2. <http://www.biblestudytools.com/history/flavius-josephus/antiquities-jews/>.

4. NTSLibrary.com, *Easton's Bible Dictionary*, online PDF, *Entry:* "Cain," page 197.

5. Flavius Josephus, *Antiquities of the Jews*, Book 1, Chapter 2, Paragraph 2. <http://www.biblestudytools.com/history/flavius-josephus/antiquities-jews/>.

6. *Strong's Concordance with Hebrew and Greek Lexicon.* EliYah, No Date. Web. Word #H3913 "LATASH" used 5x in Old Testament Text, KJV-1611. The KJV translates Strong's H3913 in the following manner: sharpen (2x), sharp (1x), whet (1x), instructer (1x).

7. *Strong's Concordance with Hebrew and Greek Lexicon.* EliYah, No Date. Web. Word #H2794 "CHORESH" used 1x in Old Testament Text, KJV-1611. The KJV translates Strong's H2794 in the following manner: artificer (1x). <http://www.eliyah.com/lexicon.html>.

8. Nichol, Francis D., *The Seventh-day Adventist Bible Commentary*, Washington, D.C. Review and Herald Publishing Assoc. 1978. <http://www.bibleinfo.com/en/questions/what-was-noahs-wifes-name>

9. Freedman, Harry, and Maurice Simon. *Midrash Rabbah, Translated into English with Notes, Glossary and Indices*. London: Soncino, 1961. p.194

10. Charles, Robert Henry (1911). "Apocryphal literature," In Chisholm, Hugh. *Encyclopedia Britannica (11th ed.)*. Cambridge University Press.

11. The Church of Jesus Christ of Latter-Day Saints, *Online Bible Dictionary*, "Pseudepigrapha," Retrieved March 28, 2014. <https://www.lds.org/scriptures/bd/pseudepigrapha>

12. Benjaminson, Chani. "How old was Moses when The Torah was given at Mount Sinai?" *Chabad-Lubavitch Media Center*. Retrieved March 28, 2014. <http://www.chabad.org/library/article_cdo/aid/476253/jewish/How-old-was-Moses-when-the-Torah-was-given.htm>

13. *Strong's Concordance with Hebrew and Greek Lexicon.* EliYah, No Date. Web. Word #H7121 "QARA" used 735x in Old Testament Text, KJV-1611. The KJV translates Strong's H7121 in the following manner: call (528x), cried (98x), read (38x), proclaim (36x), named (7x), guests (4x), invited (3x), gave (3x), renowned (3x), bidden (2x), preach (2x), misc (11x). <http://www.eliyah.com/lexicon.html>.

14. *Matthew Henry's Commentary*, Grand Rapids: Zondervan Publishing House, 1961.

15. *Strong's Concordance with Hebrew and Greek Lexicon.* EliYah, No Date. Web. Word #H3947 "LAQACH" used 965x in Old Testament Text, KJV-1611. The KJV translates Strong's H3947 in the following manner: take (747x), receive (61x), take away (51x), fetch (31x), bring (25x), get (6x), take out (6x), carry away (5x), married (4x), buy (3x), misc (26x). <http://www.eliyah.com/lexicon.html>.

16. *Strong's Concordance with Hebrew and Greek Lexicon.* EliYah, No Date. Web. Word #H3382 "YERED" used 7x in Old Testament Text, KJV-1611. The KJV translates Strong's H3382 in the following manner: Jared (5x), Jered (2x). From root word "YARAD". Strong's Hebrew Lexicon, Word #H3381 "YARAD" used 380x in Old Testament Text, KJV-1611. The KJV translates Strong's H3381 in the following manner: (come, go, etc) down (340x), descend (18x), variant (2x), fell (2x), let (1x), abundantly (1x), down by (1x), indeed (1x), put off (1x), light off (1x), out (1x), sank (1x), subdued (1x), take (1x). <http://www.eliyah.com/lexicon.html>.

17. Giorgio A. Tsoukalos, "Gods or Ancient Aliens," *MUFON*, Oct. 2010 <http://www.mufonoc.org/gods-or-ancient-aliens/>, Giorgio A. Tsoukalos, Facebook Post explaining comments from Ancient Aliens S2/E2, Nov. 5, 2010, Retrieved Sept. 17, 2014. <https://www.facebook.com/giorgiotsoukalosfans/posts/173211032690916>

Chapter 3 - There's New Kids On The Block

1. *Strong's Concordance with Hebrew and Greek Lexicon.* EliYah, No Date. Web. Word #A5894 "`IYR" (Aramaic) used 3x in Old Testament Text, KJV-1611. The KJV translates Strong's A5894 in the following manner: watcher (3x). <http://www.eliyah.com/lexicon.html>.

2. *Strong's Concordance with Hebrew and Greek Lexicon.* EliYah, No Date. Web. Word #H5782 "`UWR" (Hebrew) used 81x in Old Testament Text, KJV-1611. The KJV translates Strong's H5782 in the following manner: (stir, lift....) up (40x), awake (25x), wake (6x), raise (6x), arise (1x), master (1x), raised out (1x), variant (1x). <http://www.eliyah.com/lexicon.html>.

3. *Strong's Concordance with Hebrew and Greek Lexicon.* EliYah, No Date. Web. Word #H6491 "PAQACH" used 20x in Old Testament Text, KJV-1611. The KJV translates Strong's H6491 in the following manner: open (20x). <http://www.eliyah.com/lexicon.html>.

4. *Strong's Concordance with Hebrew and Greek Lexicon.* EliYah, No Date. Web. Word #H582 "`ENOWSH" used 564x in Old Testament Text, KJV-1611. The KJV translates Strong's H582 in the following manner: man (520x), certain (10x), husbands (3x), some (3x), merchantmen (2x), persons (2x), misc (24x). <http://www.eliyah.com/lexicon.html>.

5. The full story of Jacob wrestling with the angelic being is recorded in the Old Testament Book of Genesis, chapter 32, verses 22 through 32.

6. Taken from History Channel Production, *"Angels: Good or Evil,"* A&E Television Networks, 2003.

7. US History.org, "Early American Railroads," *U.S. History Online Textbook.* Retrieved July 28, 2014. <http://www.ushistory.org/us/25b.asp>

8. *Strong's Concordance with Hebrew and Greek Lexicon.* EliYah, No Date. Web. Word #G746 "ARCHĒ" used 58x in New Testament Text, KJV-1611. The KJV translates Strong's G746 in the following manner: beginning (40x), principality (8x), corner (2x), first (2x), misc (6x). <http://www.eliyah.com/lexicon.html>.

9. *Strong's Concordance with Hebrew and Greek Lexicon.* EliYah, No Date. Web. Word #G3613 "OIKĒTĒRION" used 2x in New Testament Text, KJV-1611. The KJV translates Strong's G3613 in the following manner: house (1x), habitation (1x). <http://www.eliyah.com/lexicon.html>.

10. *Strong's Concordance with Hebrew and Greek Lexicon.* EliYah, No Date. Web. Word #G3613 "OIKĒTĒRION" used 2x in New Testament Text, KJV-1611. The KJV translates Strong's G3613 in the following manner: house (1x), habitation (1x). <http://www.eliyah.com/lexicon.html>.

11. *Strong's Concordance with Hebrew and Greek Lexicon.* EliYah, No Date. Web. Word #G3614 "OIKIA" used 95x in New Testament Text, KJV-1611. The KJV translates Strong's G3614 in the following manner: house (92x), at home (1x), household (1x), from the house (1x). <http://www.eliyah.com/lexicon.html>.

12. *Strong's Concordance with Hebrew and Greek Lexicon.* EliYah, No Date. Web. Word #G2647 "KATALYŌ" used 17x in New Testament Text, KJV-1611. The KJV translates Strong's G2647 in the following manner: destroy (9x), throw down (3x), lodge (1x), guest (1x), come to naught (1x), overthrow (1x), dissolve (1x). <http://www.eliyah.com/lexicon.html>.

13. *Strong's Concordance with Hebrew and Greek Lexicon.* EliYah, No Date. Web. Word #G5349 "PHTHARTOS" used 6x in New Testament Text, KJV-1611. The KJV translates Strong's G5349 in the following manner: corruptible (6x). <http://www.eliyah.com/lexicon.html>.

14. *Strong's Concordance with Hebrew and Greek Lexicon.* EliYah, No Date. Web. Word #G861 "APHTHARSIA" used 8x in New Testament Text, KJV-1611. The KJV translates Strong's G861 in the following manner: incorruption (4x), immortality (2x), sincerity (2x). <http://www.eliyah.com/lexicon.html>.

15. *Strong's Concordance with Hebrew and Greek Lexicon.* EliYah, No Date. Web. Word #G2349 "THNĒTOS" used 6x in New Testament Text, KJV-1611. The KJV translates Strong's G2349 in the following manner: mortal (5x), mortality (with G3588) (1x). <http://www.eliyah.com/lexicon.html>.

16. *Strong's Concordance with Hebrew and Greek Lexicon.* EliYah, No Date. Web. Word #G110 "ATHANASIA" used 3x in New Testament Text, KJV-1611. The KJV translates Strong's G110 in the following manner: immortality (3x). <http://www.eliyah.com/lexicon.html>.

17. Christ's teaching of the resurrection acknowledged that all of mankind was eternal in nature and whereas their physical body was perishable, their essence was everlasting. Taken from Matthew 22:30. Referenced earlier in this chapter on page 100 & following under the sub-header: Of Angels and Men.

18. Post-Flood Biblical references of giants include: Numbers 13:33, Deuteronomy 2:11, Deuteronomy 2:20, Deuteronomy 3:11-13, Joshua 12:4, Joshua 13:12, Joshua 15:8, Joshua 17:15, Joshua 18:16.

19. *Strong's Concordance with Hebrew and Greek Lexicon.* EliYah, No Date. Web. Word #H3382 "YERED" used 7x in Old Testament Text, KJV-1611. The KJV translates Strong's H3382 in the following manner: Jared (5x), Jered (2x). From root word "YARAD". Strong's Hebrew Lexicon, Word #H3381 "YARAD" used 380x in Old Testament Text, KJV-1611. The KJV translates Strong's H3381 in the following manner: (come, go, etc) down (340x), descend (18x), variant (2x), fell (2x), let (1x), abundantly (1x), down by (1x), indeed (1x), put off (1x), light off (1x), out (1x), sank (1x), subdued (1x), take (1x). <http://www.eliyah.com/lexicon.html>.

20. *Strong's Concordance with Hebrew and Greek Lexicon.* EliYah, No Date. Web. Word #H2585 "CHANOWK" used 16x in Old Testament Text, KJV-1611. The KJV translates Strong's H2585 in the following manner: Enoch (9x), Hanoch (5x), Henoch (2x). Derived from the root word: CHANAK <http://www.eliyah.com/lexicon.html>.

21. *Strong's Concordance with Hebrew and Greek Lexicon.* EliYah, No Date. Web. Word #H2596 "CHANAK" used 5x in Old Testament Text, KJV-1611. The KJV translates Strong's H2596 in the following manner: dedicate (4x), train up (1x). <http://www.eliyah.com/lexicon.html>.

22. *Strong's Concordance with Hebrew and Greek Lexicon.* EliYah, No Date. Web. Word #H4962 "MATH" used 22x in Old Testament Text, KJV-1611. The KJV translates Strong's H4962 in the following manner: men (14x), few (2x), few (with H4557) (1x), friends (1x), number (1x), persons (1x), small (1x), with (1x). <http://www.eliyah.com/lexicon.html>.

23. *Strong's Concordance with Hebrew and Greek Lexicon.* EliYah, No Date. Web. Word #H7973 "SHELACH" used 8x in Old Testament Text, KJV-1611. The KJV translates Strong's H7973 in the following manner: sword (3x), weapon (2x), dart (1x), plant (1x), put them off. <http://www.eliyah.com/lexicon.html>.

24. *Strong's Concordance with Hebrew and Greek Lexicon.* EliYah, No Date. Web. Word #H8352 "SHETH" used 9x in Old Testament Text, KJV-1611. The KJV translates Strong's H8352 in the following manner: Seth (7x), Sheth (2x). <http://www.eliyah.com/lexicon.html>.

25. *Strong's Concordance with Hebrew and Greek Lexicon.* EliYah, No Date. Web. Word #H5897 "`IYRAD" used 2x in Old Testament Text, KJV-1611. The KJV translates Strong's H5897 in the following manner: Irad (2x). <http://www.eliyah.com/lexicon.html>.

26. *Strong's Concordance with Hebrew and Greek Lexicon.* EliYah, No Date. Web. Word #H4229 "MACHAH" used 36x in Old Testament Text, KJV-1611. The KJV translates Strong's H4229 in the following manner: (blot, put, etc)...out (17x), destroy (6x), wipe (4x), blot (3x), wipe away (2x), abolished (1x), marrow (1x), reach (1x), utterly (1x). <http://www.eliyah.com/lexicon.html>.

27. *Strong's Concordance with Hebrew and Greek Lexicon.* EliYah, No Date. Web. Word #H410 "`EL" used 245x in Old Testament Text, KJV-1611. The KJV translates Strong's H410 in the following manner: God (213x), god (16x), power (4x), mighty (5x), goodly (1x), great (1x), idols (1x), Immanuel (with H6005) (2x), might (1x), strong (1x). <http://www.eliyah.com/lexicon.html>.

28. Jackson, J.B., *A Dictionary of Scripture Proper Names*, Loizeaux Brothers, June 1909, pg. 53.

29. *Strong's Concordance with Hebrew and Greek Lexicon.* EliYah, No Date. Web. Word #H4962 "MATH" used 22x in Old Testament Text, KJV-1611. The KJV translates Strong's H4962 in the following manner: men (14x), few (2x), few (with H4557) (1x), friends (1x), number (1x), persons (1x), small (1x), with (1x). <http://www.eliyah.com/lexicon.html>.

30. *Strong's Concordance with Hebrew and Greek Lexicon.* EliYah, No Date. Web. Word #H410 "`EL" used 245x in Old Testament Text, KJV-1611. The KJV translates Strong's H410 in the following manner: God (213x), god (16x), power (4x), mighty (5x), goodly (1x), great (1x), idols (1x), Immanuel (with H6005) (2x), might (1x), strong (1x). <http://www.eliyah.com/lexicon.html>.

31. Jackson, J.B., *A Dictionary of Scripture Proper Names*, Loizeaux Brothers, June 1909, pg. 54.

32. *Strong's Concordance with Hebrew and Greek Lexicon.* EliYah, No Date. Web. Word #H5303 "NĚPHIYL" used 3x in Old Testament Text, KJV-1611. The KJV translates Strong's H5303 in the following manner: giant (3x). <http://www.eliyah.com/lexicon.html>.

33. *Strong's Concordance with Hebrew and Greek Lexicon.* EliYah, No Date. Web. Word #H5307 "NAPHAL" used 434x in Old Testament Text, KJV-1611. The KJV translates Strong's H5307 in the following manner: fall (318x), fall down (25x), cast (18x), cast down (9x), fall away (5x), divide (5x), overthrow (5x), present (5x), lay (3x), rot (3x), accepted (2x), lie down (2x), inferior (2x), lighted (2x), lost (2x), misc (22x). <http://www.eliyah.com/lexicon.html>.

34. *Strong's Concordance with Hebrew and Greek Lexicon.* EliYah, No Date. Web. Word #H3929 "LEMEK" used 11x in Old Testament Text, KJV-1611. The KJV translates Strong's H3929 in the following manner: Lamech (11x). <http://www.eliyah.com/lexicon.html>.

35. "Lamech." BibleStudyTools.com. No Date. Web., *Easton's Bible Dictionary*, <http://www.biblestudytools.com/dictionaries/eastons-bible-dictionary/lamech.html>

36. Jackson, J.B., *A Dictionary of Scripture Proper Names*, Loizeaux Brothers, June 1909, pg. 49.

37. *Strong's Concordance with Hebrew and Greek Lexicon*. EliYah, No Date. Web. Word #H5711 "`ADAH" used 8x in Old Testament Text, KJV-1611. The KJV translates Strong's H5711 in the following manner: Adah (8x). <http://www.eliyah.com/lexicon.html>.

38. *Strong's Concordance with Hebrew and Greek Lexicon*. EliYah, No Date. Web. Word #H2989 "YABAL" used 1x in Old Testament Text, KJV-1611. The KJV translates Strong's H2989 in the following manner: Jabal (1x). Derived from Root Word #H2988 "YABAL" used 2x in Old Testament Text, KJV-1611. The KJV translates Strong's H2988 in the following manner: stream (1x), course (1x). <http://www.eliyah.com/lexicon.html>.

39. *Strong's Concordance with Hebrew and Greek Lexicon*. EliYah, No Date. Web. Word #H3106 "YUWBAL" used 1x in Old Testament Text, KJV-1611. The KJV translates Strong's H3106 in the following manner: Jubal (1x). Derived from Root Word #H2986 "YABAL" used 18x in Old Testament Text, KJV-1611. The KJV translates Strong's H2986 in the following manner: bring (11x), carry (4x), bring forth (1x), lead forth (1x), lead (1x). <http://www.eliyah.com/lexicon.html>.

40. *Strong's Concordance with Hebrew and Greek Lexicon*. EliYah, No Date. Web. Word #H6741 "TSILLAH" used 3x in Old Testament Text, KJV-1611. The KJV translates Strong's H6741 in the following manner: Zillah (3x). <http://www.eliyah.com/lexicon.html>.

41. Flavius Josephus, *Antiquities of the Jews*, Book 1, Chapter 2, Paragraph 2.<http://www.biblestudytools.com/history/flavius-josephus/antiquities-jews/>.

42. *Strong's Concordance with Hebrew and Greek Lexicon*. EliYah, No Date. Web. Word #H5303 "NĚPHIYL" is translated "giants" in the following Bible translations: King James Version, New King James Version, Darby Translation, Webster's Bible, Latin Vulgate, possibly others. <http://www.eliyah.com/lexicon.html>.

43. *Strong's Concordance with Hebrew and Greek Lexicon*. EliYah, No Date. Web. Word #H5303 "NĚPHIYL" is translated "Nephilim" or "Nephilites" in the following Bible translations: New Living Translation, New International Version, English Standard Version, American Standard Version, New American Standard Bible, Revised Standard Version, Hebrew Names Version, possibly others. Young's Literal Translation translates Word #H5303 "NĚPHIYL" as "fallen ones." <http://www.eliyah.com/lexicon.html>.

44. *Strong's Concordance with Hebrew and Greek Lexicon.* EliYah, No Date. Web. Word #H5307 "NAPHAL" used 434x in Old Testament Text, KJV-1611. The KJV translates Strong's H5307 in the following manner: fall (318x), fall down (25x), cast (18x), cast down (9x), fall away (5x), divide (5x), overthrow (5x), present (5x), lay (3x), rot (3x), accepted (2x), lie down (2x), inferior (2x), lighted (2x), lost (2x), misc (22x). <http://www.eliyah.com/lexicon.html>.

45. Alchon, Suzanne Austin. *A Pest in the Land: New World Epidemics in a Global Perspective.* Albuquerque: U of New Mexico, 2003. Print. pg. 21.

46. Jay, Peter, "A Distant Mirror," *TIME Europe.* July 17, 2000. Vol. 156 No. 3. Monday, July 17, 2000.

47. "Historical Estimates of World Population." Census.gov.

48. *Strong's Concordance with Hebrew and Greek Lexicon.* EliYah, No Date. Web. Word #H4284 "MACHASHABAH" used 56x in Old Testament Text, KJV-1611. The KJV translates Strong's H4284 in the following manner: thought (28x), device (12x), purpose (6x), work (3x), imaginations (3x), cunning (1x), devised (1x), invented (1x), means (1x). <http://www.eliyah.com/lexicon.html>.

49. *Strong's Concordance with Hebrew and Greek Lexicon.* EliYah, No Date. Web. Word #H3336 "YETSER" used 9x in Old Testament Text, KJV-1611. The KJV translates Strong's H3336 in the following manner: imagination (5x), frame (1x), mind (1x), thing framed (1x), work (1x). <http://www.eliyah.com/lexicon.html>.

50. *Strong's Concordance with Hebrew and Greek Lexicon.* EliYah, No Date. Web. Word #H3335 "YATSAR" used 62x in Old Testament Text, KJV-1611. The KJV translates Strong's H3335 in the following manner: form (26x), potter (17x), fashion (5x), maker (4x), frame (3x), make (3x), former (2x), earthen (1x), purposed (1x). <http://www.eliyah.com/lexicon.html>.

51. *Strong's Concordance with Hebrew and Greek Lexicon.* EliYah, No Date. Web. Word #H834 "'ASHER" used 111x in Old Testament Text, KJV-1611. The KJV translates Strong's H834 in the following manner: which, wherewith, because, when, soon, whilst, as if, as when, that, until, much, whosoever, whereas, wherein, whom, whose. <http://www.eliyah.com/lexicon.html>.

52. Joshua 1:14, Joshua 8:3, Joshua 10:7, Judges 6:12, Judges 11:1, Ruth 2:1, 1st Samuel 9:1, 1st Samuel 16:18, There are a total of 158 OT references wherein the word is used. *Strong's Concordance with Hebrew and Greek Lexicon.* EliYah, No Date. Web. Word #H1368 "GIBBOWR" used 158x in Old Testament Text, KJV-1611. The KJV translates Strong's H1368 in the following manner: mighty (63x), mighty man (68x), strong (4x), valiant (3x), ... ones (4x), mighties (2x), man (2x), valiant men (2x), strong man (1x), upright man (1x), champion (1x), chief (1x), excel (1x), giant (1x), men's (1x), mightiest (1x), strongest (1x). <http://www.eliyah.com/lexicon.html>.

53. *Strong's Concordance with Hebrew and Greek Lexicon.* EliYah, No Date. Web. Word #H8034 "SHEM" used 864x in Old Testament Text, KJV-1611. The KJV translates Strong's H8034 in the following manner: name (832x), renown (7x), fame (4x), famous (3x), named (3x), named (with H7121) (2x), famous (with H7121) (1x), infamous (with H2931) (1x), report (1x), misc (10x). <http://www.eliyah.com/lexicon.html>.

54. *Strong's Concordance with Hebrew and Greek Lexicon.* EliYah, No Date. Web. Word #H5769 "`OWLAM" used 439x in Old Testament Text, KJV-1611. The KJV translates Strong's H5769 in the following manner: ever (272x), everlasting (63x), old (22x), perpetual (22x), evermore (15x), never (13x), time (6x), ancient (5x), world (4x), always (3x), alway (2x), long (2x), more (2x), never (with H408) (2x), misc (6x). <http://www.eliyah.com/lexicon.html>.

55. Swartz, Jr., B.K., "The Origin of the American Christmas Myth and Customs," *Ball State University*, Retrieved Jan. 18, 2014. <http://web.archive.org/web/20110430004539/http://www.bsu.edu/web/01bkswartz/xmaspub.html>

56. Johnson, Ken, Th.D. *Ancient Paganism: The Sorcery of the Fallen Angels.* United States: Bibliofacts Ministries, 2009. Print. pg. 34.

57. Karel van der Toorn, Bob Becking, Pieter W. van der Horst, *Dictionary of Deities and Demons in the Bible, Second Edition*, Wm. B. Eerdmans Publishing Company; Revised 2nd edition (May 30, 1999), pg. 316.

58. *Strong's Concordance with Hebrew and Greek Lexicon.* EliYah, No Date. Web. Word #H7843 "SHACHATH" used 147x in Old Testament Text, KJV-1611. The KJV translates Strong's H7843 in the following manner: destroy (96x), corrupt (22x), mar (7x), destroyer (3x), corrupters (2x), waster (2x), spoilers (2x), battered (1x), corruptly (1x), misc (11x). <http://www.eliyah.com/lexicon.html>.

59. *Strong's Concordance with Hebrew and Greek Lexicon.* EliYah, No Date. Web. Word #H1320 "BASAR" used 269x in Old Testament Text, KJV-1611. The KJV translates Strong's H1320 in the following manner: flesh (256x), body (2x), fatfleshed (with H1277) (2x), leanfleshed (with H1851) (2x), kin (2x), leanfleshed (with H7534) (1x), mankind (with H376) (1x), myself (1x), nakedness (1x), skin (1x). <http://www.eliyah.com/lexicon.html>.

60. *Strong's Concordance with Hebrew and Greek Lexicon.* EliYah, No Date. Web. Word #H6817 "TSA`AQ" used 55x in Old Testament Text, KJV-1611. The KJV translates Strong's H6817 in the following manner: cry (44x), gather together (4x), cry out (3x), at all (1x), called (1x), gathered (1x), call together (1x). <http://www.eliyah.com/lexicon.html>.

Chapter 4 - We Have A Winner!

1. Goss, Steven. "Part II: Nothing Is New And No One Looks At It," *ARTless*, no date. Web. Retrieved April 23, 2014. <http://www.theapesheet.com/archivefive/newart2.html>

2. All passages from the Book of Jasher referenced are taken from: *The Book of Jasher: Faithfully Translated (1840) from the Original Hebrew into English*. Salt Lake City: J.H. Parry, 1887. Print.

3. *Strong's Concordance with Hebrew and Greek Lexicon*. EliYah, No Date. Web. Word #H8435 "TOWLEDAH" used 39x in Old Testament Text, KJV-1611. The KJV translates Strong's H8435 in the following manner: generations (38x), birth (1x). <http://www.eliyah.com/lexicon.html>.

4. *Strong's Concordance with Hebrew and Greek Lexicon*. EliYah, No Date. Web. Word #H1755 "DOWR" used 167x in Old Testament Text, KJV-1611. The KJV translates Strong's H1755 in the following manner: generation (133x), all (18x), many (6x), misc (10x). <http://www.eliyah.com/lexicon.html>.

5. *Strong's Concordance with Hebrew and Greek Lexicon*. EliYah, No Date. Web. Word #H8549 "TAMIYM" used 91x in Old Testament Text, KJV-1611. The KJV translates Strong's H8549 in the following manner: without blemish (44x), perfect (18x), upright (8x), without spot (6x), uprightly (4x), whole (4x), sincerely (2x), complete (1x), full (1x), misc (3x). <http://www.eliyah.com/lexicon.html>.

6. *Strong's Concordance with Hebrew and Greek Lexicon*. EliYah, No Date. Web. Word #H8552 "TAMAM" used 64x in Old Testament Text, KJV-1611. The KJV translates Strong's H8552 in the following manner: consume (26x), end (9x), finished (4x), clean (3x), upright (3x), spent (3x), perfect (2x), done (2x), failed (2x), accomplish (2x), misc (8x). <http://www.eliyah.com/lexicon.html>.

7. Flavius Josephus, *Antiquities of the Jews*, Book 1, Chapter 6, Paragraph 5. <http://www.biblestudytools.com/history/flavius-josephus/antiquities-jews/>.

8. Johnson, Ken, Th.D. *Ancient Paganism: The Sorcery of the Fallen Angels*. United States: Bibliofacts Ministries, 2009, pgs. 19-20.

9. *Strong's Concordance with Hebrew and Greek Lexicon*. EliYah, No Date. Web. Word #H5799 "AZAZEL" used 4x in Old Testament Text, KJV-1611. The KJV translates Strong's H5799 in the following manner: scapegoat (4x). <http://www.eliyah.com/lexicon.html>.

10. Johnson, Ken, Th.D. *Ancient Messianic Festivals*, United States: Bibliofacts Ministries, 2012, pgs. 97-100.

11. Johnson, Ken, Th.D. *Fallen Angels*, United States: Bibliofacts Ministries, 2013, pgs. 25-26.

12. Johnson, Ken, Th.D. *Ancient Messianic Festivals*, United States: Bibliofacts Ministries, 2012, pgs. 97-100.

13. Wilford, John Noble. "Ideas and Trends: Clues Get Warm in the Search for Planet X," *New York Times*, January 30, 1983, Retrieved May 13, 2014. <http://www.nytimes.com/1983/01/30/weekinreview/ideas-and-trends-clues-get-warm-in-the-search-for-planet-x.html>

14. According to Genesis 5:27, Methuselah was 969 years of age when he died. Whereas we have quoted directly from the J.H. Parry translated version of The Book of Jasher for this reference, we accept the Old Testament documents as the final authority regarding all discrepancies.

Chapter 5 - Lions and Tigers and Bears? Seriously?

1. Buis, Alan, "Chilean Quake May Have Shortened Earth Days," *NASA News*, March 1, 2010. Retrieved May 13, 2014. <http://www.nasa.gov/topics/earth/features/earth-20100301.html>

2. Buis, Alan, "Japan Quake May Have Shortened Earth Days, Moved Axis," *NASA Jet Propulsion Laboratory: California Institute of Technology*, March 14, 2011. Retrieved May 13, 2014. <http://www.jpl.nasa.gov/news/news.php?release=2011-080>

3. Buis, Alan, "Japan Quake May Have Shortened Earth Days, Moved Axis," *NASA News & Features*, March 14, 2011. Retrieved May 13, 2014. <http://www.nasa.gov/topics/earth/features/japanquake/earth20110314.html>

4. Buis, Alan, "Japan Quake May Have Shortened Earth Days, Moved Axis," *NASA Jet Propulsion Laboratory: California Institute of Technology*, March 14, 2011. Retrieved May 13, 2014. <http://www.jpl.nasa.gov/news/news.php?release=2011-080>

5. Haraldur, Sigurdsson, "Mount Vesuvius before the Disaster," In Jashemski, Wilhelmina F., and Frederick G. Meyer. *The natural history of Pompeii*. Cambridge UK: The Press Syndicate of the University of Cambridge. 2002. pp. 29–36

6. Ray, Dewey, "Oregon volcano may be warming up for an eruption," *The Christian Science Monitor*. March 27, 1980. Retrieved May 28, 2014 <http://www.csmonitor.com/1980/0327/032754.html>

7. "Mount St. Helens: Summary," *United States Geological Survey*. February 12, 2013. Retrieved May 26, 2014. <http://volcanoes.usgs.gov/volcanoes/st_helens/>

8. Harris, Stephen L. *Fire Mountains of the West: The Cascade and Mono Lake Volcanoes.* Missoula, MT: Mountain Pub., 1988. Print. pgs 208-209

9. Engelhardt, H. Tristram, and Arthur L. Caplan. *Scientific Controversies: Case Studies in the Resolution and Closure of Disputes in Science and Technology.* Cambridge: Cambridge UP, 1987. Print. pgs 210-211.

10. Glen, William. *The Road to Jaramillo: Critical Years of the Revolution in Earth Science.* Stanford, CA: Stanford UP, 1982. Print. pgs 4-5. AND Runcorn, S. K. "Paleomagnetic comparisons between Europe and North America," *Proceedings of The Geologists Association*. Canada. 1956. pgs 77–85.

11. Carey, S. W. (1958). "The tectonic approach to continental drift" In *Carey, S.W. Continental Drift—A Symposium,* held in March 1956. Hobart: Univ. of Tasmania. pp. 177–363. AND Carey, S. Warren. *The Expanding Earth.* Amsterdam: Elsevier Scientific Pub., 1976. Print. pgs. 311-349.

12. Read, Herbert Harold, and Janet Watson. *Introduction to Geology.* London: Macmillan, 1975. Print. pgs 13–15.

13. Hess, H. H. "History of Ocean Basins". Engel, A. E. J. *Petrologic Studies; a Volume in Honor of A.F. Buddington.* Boulder, CO: Geological Society of America. 1962. Print. pgs. 599–620.

14. Barrell, J. "The Strength of the Earth's Crust." *Journal of Geology* 22.4 (1914): 289-314. Print.

15. Müller, R. Dietmar, and Maria Sdrolias. "Age, Spreading Rates, and Spreading Asymmetry of the World's Ocean Crust." *Geochemistry Geophysics Geosystems* 9.4 (2008): Web. Retrieved June 3, 2014. <http://www.earthbyte.org/people/dietmar/Pdf/Muller_etal_age_rate_asym_G3_2008.pdf>.

16. Turcotte, Donald Lawson., and Gerald Schubert. *Geodynamics. 2nd ed.* Cambridge: Cambridge UP, 2002. Print. pgs 1-21.

17. Ogrisseg, Jeff. "Dogmas May Blinker Mainstream Scientific Thinking." *The Japan Times* [Tokyo] 22 Nov. 2009, Life sec.: Web. Retrieved June 8, 2014. <http://www.japantimes.co.jp/life/2009/11/22/general/dogmas-may-blinker-mainstream-scientific-thinking/#.VFeFePnF98E>

18. NASA/Jet Propulsion Laboratory. "It's a small world, after all: Earth is not expanding, NASA research confirms." *Science Daily.* 17 August 2011. Retrieved June 8, 2014. <www.sciencedaily.com/releases/2011/08/110817120527.htm>.

19. "Expanding Earth." *Wikipedia.* Wikimedia Foundation, (June 2014). Web. Retrieved June 8, 2014. <http://en.wikipedia.org/wiki/Expanding_Earth#Different_forms_of_the_hypothesis>.

20. Carey, S. Warren. *The Expanding Earth.* Amsterdam: Elsevier Scientific Pub., 1976. Print. 448 pp.

21. Carey, S. Warren. *Earth, Universe, Cosmos.* Hobart, Tas.: Geology Dept., U of Tasmania, 1996. Print. pg 131.

22. *Strong's Concordance with Hebrew and Greek Lexicon.* EliYah, No Date. Web. Word #H8414 "TOHUW" used 20x in Old Testament Text, KJV-1611. The KJV translates Strong's H7227 in the following manner: vain (4x), vanity (4x), confusion (3x), without form (2x), wilderness (2x), nought (2x), nothing (1x), empty place (1x), waste (1x). <http://www.eliyah.com/lexicon.html>.

23. *Strong's Concordance with Hebrew and Greek Lexicon.* EliYah, No Date. Web. Word #H922 "BOHUW" used 3x in Old Testament Text, KJV-1611. The KJV translates Strong's H922 in the following manner: void (2x), emptiness (1x). <http://www.eliyah.com/lexicon.html>.

24. *Strong's Concordance with Hebrew and Greek Lexicon*. EliŸah, No Date. Web. Word #H7227 "RAB" used 458x in Old Testament Text, KJV-1611. The KJV translates Strong's H7227 in the following manner: many (190x), great (118x), much (36x), captain (24x), more (12x), long (10x), enough (9x), multitude (7x), mighty (5x), greater (4x), greatly (3x), misc (40x). <http://www.eliyah.com/lexicon.html>.

25. "Giorgio Tsoukalos on Angels." *YouTube*. YouTube, 24 Sept. 2011. Web. 13 June 2014. <http://www.youtube.com/watch?v=SUxGzC2WRss>.

26. "Laws of Thermodynamics." *Wikipedia*. Wikimedia Foundation, 18 June 2014. Web. Retrieved June 18, 2014. <http://en.wikipedia.org/wiki/Laws_of_thermodynamics#First_law>.

27. Lemaître, G. (1927). "Un univers homogène de masse constante et de rayon croissant rendant compte de la vitesse radiale des nébuleuses extragalactiques," *Annals of the Scientific Society of Brussels* 47A: 41.(French) (Translated in: Lemaître, G. (1931). AND "A Homogeneous Universe of Constant Mass and Growing Radius Accounting for the Radial Velocity of Extragalactic Nebulae". *Monthly Notices of the Royal Astronomical Society* 91: 483–490).

28. Livio, M.; Riess, A. (2013). "Measuring the Hubble constant". *Physics Today* 66 (10): 41.

29. Coles, Peter. *The Routledge Critical Dictionary of the New Cosmology*. New York: Routledge, 1999. Print. pg 202.

30. Friedman, A.A. (1922). "Über die Krümmung des Raumes," *Zeitschrift für Physik* 10 (1): 377-386. (German) (English translation in: Friedman, A. (1999). "On the Curvature of Space," *General Relativity and Gravitation* 31 (12): 1991–2000.)

31. *Ibid*. Lemaître, G. (1927).

32. Taylor, J. H.; Weisberg, J. M. (1989). "Further experimental tests of relativistic gravity using the binary pulsar PSR 1913 + 16". *Astrophysical Journal* 345: 434–450.

33. Weisberg, J. M.; Nice, D. J.; Taylor, J. H. (2010). "Timing Measurements of the Relativistic Binary Pulsar PSR B1913+16". *Astrophysical Journal* 722: 1030–1034.

34. Derry, Gregory N. *What Science Is and How It Works*. Princeton, NJ: Princeton UP, 1999. Print. pg 167.

35. Roy, Bimalendu Narayan. *Fundamentals of Classical and Statistical Thermodynamics*. West Sussex, England: John Wiley, 2002. Print. pg 58.

36. <http://www.ngdc.noaa.gov/mgg/image/crustageposter.gif>

37. <http://www.geo.cornell.edu/geology/classes/Geo101/graphics/ocean_crust_age.gif> from Cornell University.

38. "ITIS Hierarchical Report." *ITIS Hierarchical Report*. Updated Sept. 2014. Web. Retrieved Sept. 5, 2014. <http://www.itis.gov/hierarchy.html>.

39. "Animal Classification." - Reference. no publisher. no date. Web. Retrieved Sept. 2 2014. <http://a-z-animals.com/reference/animal-classification/>.

40. "Examples of Arthropods." *YourDictionary*. no publisher. no date. Web. Retrieved Sept. 2 2014. <http://examples.yourdictionary.com/examples/examples-of-arthropods.html>.

41. "Microbiotheria." *Animal Diversity Web*. no publisher. no date. Web. Retrieved Sept. 2 2014. <http://animaldiversity.ummz.umich.edu/accounts/Microbiotheria/>.

42. Brownlee, John. "Infographic: How Dogs Evolved." *Co.Design*. Fast Company, Jan. 17, 2014. Web. Retrieved April 8, 2014. <http://www.fastcodesign.com/3025003/infographic-of-the-day/how-dogs-evolved>.

43. Handwerk, Brian. "House Cat Origin Traced to Middle Eastern Wildcat Ancestor." *National Geographic*. National Geographic Society, June 28, 2007. Web. Retrieved April 8, 2014. <http://news.nationalgeographic.com/news/2007/06/070628-cat-ancestor.html>.

44. Mott, Maryann. "Cats Climb New Family Tree." *National Geographic*. National Geographic Society, Jan. 11, 2006. Web. Retrieved April 8, 2014. <http://news.nationalgeographic.com/news/2006/01/0111_060111_cat_evolution.html>.

45. *Strong's Concordance with Hebrew and Greek Lexicon*. EliYah, No Date. Web. Word #H5437 "CABAB" used 154x in Old Testament Text, KJV-1611. The KJV translates Strong's H7227 in the following manner: (stood, turned, etc...) about (54x), compass (41x), turn (34x), turn away (4x), remove (3x), returned (2x), round (2x), side (2x), turn aside (2x), turn back (2x), beset (2x), driven (2x), compass in (2x), misc (8x). <http://www.eliyah.com/lexicon.html>.

46. Wood, Todd Charles., and Paul A. Garner. *Genesis Kinds: Creationism and the Origin of Species*. Eugene, Or.: Wipf & Stock, 2009. Print. pg 16.

47. "Sacrifice: Quality of Offerings." *Jewish Encyclopedia*, 2011. Web. ¶ 2. Retrieved April 17, 2014. <http://www.jewishencyclopedia.com/articles/12984-sacrifice,%20Sacrifice:%20Qualities%20of%20Offerings>.

48. *Ibid*.

49. Johnson, Ken, Th.D. *Ancient Paganism: The Sorcery of the Fallen Angels*. United States: Bibliofacts Ministries, 2009. Print. pg 30.

Chapter 6 - What's Causin' All This?

1. "USGS FAQs - Faults - Where Are the Fault Lines in the Eastern United States (east of the Rocky Mountains)?" *U.S. Geological Survey*, 15 Oct. 2014. Web. Retrieved Nov. 3, 2014. <http://www.usgs.gov/faq/categories/9838/3399>.

2. Cain, Fraser. "How Mountains Are Formed." *Universe Today*, 23 Apr. 2009. Web. ¶ 2. Retrieved June 24, 2014. <http://www.universetoday.com/29833/how-mountains-are-formed>.

3. Britannica Editors. *Encyclopedia Britannica Online*. Encyclopedia Britannica, 24 Feb. 2011. Web. Retrieved June 24, 2014. <http://www.britannica.com/blogs/2011/02/how-fault-lines-form/>.

4. Meredith, Charlotte. "Preserved Ice Age Mammoth Found with FLOWING BLOOD Boosts Bid to Clone Prehistoric Beast." *Daily Express Tech RSS*. 30 May 2013. Web. Retrieved June 24, 2014. <http://www.express.co.uk/life-style/science-technology/403691/Preserved-Ice-Age-mammoth-found-with-FLOWING-BLOOD-boosts-bid-to-clone-prehistoric-beast>.

5. Larmer, Brook. "Mammoth Tusk Hunters." *National Geographic Magazine*, Apr. 2013. Web. Retrieved June 24, 2014. <http://ngm.nationalgeographic.com/2013/04/125-mammoth-tusks/larmer-text>.

6. *Ibid*. Meredith.

7. Adams, Cecil. "Prehistoric, It's What's for Dinner: Have Explorers Had Feasts of Woolly Mammoth?" *The Straight Dope*. 14 Sept. 2007. Web. Retrieved June 27, 2014. <http://www.straightdope.com/columns/read/2725/prehistoric-its-whats-for-dinner>.

8. Crawford, John Martin, and V. I. Kovalevsky. *The Industries of Russia. Vol. 3*. St. Petersburg: Trenke & Fusnot, Printers, 1898. Print., pg. 53

9. Hellen, Nicholas. "Scientist Finds Frozen Prehistoric 'Zoo' In Siberian Ice." *Sightings*, 5 Mar. 2000. Web. Retrieved July 2, 2014. <http://www.rense.com/ufo6/prehist.htm>.

10. "Last Glacial Maximum." *Wikipedia*. Wikimedia Foundation, June 2014. Web. 03 July 2, 2014. <http://en.wikipedia.org/wiki/Last_Glacial_Maximum#North_America>.

11. Falcon-Lang, Howard. "Secrets of Antarctica's Fossilized Forests." *BBC News: Science & Environment*. Royal Holloway, London, 8 Feb. 2011. Web. Retrieved July 5, 2014. <http://www.bbc.co.uk/news/science-environment-12378934>.

12. Nilsson, Tage. *The Pleistocene: Geology and Life in the Quaternary Ice Age*. Dordrecht, Holland: D. Reidel Pub., 1983. Print., pgs 223–233. AND Stuart, A. J. *On the Tracks of Ice Age Mammals*. Cambridge, MA: Harvard University Press, 1985. Print. pg 24.

13. Stuart, A. J. *Pleistocene Vertebrates in the British Isles*. London: Longman, 1982. Print. pg 52.

14. Pfizenmayer, Eugen Wilhelm, and Muriel D. Simpson. *Siberian Man and Mammoth*. London: Blackie & Son, 1939. Print. pgs 46–61.

15. "List of Deserts by Area." *Wikipedia*. Wikimedia Foundation, July 2014. Web. Retrieved July 17, 2014. <http://en.wikipedia.org/wiki/List_of_deserts_by_area>.

16. Cain, Fraser. "What Percent of Earth Is Water?" *Universe Today*, 31 May 2010. Web. Retrieved July 15, 2014. <http://www.universetoday.com/65588/what-percent-of-earth-is-water/>.

17. "What Is a Desert?" *U.S. Geological Survey*, 18 Dec. 2001. Web. Retrieved July 15, 2014. <http://pubs.usgs.gov/gip/deserts/what/>.

18. "Chicxulub." *University of New Brunswick*, no date. Web. Retrieved July 17, 2014. <http://www.passc.net/EarthImpactDatabase/chicxulub.html>.

19. Hildebrand, Alan R.; Penfield, Glen T.; Kring, David A.; Pilkington, Mark; Zanoguera, Antonio Camargo; Jacobsen, Stein B.; Boynton, William V. (September 1991). "Chicxulub Crater; a possible Cretaceous/Tertiary boundary impact crater on the Yucatan Peninsula, Mexico." *Geology* 19 (9): 867–871. Retrieved July 14, 2014. <http://geology.geoscienceworld.org/content/19/9/867.abstract>

20. "List of Impact Craters on Earth." *Wikipedia*. Wikimedia Foundation, 11 Feb. 2014. Web. Retrieved July 14, 2014. <http://en.wikipedia.org/wiki/List_of_impact_craters_on_Earth>.

21. Barringer, J.P. "J. P. Barringer's Acceptance Speech." *Meteoritics*, volume 28, page 9 (1993). SAO/NASA Astrophysics Data System (ADS). Retrieved July 15, 2014. <http://articles.adsabs.harvard.edu//full/1993Metic..28....9B/0000009.000.html>.

22. "The History of the Crater." *Barringer Crater Company*, no date. Web. Retrieved July 15, 2014. <http://www.barringercrater.com/about/>.

23. "List of Impact Craters on Earth." *Wikipedia*. Wikimedia Foundation, 11 Feb. 2014. Web. Retrieved July 14, 2014. <http://en.wikipedia.org/wiki/List_of_impact_craters_on_Earth>.

24. *Ibid.*

25. Pfeiffer, Eric. "Ancient Meteorite Standing Between One Iowa Town and Its Water Supply." *Yahoo! News*. Yahoo!, 17 Feb. 2012. Web. Retrieved July 15, 2014. <http://news.yahoo.com/blogs/sideshow/ancient-meteor-standing-between-one-iowa-town-water-154639667.html>.

26. "List of Impact Craters on Earth." *Wikipedia*. Wikimedia Foundation, 11 Feb. 2014. Web. Retrieved July 14, 2014. <http://en.wikipedia.org/wiki/List_of_impact_craters_on_Earth>.

27. Atkinson, Nancy. "Impressive Craters on Earth." *Universe Today*, 10 Nov. 2008. Web. Retrieved July 16, 2014. <http://www.universetoday.com/19616/earths-10-most-impressive-impact-craters/>.

28. Farinella, P., L. Foschini, Ch. Froeschlé, R. Gonczi, T. J. Jopek, G. Longo, and P. Michel. "Probable Asteroidal Origin of the Tunguska Cosmic Body." *Astronomy & Astrophysics* 377 (17 July 2001): 1081-097. Web. Retrieved July 15, 2014. <http://www-th.bo.infn.it/tunguska/aah2886.pdf>.

29. Lyne, J. E., and Michael Tauber. "The Tunguska Event." no publisher, no date. Web. Retrieved July 15, 2014. <http://web.utk.edu/~comet/papers/nature/TUNGUSKA.html>.

30. Shoemaker, Eugene M. "Asteroid and Comet Bombardment of the Earth." *Annual Review of Earth and Planetary Sciences* 11.1 (1983): 461-94. Web. Retrieved July 17, 2014. <http://www.annualreviews.org/doi/abs/10.1146/annurev.ea.11.050183.002333>.

31. Longo, Giuseppe. "The Tunguska event." Found in Bobrowsky, Peter T., and H. Rickman. *Comet/asteroid Impacts and Human Society: An Interdisciplinary Approach*. Berlin: Springer, 2007. Print. pgs 303–330.

32. *Ibid.*

33. Popova, Olga P.; Jenniskens, Peter; Emel'yanenko, Vacheslav; et al. (2013). "Chelyabinsk Airburst, Damage Assessment, Meteorite Recovery, and Characterization." *Science* 342 (6162): 1069–1073. doi:10.1126/science.1242642. Archived from the original on 2014-01-25. Retrieved July 17, 2014. <http://cams.seti.org/Popova2013-ms.pdf>.

34. *Ibid.*

35. Schiermeier, Quirin. "Risk of Massive Asteroid Strike Underestimated." *Nature.com*. Nature Publishing Group, 6 Nov. 2013. Web. Retrieved July 17, 2014. <http://www.nature.com/news/risk-of-massive-asteroid-strike-underestimated-1.14114>.

36. McClure, Bruce, and Deborah Byrd. "EarthSky's Meteor Shower Guide for 2014 | EarthSky.org." *EarthSky*. no date. Web. Retrieved July 18, 2014. <http://earthsky.org/astronomy-essentials/earthskys-meteor-shower-guide>.

37. Steigerwald, William A. "Polar Spacecraft Images Support Theory of Interplanetary Snowballs Spraying Earth's Upper Atmosphere." *NASA*. Greenbelt, MD, 28 May 1997. NASA news release 97-112. Web. Retrieved July 18, 2014. <http://www.nasa.gov/home/hqnews/1997/97-112.txt>.

38. "Electromagnetic Spectrum." *NASA's Imagine The Universe!* NASA. Goddard Space Flight Center, 19 Feb. 2014. Web. Retrieved July 19, 2014. <http://imagine.gsfc.nasa.gov/docs/science/know_l1/emspectrum.html>.

39. Leger, Marc. "Why the Sun Can Harm You and WiFi Can't (and How Microwave Ovens Cook Your Food)." *Atoms and Numbers*. no publisher. 24 June 2013. Web. Retrieved July 19, 2014. <http://www.atomsandnumbers.com/2013/why-the-sun-can-harm-you-and-wifi-cant-and-how-microwave-ovens-cook-your-food/>.

40. "Resources for You (Radiation-Emitting Products)." *Microwave Oven Radiation. U.S. Department of Health and Human Services*, no date. Web. Retrieved July 19, 2014. <http://www.fda.gov/radiation-emittingproducts/resourcesforyouradiationemittingproducts/ucm252762.htm>.

41. "Introduction to Solar Energy." *Passive Solar Heating & Cooling Manual*. Rodale Press, Inc., 1980. Web. Retrieved July 20, 2014. <http://www.azsolarcenter.org/tech-science/solar-architecture/passive-solar-design-manual/passive-solar-design-manual-intro.html>.

42. "How Night Vision Works." *YouTube*. American Technologies Network, 24 Mar. 2010. Web. Retrieved July 21, 2014. <https://www.youtube.com/watch?v=yw1ByhaSvHo>.

43. *Ibid.* "Introduction to Solar Energy."

44. Fu, Qiang. Prentice-Hall. *RADIATION (SOLAR)* pg 1859. Elsevier Science Ltd., University of Washington, Seattle, WA., 2003. Web. Retrieved July 20, 2014. <http://curry.eas.gatech.edu/Courses/6140/ency/Chapter3/Ency_Atmos/Radiation_Solar.pdf>.

45. "UV Radiation." *U.S. Environmental Protection Agency*, June 2010. Web. Retrieved July 20, 2014. <http://www.epa.gov/sunwise/doc/uvradiation.html>.

46. "Solar Spectral Irradiance: Air Mass 1.5." *Solar Spectral Irradiance: Air Mass 1.5*. American Society for Testing and Materials (ASTM), no date. Web. Retrieved July 20, 2014. <http://rredc.nrel.gov/solar/spectra/am1.5/>.

47. "Health Effects of UV Radiation." *U.S. Environmental Protection Agency*, 16 Mar. 2014. Web. Retrieved July 23, 2014. <http://www2.epa.gov/sunwise/health-effects-uv-radiation>.

48. Attwood, David T. *Soft X-rays and Extreme Ultraviolet Radiation: Principles and Applications*. Cambridge: Cambridge UP, 2000. Print. pg 2.

49. "X-ray: Properties." *Wikipedia*. Wikimedia Foundation, no date. Web. Retrieved July 23, 2014. <http://en.wikipedia.org/wiki/X-ray#Properties>.

50. "X-ray: Adverse Effects." *Wikipedia*. Wikimedia Foundation, no date. Web. Retrieved July 23, 2014. <http://en.wikipedia.org/wiki/X-ray#Adverse_effects>.

51. Hodgman, Charles D., ed. *CRC Handbook of Chemistry and Physics, 44th Edition*. USA: Chemical Rubber Company, 1961. Print. pg 2850.

52. "Gamma-rays." *NASA*, 27 Mar. 2007. Web. Retrieved July 23, 2014. <http://science.hq.nasa.gov/kids/imagers/ems/gamma.html>.

53. Villanueva, John Carl. "Radiation from the Sun." *Universe Today*, 19 Mar. 2010. Web. Retrieved July 24, 2014. <http://www.universetoday.com/60065/radiation-from-the-sun/>.

54. Moskalenko, Igor, Tory Porter, and Seth Digel. "Gamma Rays from the Sun: A New Way for Looking at the Solar System." *SLAC Today*, 31 Oct. 2006. Web. Retrieved July 23, 2014. <http://today.slac.stanford.edu/feature/gammaraysfromthesun.asp>.

55. Mills, John P., Ph.D. "Radiation." *About.com*, no date. Web. Retrieved July 24, 2014. <http://space.about.com/od/astronomydictionary/g/Radiation.htm>.

56. "Ultraviolet Radiation." *National Science Foundation Polar Programs UV Monitoring Network*, Biospherical Instruments Inc., no date. Web. Retrieved July 25, 2014. <http://uv.biospherical.com/student/page3.html>.

57. "A Time-Lapse Map of Every Nuclear Explosion Since 1945 - by Isao Hashimoto." *YouTube*. A Concerned Human, 24 Oct. 2010. Web. Retrieved July 25, 2014. <http://www.youtube.com/watch?v=LLCF7vPanrY>.

58. *Strong's Concordance with Hebrew and Greek Lexicon*. EliYah, No Date. Web. Word #H7673 "SHABATH" used 71x in Old Testament Text, KJV-1611. The KJV translates Strong's H7673 in the following manner: cease (47x), rest (11x), away (3x), fail (2x), celebrate (1x), misc (7x). <http://www.eliyah.com/lexicon.html>.

59. *Strong's Concordance with Hebrew and Greek Lexicon*. EliYah, No Date. Web. Word #H2896 "TOWB" used 559x in Old Testament Text, KJV-1611. The KJV translates Strong's H2896 in the following manner: good (361x), better (72x), well (20x), goodness (16x), goodly (9x), best (8x), merry (7x), fair (7x), prosperity (6x), precious (4x), fine (3x), wealth (3x), beautiful (2x), fairer (2x), favour (2x), glad (2x), misc (35x). <http://www.eliyah.com/lexicon.html>.

60. *Strong's Concordance with Hebrew and Greek Lexicon*. EliYah, No Date. Web. Word #H8318 "SHERETS" used 15x in Old Testament Text, KJV-1611. The KJV translates Strong's H8318 in the following manner: creeping thing (11x), creep (2x), creature (1x), move (1x). <http://www.eliyah.com/lexicon.html>.

61. *Strong's Concordance with Hebrew and Greek Lexicon*. EliYah, No Date. Web. Word #H5315 "NEPHESH" used 753x in Old Testament Text, KJV-1611. The KJV translates Strong's H5315 in the following manner: soul (475x), life (117x), person (29x), mind (15x), heart (15x), creature (9x), body (8x), himself (8x), yourselves (6x), dead (5x), will (4x), desire (4x), man (3x), themselves (3x), any (3x), appetite (2x), misc (47x). <http://www.eliyah.com/lexicon.html>.

62. Lindelof, Damon, and Carlton Cuse. "Transcript: Season 5, Episode 6, '316'" *LOSTPEDIA: The LOST Encyclopedia*. No Posting Date. Web. Retrieved June 24, 2014. <http://lostpedia.wikia.com/wiki/316_transcript>.

Chapter 7 - A Visit to the Clue Store

1. *Strong's Concordance with Hebrew and Greek Lexicon.* EliYah, No Date. Web. Word #H8064 "SHAMAYIM" used 420x in Old Testament Text, KJV-1611. The KJV translates Strong's H8064 in the following manner: heaven (398x), air (21x), astrologers (with H1895) (1x). <http://www.eliyah.com/lexicon.html>.

2. "How Big Is Earth?" *Space.com.* Ed. Tim Sharp. 17 Sept. 2012. Web. Retrieved July 26, 2014. <http://www.space.com/17638-how-big-is-earth.html>.

3. Cain, Fraser. "Circumference of the Earth." *Universe Today.* 2 Mar. 2009. Web. Retrieved July 26, 2014. <http://www.universetoday. com/26461/circumference-of-the-earth/>.

4. Rosenberg, Matt. "Basic Earth Facts: 22 Essential Facts You Need to Know About The Planet Earth." *About.com.* no date. Web. Retrieved July 26, 2014. <http://geography.about.com/od/learnabouttheearth/a/earthfacts.htm>.

5. "How Much Water Is in the Ocean?" *National Ocean Service*, NOAA, no date. Web. Retrieved July 26, 2014. <http://oceanservice.noaa.gov/facts/occanwater.html>.

6. *Ibid.*

7. Oskin, Becky. "Mariana Trench: The Deepest Depths." *LiveScience.* TechMedia Network, Entry updated 08 Oct. 2014. Web. Originally Retrieved July 26, 2014. Update confirmed Nov. 5, 2014. <http://www.livescience.com/23387-mariana-trench.html>.

8. Harder, Ben. "Inner Earth May Hold More Water Than the Seas." *National Geographic News.* National Geographic Society, 7 Mar. 2002. Web. Retrieved July 27, 2014. <http://news.nationalgeographic.com/news/2002/03/0307_0307_waterworld.html>.

9. Than, Ker. "Why Giant Bugs Once Roamed the Earth." *National Geographic News.* National Geographic Society, 08 Aug. 2011. Web. Retrieved July 28, 2014. <http://news.nationalgeographic.com/news/2011/08/110808-ancient-insects-bugs-giants-oxygen-animals-science/>.

10. Ortlieb, Edward P., and Richard Cadice. *Fossils & Prehistoric Life: Grades 5-9.* Milliken Publishing Company, 1986. Print, pg iv. <http://www.amazon.com/gp/product/1558630902/ref=ox_sc_act_title_1?ie=UTF8&psc=1&smid=ATVPDKIKXODER>.

11. "ESA's Magnetic Field Mission Swarm." *European Space Agency.* no date. Web. Retrieved July 29, 2014. <http://www.esa.int/Our_Activities/Observing_the_Earth/The_Living_Planet_Programme/Earth_Explorers/Swarm/ESA_s_magnetic_field_mission_Swarm>.

12. Hall, J. M., and P. T. Robinson. "Deep Crustal Drilling in the North Atlantic Ocean." *Science* 204.4393 (11 May 1979): 573-586. Web. Retrieved July 28, 2014. <http://www.sciencemag.org/content/204/4393/573.short>.

13. Wickham, Chris. "Lost in Migration: Earth's Magnetic Field Overdue a Flip." *Reuters*. Thomson Reuters, 03 Oct. 2012. Web. Retrieved July 29, 2014. <http://www.reuters.com/article/2012/10/03/us-science-earth-magneticfield-idUSBRE8920X620121003>.

14. Vail, Isaac N. *The Waters above the Firmament*. Santa Barbara, CA: Stonehenge Viewpoint, 1987. Print. 174 pgs. <http://www.amazon.com/WATERS-ABOVE-FIRMAMENT-Isaac-Vail/dp/B001BFKS1Y/ref=sr_1_1?ie=UTF8&qid=1415194818&sr=8-1&keywords=B001BFKS1Y>

15. Baugh, Carl E., "Crystalline Canopy Theory." *Creation Evidence Museum of Texas Online*, no date. Web. Retrieved July 30, 2014. <http://184.154.224.5/~creatio1/index.php?option=com_content&task=view&id=74>.

16. Brown, Walter T. *In the Beginning: Compelling Evidence for Creation and the Flood, 8th ed*. Phoenix, AZ: Center for Scientific Creation, 2008. Print. pgs 362-370.

17. Flavius Josephus, *Antiquities of the Jews*, Book 1, Chapter 1, Paragraph 1. <http://www.biblestudytools.com/history/flavius-josephus/antiquities-jews/>.

18. Flavius Josephus, *Antiquities of the Jews*, Book 1, Chapter 2, Paragraph 3. <http://www.biblestudytools.com/history/flavius-josephus/antiquities-jews/>.

19. Scofield, C.I. Ed. *The Scofield Reference Bible: Authorized Version*. New York: For Oxford UP, American Branch, 1909. Print. pg 1317.

20. "Kuiper Belt & Oort Cloud: Read More." *Solar System Exploration*. NASA, no date. Web. Retrieved July 30, 2014. <http://solarsystem.nasa.gov/planets/profile.cfm?Object=KBOs&Display=OverviewLong>.

21. Delft University of Technology. "New Insights Into Origin Of Earth's Magnetic Field." *ScienceDaily*, 10 March 2007. Retrieved July 30, 2014. <www.sciencedaily.com/releases/2007/03/070309103129.htm>.

22. Barnes, T. G. "Decay of the Earth's Magnetic Moment and the Geochronological Implications," *Creation Research Society Quarterly* 8 (June 1971) pgs 24-29. Retrieved July 30, 2014.

23. Humphreys DR, "The Creation of the Earth's Magnetic Field," *Creation Research Society Quarterly*, 20(2): pgs 89-94. Creation Research Society, Sept. 1983. Retrieved July 30, 2014.

24. Humphreys, D. Russell, Ph.D. "The Creation of Planetary Magnetic Fields." *Creation Research Society Quarterly*, 21(3). Creation Research Society, Dec. 1984. Web. Retrieved July 30, 2014. <http://www.creationresearch.org/crsq/articles/21/21_3/21_3.html>

25. University of British Columbia. "Magnetic Fingerprint of Our Galaxy Revealed." *ScienceDaily*, May 6, 2014, Retrieved July 30, 2014. <www.sciencedaily.com/releases/2014/05/140506120240.htm>.

26. Bergman, Jennifer. "History of Observation of Noctilucent Clouds." *Windows to the Universe*. National Earth Science Teachers Association, 17 Aug. 2004. Web. 05 Nov. 2014. Retrieved August 2, 2014. <http://www.windows2universe.org/earth/Atmosphere/NLC_history.html>.

27. "Noctilucent Clouds." *University of Albany*. no date. Web. Retrieved August 2, 2014. <http://www.albany.edu/faculty/rgk/atm101/nlc.htm>.

28. Gadsden, Michael, and Pekka Parviainen. *OBSERVING NOCTILUCENT CLOUDS* (2006): 39 pages. The International Association Of Geomagnetism & Aeronomy. Web. Retrieved August 2, 2014. <http://www.iugg.org/IAGA/iaga_pages/pdf/ONC_Sep06.pdf>.

29. Militzer, Burkhard, and Hugh F. Wilson. "New Phases of Water Ice Predicted at Megabar Pressures." *Physical Review Letters* 195701st ser. 105.19 (2010): 4 pgs. The American Physical Society, 2 Nov. 2010. Web. Retrieved August 2, 2014. <http://arxiv.org/pdf/1009.4722.pdf>.

30. McMahon, Jeffery M. "Ground-State Structures of Ice at High-Pressures." *Physical Review B* 220104(R) 84.22 (2010): 10 pgs. The American Physical Society, 13 Dec. 2011. Web. Retrieved August 2, 2014. <http://arxiv.org/pdf/1106.1941.pdf>.

31. Coffey, Jerry. "How Old Is the Solar System?" *Universe Today*. 16 July 2008. Web. Retrieved August 3, 2014. <http://www.universetoday.com/15575/how-old-is-the-solar-system/>.

32. Cain, Fraser. "Interesting Facts About Mercury." *Universe Today*. 29 Apr. 2008. Web. Retrieved August 3, 2014. <http://www.universetoday.com/13944/interesting-facts-about-mercury/>.

33. "Mercury." *Solar System Exploration*. NASA, no date. Web. Retrieved August 3, 2014. <http://solarsystem.nasa.gov/faq/index.cfm?Category=Mercury>.

34. Cain, Fraser. "Interesting Facts About Venus." *Universe Today*, 5 May 2008. Web. Retrieved August 3, 2014. <http://www.universetoday.com/14070/interesting-facts-about-venus/>.

35. "Venus: FAQ." *Solar System Exploration*. NASA, no date. Web. Retrieved August 3, 2014. <http://solarsystem.nasa.gov/planets/profile.cfm?Object=Venus&Display=FAQ>.

36. Strom, Robert G., Gerald G. Schaber, and Douglas D. Dawson. "The Global Resurfacing of Venus." *Journal of Geophysical Research* 99.E5 (1994): pgs 10899-10926. 25 May 1994. Web. Retrieved August 3, 2014. <http://www.astro.queensu.ca/~tjb/het618/nathan/94JE00388.pdf>

37. "Earth's Moon: Overview." *Solar System Exploration.* NASA, no date. Web. Retrieved August 3, 2014. <http://solarsystem.nasa.gov/planets/profile.cfm?Object=Moon>.

38. Cain, Fraser. "Interesting Facts about the Moon." *Universe Today*, 24 Oct. 2008. Web. Retrieved August 3, 2014. <http://www.universetoday.com/20050/10-interesting-facts-about-the-moon/>.

39. "Mars: Overview." *Solar System Exploration.* NASA, no date. Web. Retrieved August 3, 2014. <http://solarsystem.nasa.gov/planets/profile.cfm?Object=Mars>.

40. Cain, Fraser. "Interesting Facts About Planet Mars." *Universe Today*, 5 June 2008. Web. Retrieved August 3, 2014. <http://www.universetoday.com/14853/interesting-facts-about-planet-mars/>.

41. "Twelve Observations of Mars." *Kepler's Discovery*, 2007. Web. Retrieved August 3, 2014. <http://www.keplersdiscovery.com/CorrectedTable.html>.

42. Coffey, Jerry. "Asteroid Belt." *Universe Today*, 18 June 2009. Web. Retrieved August 5, 2014. <http://www.universetoday.com/32856/asteroid-belt/#ixzz2xLqBkIFa>.

43. "Trojan Asteroids." *Cosmos, The SAO Encyclopedia of Astronomy.* Swinburne University of Technology, no date. Web. Retrieved August 5, 2014. <http://astronomy.swin.edu.au/cosmos/T/Trojan+Asteroids>.

44. Romanishin, William, Ph.D. "Hildas and Trojans - Dancing with Jupiter." *Wm. Romanishin, Ph.D.*, no date. Web. Retrieved August 6, 2014. <http://hildaandtrojanasteroids.net/>.

45. Bate, Roger, Donald D. Mueller, and Jerry E. White. *Fundamentals of Astrodynamics.* New York: Dover Publications, 1971. Print. pg 385.

46. Moulton, Forest Ray. *An Introduction to Celestial Mechanics ... Second Revised Edition.* Ch. 9. Macmillan Co.: New York: Macmillan &: London, 1914. Print.

47. Armagnac, Alan P. "How They Trailed a New Planet." *Popular Science Monthly* (June 1930): 27-28+123-125. Found in Modern Mechanix: Yesterday's Tomorrow Today. Web. Retrieved August 7, 2014. <http://blog.modernmechanix.com/how-they-trailed-a-new-planet/>.

48. *Ibid.* pg. 123.

49. *Ibid.* pg. 28.

50. Cain, Fraser. "Why Pluto Is No Longer a Planet." *Universe Today*, 5 Jan. 2012. Web. Retrieved August 7, 2014. <http://www.universetoday.com/13573/why-pluto-is-no-longer-a-planet/>.

51. Wilford, John Noble. "CLUES GET WARM IN THE SEARCH FOR PLANET X." *The New York Times: Ideas and Trends*, 30 Jan. 1983. Web. August 8, 2014. <http://www.nytimes.com/1983/01/30/weekinreview/ideas-and-trends-clues-get-warm-in-the-search-for-planet-x.html>.

52. Fisher, Arthur. "Tenth Planet Found?" *Popular Science Monthly* (July 1972): 42. Web. Retrieved August 8, 2014. <http://books.google. com/books?id=WZ6okH8FCs4C&pg=PA42&lpg=PA42&dq=Science Newsfront: Tenth Planet Found?&Source=bl&ots=khjbiKHsje&sig=UNGSyU1MMI5N92ksRrheM dVVTL4&hl=en&sa=x&ei=K2FbVNSo A8LIsASiqlK4Aw&ved=0CCAQ6AEwAA#v=onepage&q=Science Newsfront: Tenth Planet Found?&f=false>.

53. "The Outer Planets: Missions: Pioneer 10 & 11." *LASP: University of Colorado at Boulder*, 2007. Web. Retrieved August 9, 2014. <http:// lasp.colorado.edu/education/outerplanets/missions_pioneers.php>.

54. *Ibid.*

55. "Voyager: The Interstellar Mission." *NASA, Jet Propulsion Laboratory, California Institute of Technology*, no date. Web. Retrieved August 9, 2014. <http://voyager.jpl.nasa.gov/mission/fastfacts.html>.

56. O'Tool, Thomas. "Possibly as Large as Jupiter: Mystery Heavenly Body Discovered." *The Washington Post* [Washington, DC] 30 Dec. 1983, First ed., sec. A: 1A, con't on 14A. Print. Retrieved Dec. 11, 2014. <http://planet-x.150m.com/washpost.html>.

57. O'Neill, Ian. "2012: No Planet X." *Universe Today*. 25 May 2008. Web. Retrieved Dec. 11, 2014. <http://www.universetoday. com/14486/2012-no-planet-x/>.

Chapter 8 - The End Of All Flesh

1. *Strong's Concordance with Hebrew and Greek Lexicon*. EliYah, No Date. Web. Word #G1411 "DYNAMIS" used 120x in New Testament Text, KJV-1611. The KJV translates Strong's G1411 in the following manner: power (77x), mighty work (11x), strength (7x), miracle (7x), might (4x), virtue (3x), mighty (2x), misc (9x). <http://www.eliyah.com/ lexicon.html>.

2. *Strong's Concordance with Hebrew and Greek Lexicon*. EliYah, No Date. Web. Word #G4531 "SALEUŌ" used 15x in New Testament Text, KJV-1611. The KJV translates Strong's G4531 in the following manner: shake (10x), move (1x), shake together (1x), that are shaken (1x), which cannot be shaken (with G3361) (1x), stir up (1x). <http://www. eliyah.com/lexicon.html>.

3. Bobrowsky, Peter T., and Hans Rickman. "Chapter 2: The Archaeology and Anthropology of Quaternary Period Cosmic Impact, by W. Bruce Masse." Found in: *Comet/asteroid Impacts and Human Society: An Interdisciplinary Approach*. Berlin: Springer, 2007. 50-51. Print.

4. "Tour of St. Francis of Assisi Church." *St. Francis of Assisi Catholic Parish*, Staunton, Virginia, 26 July 2014. Web. August 11, 2014. <http://stfrancisparish.org/tour5.html>.

5. *Strong's Concordance with Hebrew and Greek Lexicon*. EliYah, No Date. Web. Word #G3173 "MEGAS" used 195x in New Testament Text, KJV-1611. The KJV translates Strong's G3173 in the following manner: great (150x), loud (33x), misc (12x). <http://www.eliyah.com/lexicon.html>.

6. "Earth and Moon Angular Sizes." no date. 2 pgs. *Space Math*. NASA. Goddard Space Flight Center. Web. Retrieved August 13, 2014. <http://stardustnext.jpl.nasa.gov/education/pdfs/Deep3.pdf>.

7. Rogers, John H. "Origins of the Ancient Constellations: I. The Mesopotamian Traditions." *Journal of the British Astronomical Association* 108.1 (Feb. 1998): 9-28. Web. Retrieved August 13, 2014. <http://adsabs.harvard.edu/full/1998JBAA..108....9R>.

8. Soderman/NLSI Staff. "The Draconid Meteor Shower." *Solar System Exploration Research Virtual Institute*. SSERVI, no date. Web. Retrieved August 15, 2014. <http://sservi.nasa.gov/articles/draconid-meteor-shower>.

9. Phillips, Graham. *The End of Eden: The Comet That Changed Civilization*. Rochester, VT: Bear, 2007. Print. pg. 158.

10. de Rachewiltz, Boris. *An Introduction to Egyptian Art*. London: Spring, 1960. Print. pgs 56-59.

11. *Ibid*. Phillips, pg. 159.

12. *Ibid*. Phillips, pg. 157.

13. Chuanxin, Xiong, "The Number 2 and Number 3 Han Tombs at Mawangdui," *Changsha, Volume 1*, Beijing: Cultural Relics Publishing House, 2004, pgs. 106-123.

14. *Ibid*. Phillips, pg. 158.

15. *Ibid*. Phillips, mid-book images.

16. *Ibid*. Phillips, pgs. 170-186.

17. *Ibid*. de Rachewiltz, pgs 56-59.

18. *Ibid*. Phillips, pg. 160.

19. Mobberley, Martin. *Hunting and Imaging Comets*. New York, NY: Springer, 2011. Print. The Patrick Moore Practical Astronomy Series. pg 44.

20. Keay, Colin. "Explanation of Auroral Sounds." *IPS: Radio and Space Weather Services*. Australian Government Bureau of Meteorology, 2014. Web. Retrieved August 18, 2014. <http://www.ips.gov.au/Educational/1/1/2>.

21. Cain, Fraser. "Interesting Facts About Saturn." *Universe Today*, 10 June 2013. Web. Retrieved August 18, 2014. <http://www.universetoday.com/15418/interesting-facts-about-saturn/>.

22. Nave, R. "Buoyancy." *HyperPhysics*. Georgia State University, 23 July 2007. Web. Retrieved August 19, 2014. <http://hyperphysics.phy-astr.gsu.edu/Hbase/pbuoy.html>.

23. "Inverse Square Law." *The Physics Classroom*, 2014. Web. Retrieved Sept. 23, 2014. <http://www.physicsclassroom.com/class/estatics/Lesson-3/Inverse-Square-Law>.

24. "Crab Nebula Exploded in 1054." *Astronomy Magazine*, 8 June 2007. Web. Retrieved August 21, 2014. <http://www.astronomy.com/news-observing/news/2007/06/crab%20nebula%20exploded%20in%201054>.

25. Breen, A., and D. McCarthy. "A Re-evaluation of the Eastern and Western Records of the Supernova of 1054." *Vistas in Astronomy* 39.3 (1995): 363-79. Web. Retrieved August 21, 2014. <http://www.sciencedirect.com/science/article/pii/0083665695966199S>.

26. Livingston, David, Th.D. "The Date of Noah's Flood: Literary and Archaeological Evidence." *David Livingston*, 2003. Web. Retrieved August 21, 2014. <http://davelivingston.com/flooddate.htm>.

27. Austin, Steven A., Gordon W. Franz, and Eric G. Frost. "Amos's Earthquake: An Extraordinary Middle East Seismic Event of 750 B.C." *International Geology Review* 42.7 (2000): 657-71. Web. Retrieved August 21, 2014. <http://www.tandfonline.com/doi/abs/10.1080/00206810009465104?journalCode=tigr20#.VFu-T_nF98E>.

28. Rawlinson, Henry Creswicke. "The Assyrian Canon Verified by the Record of a Solar Eclipse, B.C. 763." *The Athenaeum: Journal of Literature, Science and the Fine Arts* 2064 (May 1867): 660-61. Web. Retrieved August 21, 2014. <http://pages.rediff.com/assyrian-eclipse/1620147>.

29. "Phlegon." *Never Thirsty*. Like The Master Ministries, n.d. Web. 06 Nov. 2014. Retrieved August 21, 2014. <http://www.neverthirsty.org/pp/historical-secular-quotes-about-jesus/phlegon.html>.

30. Van Voorst, Robert E. *Jesus Outside the New Testament: An Introduction to the Ancient Evidence*. Grand Rapids, MI: W.B. Eerdmans Pub., 2000. Print.. pp 19–20

31. Buis, Alan, "Japan Quake May Have Shortened Earth Days, Moved Axis," *NASA Jet Propulsion Laboratory: California Institute of Technology*, March 14, 2011. Retrieved May 13, 2014. <http://www.jpl.nasa.gov/news/news.php?release=2011-080>

32. Weiss, Nigel. "Dynamos in Planets, Stars and Galaxies." *Astronomy and Geophysics* 43.3 (2002): 3.09-.15. Web. Retrieved August 22, 2014. <http://astrogeo.oxfordjournals.org/content/43/3/3.9.full>.

33. Redd, Nola Taylor. "Valles Marineris: Facts About the Grand Canyon of Mars." *Space.com*, 29 Mar. 2013. Web. Retrieved August 23, 2014. <http://www.space.com/20446-valles-marineris.html>.

34. *Ibid*. Redd.

35. Thornhill, Wal. "Mars and the Grand Canyon." *The Electric Universe*. Holoscience.com, 24 Oct. 2001. Web. Retrieved August 23, 2014. <http://www.holoscience.com/wp/mars-and-the-grand-canyon/>.

36. Coffey, Jerry. "Earth's Orbit Around The Sun." *Universe Today*, 30 Mar. 2010. Web. Retrieved August 24, 2014. <http://www.universetoday.com/61202/earths-orbit-around-the-sun/>.

37. Cain, Fraser. "How Fast Does the Earth Rotate?" *Universe Today*, 20 May 2013. Web. Retrieved August 24, 2014. <http://www.universetoday.com/26623/how-fast-does-the-earth-rotate/>.

38. Clark, John Owen Edward. *The Essential Dictionary of Science*. New York: Barnes & Noble, 2004. Print.

Chapter 9 - When The Dust Settles, It's Underwater

1. *Strong's Concordance with Hebrew and Greek Lexicon*. EliYah, No Date. Web. Word #H1368 "GIBBOWR" used 158x in Old Testament Text, KJV-1611. The KJV translates Strong's H1368 in the following manner: mighty (63x), mighty man (68x), strong (4x), valiant (3x), ... ones (4x), mighties (2x), man (2x), valiant men (2x), strong man (1x), upright man (1x), champion (1x), chief (1x), excel (1x), giant (1x), men's (1x), mightiest (1x), strongest (1x). <http://www.eliyah.com/lexicon.html>.

2. *Strong's Concordance with Hebrew and Greek Lexicon*. EliYah, No Date. Web. Word #H1396 "GABAR" used 25x in Old Testament Text, KJV-1611. The KJV translates Strong's H1396 in the following manner: prevail (14x), strengthen (3x), great (2x), confirm (1x), exceeded (1x), mighty (1x), put (1x), stronger (1x), valiant (1x). <http://www.eliyah.com/lexicon.html>.

3. Various online resources provide this information. None permit exact reproduction of the data. Search Term: Average Draft of Cargo Ship.

4. Most often referred to as Jacob, his name was officially changed to Israel by the angelic being with whom he wrestles in Genesis 32:28. This name change is also referenced in Chapter 3 of this book.

5. *Strong's Concordance with Hebrew and Greek Lexicon*. EliYah, No Date. Web. Word #H5674 "`ABAR" used 559x in Old Testament Text, KJV-1611. The KJV translates Strong's H5674 in the following manner: (pass, went, ...) over (174x), pass (108x), (pass, ect...) through (58x), pass by (27x), go (26x), (put, pass, etc...) away (24x), pass on (19x), misc (123x). <http://www.eliyah.com/lexicon.html>.

6. *Strong's Concordance with Hebrew and Greek Lexicon*. EliYah, No Date. Web. Word #H4390 "MALE'" used 249x in Old Testament Text, KJV-1611. The KJV translates Strong's H4390 in the following manner: fill (107x), full (48x), fulfil (28x), consecrate (15x), accomplish (7x), replenish (7x), wholly (6x), set (6x), expired (3x), fully (2x), gather (2x), overflow (2x), satisfy (2x), misc (14x). <http://www.eliyah.com/lexicon.html>.

7. Ogilvie, Jen. "Book of the Dead: A Commentary on the British Museaum Exhibition." *Fortean Times: The World of Strange Phenomena*, Nov. 2010. Web. Retrieved August 27, 2014. <http://www.forteantimes. com/features/commentary/4654/book_of_the_dead.html>.

8. Taylor, John H., ed. *Ancient Egyptian Book of the Dead: Journey through the Afterlife*. London: British Museum, 2010. Print. pgs 54-55. <http://www.amazon.com/Journey-Through-Afterlife-Ancient-Egyptian/ dp/0674072391>

9. Johnson, Ken, Th.D. *Ancient Post-flood History*. United States: Bibliofacts Ministries, 2010. Print. pg. 152.

10. *Ibid*. Johnson, pg. 153.

11. Dunn, Jimmy. "Imhotep, Doctor, Architect, High Priest, Scribe and Vizier to King Djoser." *About Egyptian Pyramids*. TourEgypt.com, 24 Oct. 2011. Web. Retrieved August 26, 2014. <http://www.touregypt.net/ featurestories/imhotep.htm>.

12. *Ibid*. Ogilvie.

13. Wilson, K. "Neb Ankh." Found in: Asante, Molefi Kete, and Ama Mazama. *Encyclopedia of African Religion*. Thousand Oaks, CA: SAGE, 2009. 445-46. Print.

14. Grajetzki, Wolfram. *Burial Customs in Ancient Egypt: Life in Death for Rich and Poor*. London: Duckworth, 2003. Print. pgs 7-14.

15. Budge, E. A. Wallis. *The Gods of the Egyptians: Studies in Egyptian Mythology — Volume 1*. New York: Dover Publications, 1969. Originally published London: Methuen in 1904. pg. 418

16. *Ibid*. Ogilvie.

17. See Timeline Chart pg. 395

18. See Timeline Chart pg. 395

19. Anderson, Stephen R. "How Many Languages Are There in the World?" *Linguistic Society of America*, 2012. Web. Retrieved Sept. 8, 2014. <http://www.linguisticsociety.org/content/how-many-languages-are- there-world>.

20. Palmer, Brian. "Are There Really Just Five Racial Groups?" *Slate Magazine*, 17 May 2012. Web. Retrieved Sept. 8, 2014. <http://www. slate.com/articles/news_and_politics/explainer/2012/05/white_ american_babies_are_now_in_the_minority_why_does_the_census_ divide_people_by_race_anyway_.html>.

About the Author

Born in Jacksonville, Florida, Mark graduated in 1982 from the Arlington Baptist College in Arlington, Texas, with a Bachelor of Science degree. He is an accomplished public speaker and regularly moderates motivational and business themed seminar events. He is also the founder and president of Splinter In The Mind's Eye Publishing.

You can follow him on Facebook @ Splinter In The Minds Eye or on Twitter @mindseyemark or find his profile on LinkedIn.

Other Books By This Author

Coming in the summer of 2015, *MY END OF THE CIRCLE* takes an investigative look at additional evidence regarding number of topics that surfaced during the research and writing of *END THE BEGINNING*. The book revisits some of the sleeping dogs that got nudged along the way, but were never really taken for a walk. Some of those dogs include:

- Did Adam & Eve have children before the fall?

- The sin nature of man. Is everyone born into sin?

- Is there more to the story about the sacrifice in Eden?

- Was the serpent in Eden really a snake?

- If Job was a real person, when did he live?

- Where did Enoch go when God took him?

- Does seeing the universe as an enclosed system matter?

- Was the animal kingdom different before the flood?

- How did the food source change after the flood?

- What was a birthright and did every family have one?

CPSIA information can be obtained at www.ICGtesting.com
Printed in the USA
BVOW07s1723230215

388932BV00001B/60/P